A CULTURE OF FAITH

A Culture of Faith
*Evangelical Congregations
in Canada*

SAM REIMER
and
MICHAEL WILKINSON

McGill-Queen's University Press
Montreal & Kingston • London • Ithaca

© McGill-Queen's University Press 2015

ISBN 978-0-7735-4503-8 (cloth)
ISBN 978-0-7735-4504-5 (paper)
ISBN 978-0-7735-9713-6 (ePDF)
ISBN 978-0-7735-9714-3 (ePUB)

Legal deposit second quarter 2015
Bibliothèque nationale du Québec

Printed in Canada on acid-free paper that is 100% ancient forest free
(100% post-consumer recycled), processed chlorine free

This book has been published with the help of a grant from the Canadian
Federation for the Humanities and Social Sciences, through the Awards to
Scholarly Publications Program, using funds provided by the Social Sciences
and Humanities Research Council of Canada.

McGill-Queen's University Press acknowledges the support of the Canada Council
for the Arts for our publishing program. We also acknowledge the financial support
of the Government of Canada through the Canada Book Fund for our publishing
activities.

Library and Archives Canada Cataloguing in Publication

Reimer, Sam, author
A culture of faith : evangelical congregations in
Canada / Sam Reimer and Michael Wilkinson.

Includes bibliographical references and index.
Issued in print and electronic formats.
ISBN 978-0-7735-4503-8 (bound). – ISBN 978-0-7735-4504-5 (pbk.). –
ISBN 978-0-7735-9713-6 (ePDF). – ISBN 978-0-7735-9714-3 (ePUB)

1. Evangelicalism–Canada. 2. Religious gatherings–Canada.
3. Religious gatherings–Christianity. 4. Church attendance–Canada.
5. Christian sociology–Canada. I. Wilkinson, Michael, 1965–, author
II. Title.

BR1642.C3R42 2015   277.108'3   C2014-908222-3
                                       C2014-908223-1

Contents

Tables and Figures / vii

Acknowledgments / xi

Introduction / 3

1 Evangelicalism in Canada / 15

2 On Cultures and Subcultures / 37

3 The Demographics of Evangelical Congregations / 67

4 Priorities and Purposes / 90

5 Programs and Identity / 111

6 Leadership and Pastoral Well-Being / 134

7 Youth and Children / 158

8 Financing Evangelical Congregations / 182

Conclusion / 202

Appendix / 211

Notes / 243

References / 261

Index / 281

Tables and Figures

TABLES

1.1 Beliefs and weekly (or more often) attendance of Canadians across Christian traditions, 2005 / 18

1.2 Number of congregations and average number of weekly attendees for selected Christian denominations in Canada / 20

2.1 Canadians' church attendance, 1985–2010 / 49

2.2 Canadians who claimed to attend church weekly or more often, by religious tradition, 1975–2005 / 50

3.1 Evangelical congregations reporting increased (and decreased) church attendance and other membership changes since 2007, by denomination / 70

3.2 Increase or decrease in total (median) receipted gifts, by denomination, from 2000 to 2009 / 72

3.3 Number of evangelical congregations and weekly attendance, by denomination, 2008 / 76

3.4 Attributes of small and large congregations, all Christian traditions / 77

3.5 Number and age of evangelical congregations, by denomination / 78

3.6 Attributes of old and young evangelical congregations / 79

3.7 Evangelical congregations (ECs), Canadian provinces and territories / 82

3.8 Demographic attributes of evangelical congregations, by denomination / 84

3.9 Number of minority congregations, by denomination / 87

4.1 Number of times an evangelical pastor preached on the following topics in the previous six months / 93

4.2 Pastors' perception of lay leaders' awareness of the congregation's mission and goals, rural and urban evangelical congregations / 100

4.3 Very high priorities reported by evangelical congregations, by denomination / 102

4.4 Factor analysis of priorities of evangelical congregations / 106

4.5 Correlations with priority orientations – activist, traditional, and moderate – of evangelical congregations / 108

5.1 Internal programs of evangelical congregations, by denomination / 116

5.2 Service activities for the benefit of people outside the congregation, by denomination / 122

5.3 Common types of outreach or evangelistic activities, by denomination / 124

5.4 Less common types of outreach or evangelistic activities, by denomination / 125

5.5 Cooperation of evangelical congregations (ECs) with various other congregations and organizations, by denomination / 126

5.6 Identity descriptors of evangelical churches, as reported by pastors, by denomination / 131

6.1 Women pastors in the Pentecostal Assemblies of Canada and in the Convention of Atlantic Baptist Churches / 141

6.2 Ancestry of pastors of evangelical congregations in Canada / 142

6.3 Theological and non-theological educational achievement of evangelical lead pastors, by denomination / 143

6.4 Job satisfaction scores for evangelical pastors in Canada / 149

6.5 Canadian evangelical pastors' self-perceived areas of strength and weakness / 150

6.6 Evangelical pastors' self-perceived areas of strength and weakness correlated with job satisfaction scale / 153

6.7. Congregation satisfied with its pastor and pastor's job satisfaction, by pastor age groups / 155

7.1 Events for youth and children offered weekly by evangelical congregations / 162

7.2 Events for youth and children offered by evangelical congregations in the previous twelve months / 164

7.3 Description of those attending youth events offered by evangelical congregations / 166

7.4 Description of those attending children's events offered by evangelical congregations / 167

7.5 Religious affiliation of young Canadian adults "raised Christian," by childhood family religious affiliation / 170

7.6 Retention and switching rates of younger/emerging adults by Christian tradition, Canada–USA comparison / 172

7.7 Attendance at religious services of young Canadian adults "raised Christian," by childhood family religious affiliation / 173

7.8 Religious experiences of young Canadian adults "raised evangelical," by attendance at religious services / 175

7.9 Young Canadian adults "raised Christian" who attend weekly or more, by parents' attendance (non-divorced parents only) / 178

7.10 Religious practices of young Canadian adults "raised evangelical," by parental religious practices / 179

8.1 Generosity in relation to evangelical church attendance / 187

8.2 Correlations with perceived financial vitality, evangelical congregations / 192

8.3 Annual change in giving in relation to perceived financial health, evangelical congregations / 193

8.4. Median tax-receipted gifts and total revenue by Christian tradition, 2000 and 2010 / 196

8.5 Median expenditures 2000–10 by Christian tradition, select charitable information return expenditure lines / 198

A1 Congregational incomes, CRA and CECS data / 214

A2 Congregational frequency counts by denomination and tradition / 217

FIGURES

3.1 Number of churches in evangelical denominations, 1971–2010 / 74

6.1 Number of seminary students in Association of Theological Schools in Canada / 138

8.1 Median tax-receipted gifts (line 4500) 2000–09 by denomination in 2000 dollars / 194

A1 Response rates flowchart / 213

Acknowledgments

Many people contributed to this project and deserve recognition, far more than we are able to give here. First, we want to thank the denominational leaders and administrative staff of the Convention Baptist, Christian and Missionary Alliance, Pentecostal Assemblies of Canada, Mennonite Brethren, and Christian Reformed Church who participated in the interviews, promoted our project in their constituencies, and sent us statistics about their denominations. The fifty pastors who provided face-to-face interviews and the 478 pastors who responded to a lengthy telephone interview deserve special thanks. Without their willingness to participate, this book would not exist. We also benefited from the work of Andrew Grenville and Joel Thiessen who completed face-to-face interviews with pastors in Toronto and Calgary, respectively. Advitek, Inc. of Toronto completed the telephone interviews in French and English in a timely and professional manner.

Funding for this research came primarily from the Evangelical Fellowship of Canada's Centre for Research on Canadian Evangelicalism, and some findings from our data were published in their online journal, *Church & Faith Trends* (www.evangelicalfellowship. ca/cft). We could not have completed this project without their generous support, including that of John Stackhouse, Jr, who offered insight and assistance at the beginning of this project. Crandall University and Trinity Western University contributed to the administration of the project, especially the Trinity Western Research Office and the work of Sue Funk. We also gratefully acknowledge the funding for publication by the Awards to Scholarly Publications Program (ASPP) from the Federation for the Humanities and Social Sciences.

The Religion and Diversity Project led by Lori Beaman also funded a presentation we made on these data in Cambridge, England.

Rick Hiemstra helped us with chapter 8 on financing evangelical congregations. Rick has worked tirelessly to create a dataset of Christian churches from the Canadian Revenue Agency's publicly available T3010 data. Using these data, Rick ran most of the tables in chapter 8 and helped with the writing. The same can be said of James Penner, lead researcher on the Church and Faith Study of Young Adults (better known as the Hemorrhaging Faith Study), who provided us with much of the data for chapter 7 on Youth and Children; James also contributed to the writing of this chapter. We are very appreciative of their considerable contributions. Reginald Bibby shared freely with us his Project Canada datasets, which include national surveys gathered every five years from 1975 to 2005. As the reader will see, these data are prominent in this book, both when we cite Bibby and when we analyze the data ourselves.

McGill-Queen's University Press was also very supportive. We wish to particularly thank senior editor Kyla Madden for her assistance and the excellent editing skills of Kate Baltais who improved this manuscript considerably. We received helpful comments on earlier drafts of this book from David Eagle, Joel Thiessen, Rick Hiemstra, and Peter Beyer. The work of the anonymous reviewers also sharpened our arguments and enabled us to clarify our thinking on the role of evangelical congregations in Canada.

Finally, we want to thank our families for their support. We could not do what we do without you. To Mary Beth and Valerie, be assured of our gratitude and enduring love. To our children, we dedicate this book to you, in the hope that you will find communities of faith of your own.

A CULTURE OF FAITH

Introduction

In his book, *It's a New Day* (2012), leading sociologist of religion Reginald Bibby argues that religion is not going away in Canada, but it is changing. In spite of the predictions of secularization theorists, religion will continue to uphold its significant presence in Canada, although previously prominent groups will recede while other groups will come to the fore. In this reshuffling, the groups that are growing rapidly are the immigrant world religions – Muslims, Hindus, Sikhs, Buddhists – and those with no religion. According to Bibby, these world religions have grown from representing 3 per cent of the Canadian population in 1931 to 8 per cent in 2009. The proportion of those who claim no religion has grown from 1 per cent in 1931 to 25 per cent in 2009. The Christian traditions will continue to hold the allegiance of the vast majority of Canadians in the foreseeable future, but some groups are in decline. Roman Catholics are steady around 40 per cent and evangelicals are up slightly to just over 10 per cent of the population.[1] Declining are the mainline Protestants, from around 50 per cent in 1931 to less than 20 per cent today (34). One wonders if they are "mainline" anymore.[2] The number of Catholics in Quebec is rapidly declining as well.

Along with changes in the rank order of religious traditions in Canada, Bibby also points to a significant decline in institutional participation. Again using Bibby's numbers, 60 per cent of Canadians claimed to attend religious services weekly in 1945, and by 2005, only 25 per cent claimed weekly attendance (2012, 5). One reason for much of this decline is that many in the baby boomer generation – those born between 1946 and 1964 – abandoned religious institutions. Bibby's focus on changes in the religious landscape in Canada reflects the relative fortunes of the congregations within each tradition. Only a small proportion of mainline Protestants and Quebec Catholics attend church regularly, and many of their congregations are closing or struggling to survive. In comparison, roughly half of evangelical affiliates are in church on any given Sunday, and their number of congregations is holding steady. The future trajectory of each tradition is linked to its congregations.

This book is about the Christian tradition that researchers agree is showing the most institutional resiliency: the evangelical Protestants. More specifically, our purpose is to describe evangelical Protestant congregations in Canada. While we provide a "bird's-eye" view of these churches as a whole, we also peer inside them to look at their budgets, leadership, programs, outreach, and the people in the pews. The insider's view comes mainly from the pastors that lead them.

While our main purpose is describing evangelical churches, a thread of congregational vitality runs through this book. Why have evangelical congregations shown resilience in a milieu of declining institutional religiosity? We use terms like "institutional vitality," "strength," or "resiliency" often in this book to refer to evangelical congregations. We do not use the term "normatively," suggesting that evangelical congregations are better or closer to what "should be." Rather, by "institutional vitality" we mean numerical growth or decline (like number of attendees or number of churches), the levels of giving and volunteering of adherents, the percentage of youth that are retained, the growth or decline in the number of qualified clergy, and other quantifiable indicators that we elaborate below. We also frame our discussion in comparison with the other Canadian Christian traditions, primarily mainline Protestants and Roman Catholics. The point is that evangelical churches often evince institutional vitality in comparison with Catholics, and particularly in comparison with mainline Protestants. We are not suggesting that evangelical churches are vital or strong in some absolute sense.

This is not the first book about Christian churches in Canada; starting with S.D. Clark's *Church and Sect in Canada* (1948) to Bibby's *Restless Churches* (2004), scholars have studied congregations, whose church spires mark the visible centre of many Canadian communities. However, there has been little recent scholarship on Canadian churches, though they remain important to millions of Canadians even if their cultural importance has declined over time.

We seek to fill this void with (to the best of our knowledge) the first multidenominational, sociological study of evangelical congregations in Canada. An additional unique contribution of this book is that it studies the characteristics of the congregations themselves. Our focus is not the religious individual, nor the impact the congregation can potentially have on society (which have been Bibby's foci, see, e.g., 2004, 2011). We hope that our efforts will inspire other studies of congregations in Canada.

DEFINING EVANGELICAL CONGREGATIONS

Depending on how one defines "evangelical," the proportion of Canadians who are evangelicals can range from as low as 8 per cent to as high as 16 per cent. The two classic examples include Bibby's research, which defines evangelicals as conservative Protestants who attend church and participate with their denominations and congregations (1987, 1993, 2004). The higher figure focuses on beliefs, and the best example is George Rawlyk's book *Is Jesus Your Personal Saviour?* (1996). Rawlyk reported, "Some *16 per cent* of Canadians are evangelicals, ardent churchgoers with salient foundational beliefs including conversion, biblicism, crucicentrism, and activism" (115, original emphasis). What accounts for this difference?

When Rawlyk conducted his study he explored the incidence of "evangelicalism" among the full range of Protestant denominations including the United Church of Canada and the Anglican Church as well as the Roman Catholic Church. No doubt there are Christians who affiliate with "mainline" Protestant churches that hold beliefs and practices like those who attend "conservative" Protestant denominations. Similarly, there are most likely people who attend "evangelical" congregations that share more progressive or "liberal" views like those in the United Church. Rawlyk also discovered there were a significant number of Roman Catholics in his research that he identified as evangelical because of their evangelical beliefs and practices. However, we limited our study to the congregations of five evangelical denominations that self-identify as evangelical, primarily, but not limited by, their association with the Evangelical Fellowship of Canada.

John G. Stackhouse, Jr (2007) says there are two ways of defining "evangelical." The first is based on British historian David

Bebbington's quadrilateral. Bebbington (1989) focuses on four central characteristics that mark evangelicalism historically: (1) crucicentrism (the centrality of Christ's salvific work on the cross), (2) biblicism (an emphasis on the authority of the Bible), (3) conversionism (a conversion experience), and (4) activism (an active faith that includes evangelism and congregational participation). A second definition, according to Stackhouse, focuses on evangelicalism as individuals or institutional bodies with historical connections to eighteenth-century revivals. In the nineteenth century, this movement included Protestant denominations like the Baptists, some Presbyterians, some Anglicans, and much of the current United Church. Stackhouse includes one other criterion from the historian George Marsden, namely, transdenominationalism, which highlights the cooperation of evangelical Protestants across denominational lines, especially as it relates to activism and evangelism (also see Stackhouse, 1993).

We acknowledge evangelicalism as a movement or subculture within Protestantism organized around a set of beliefs, practices, and transdenominational relations (see Reimer, 2003). Congregations are important organizing features for religion generally and for evangelical Protestants specifically. Congregations are evangelical if they are part of an evangelical Protestant denomination. Those churches that are independent or part of (non-denominational) intercongregational networks can be considered evangelical if they fit Bebbington's quadrilateral. If a congregation has a membership or affiliation with a transdenominational organization, like the Evangelical Fellowship of Canada, it can be considered evangelical. Last, a congregation may be evangelical if it identifies itself as evangelical.[3] The denominations and congregations in this study are all evangelical by three, if not all four, definitional criteria.

After explaining what we mean by evangelical, we turn our focus to defining congregations. Most of these congregations are housed within denominations, although independent congregations are on the rise. As a result, there is some debate over the future vitality of denominations. However they have not disappeared but continue to be an important feature of religion (Wuthnow, 1988; Miller, 1997; Roozen and Nieman, 2005). Bruce Guenther (2008a) argues that historians have not studied Canadian denominations in great detail and evangelical Protestant denominations, specifically, are understudied compared with those in the United States. Furthermore, as Guenther states, "The vast majority of evangelical Protestants practice their faith in congregations that are connected in some way to a larger denominational body. Without giving some attention to the organizational structures that contribute to a sense of identity, that define beliefs and convictions, and that help give expression to priorities and practices, it is not possible to understand fully the diversity among twentieth-century evangelical Protestants in Canada and around the world" (163).

Central to denominational life is the local congregation. James F. Hopewell (1987) offers the following definition, "A congregation is a group that possesses a special name and recognized members who assemble regularly to celebrate a more universally practiced worship but who communicate with each other sufficiently to develop intrinsic patterns of conduct, outlook, and story" (12–13). The cultural dynamics of congregations are expressed in a narrative form that gives meaning and order to parishioners. Furthermore, the cultural aspects of congregations are important sociological factors that continue to shape their study. Mark Chaves (2004) argues that the cultural production of congregations is by far the most important contribution to society, even more so than political or social action.

Stephen Warner (1988) argues for the study of congregations as case studies for understanding religious life. His study of evangelicals and liberals in California illustrates well his congregational principle of religious organization, which allows researchers to see variation between and within denominations precisely because of the voluntary nature of religion. Warner (1993, 1994) insists on the centrality of congregations arguing that religious life is de facto congregational. For Warner (1994), the local congregation is the central organization for religious life because it is the primary place for social and religious interaction. Denominations are typically staffed by religious professionals and perform work for the organization at the national or regional level. Congregations, on the other hand, are local, voluntary communities, concerned with worship, religious education, mission, stewardship, and fellowship (63–7).

In keeping with this emphasis on congregational culture, also seen in Chaves (2004) and others (e.g., Ammerman, 1997; 2005), we use a sociology of culture approach in our analysis of evangelical congregations. This approach sees congregations as producers of culture. That is, congregations create their own ways of doing things, their own identity, rituals, and stories that make each congregation unique. Yet, there are also similarities between congregations because they draw elements of their culture from (Canadian) society, from their (evangelical) tradition, and from their denomination (Ammerman 1997). Thus, while congregations are unique because of their unique history, local context, and the unique blend of people that make them up, they also share a "family resemblance" to other churches. The degree to which they resemble the broader society – often called "accommodation" or "conforming to the world"[4] – is very important for evangelicals. They want to maintain their distinctiveness, aligning themselves more closely with biblical standards than societal norms. As a result, evangelicals form subcultures within the broader culture, guarding themselves against accommodation through symbolic, subcultural boundaries. All these themes are described in detail in chapter 2.

CHURCH ATTENDANCE

In *It's a New Day*, Bibby sees arrested congregational decline and new hope for the churches.[5] We are somewhat less sanguine, and see continued (although possibly slower) decline. Part of this difference is related to Bibby's focus on monthly, instead of weekly, attendance. He argues monthly attendance is more realistic because of the increased busyness of the lives of Canadians, particularly resulting from a colossal increase in the percentage of women working outside the home. In Bibby's words, "For peculiar reasons, researchers and practitioners have continued to use 'weekly' attendance as the gold standard for religious involvement" (2012, 27) and that is why researchers have "misread" Canada's religious situation.

We have great respect for Bibby and his work, but we think that weekly, not monthly, attendance is a better measure for institutional commitment, because the distinction is significant between those who claim weekly (or more often than weekly) and less than weekly attendance. The importance is to understand what people mean when on a survey they say they "attend weekly." Clearly, most do not mean that they never miss a Sunday: illness, snow days, vacation, work-related travel, weekend sporting events for children, and so on ensure that few Canadians attend a religious service every single week. Research shows that survey respondents in Canada exaggerate their church attendance, claiming to have attended a service in the past seven days when, in fact, they did not (Hadaway and Marler, 1997; Brenner, 2012; Eagle, 2011). Using the 2005 Canadian General Social Survey, Brenner (2012) found that less than half of those who claimed to attend a religious service "at least once a week" actually attended based on time diary accounts. That is, while 19 per cent of Canadians claimed to be weekly attendees, only 9 per cent were in church. If we add those who attend less than weekly (3%), time diary accounts show only about 12 per cent of Canadians actually attended (Brenner, 2012). It is for this reason that we think that weekly church attendance in Canada really represents between 10 and 15 per cent of the population.

So what do people mean when they say they attend church "every week"? Research suggests that people are not trying to lie; they are interpreting the question in a way that is consonant with their religious identity, not their actual behaviour. Those who say that religion is important to their lives are much more likely to overreport their attendance than those for whom religion is not important, so they truthfully answer survey questions based on their self-understanding that they are indeed religiously committed people. Hadaway, Chaves and Marler (1998) state, "Overreporting is generated by the combination of a respondent's desire to report *truthfully* his or her identity as a religious, church-going person and the perception that the attendance question is really about this identity rather than about *actual attendance*" (127, original emphasis). Claiming weekly attendance, then, is partly about religious identity, indicating that those who claim less than weekly attendance are evincing a weaker religious identity.[6]

Furthermore, other measures of institutional commitment, like voluntarism and giving money, show that weekly attendance verses non-weekly attendance is the watershed distinction. For example, McKeown et al. (2004) found that the average annual donation of Canadians who claim weekly attendance was $577, roughly twice that of monthly attendees ($286). By comparison, those who attend rarely ($166) and never ($145) gave less yet (5). Similarly, those who claim to be very religious (identity) gave $618 on average annually, compared with only $271 by those who said they were somewhat religious (5). Volunteering also shows that the important gap is between weekly and monthly attendees and those who are very religious versus somewhat religious. Weekly attendees volunteered 202 hours annually on average, which is similar to those who are very religious (200 hours). Those who attend monthly volunteered 154 hours annually, which is very close to those who attend rarely (146 hours) or never (148 hours). Those who say they are somewhat religious report similar numbers of annual volunteer hours (163) to those who are not very religious (145 hours) or not religious at all (149 hours) (McKeown et al., 2004, 10). The same can be said of religiously informed attitudes, like attitudes regarding homosexuality or abortion. For example, Bibby's Project Canada 2005 data show that weekly and more than weekly attendees are more likely to say homosexual sexual relations are always wrong (72.3% and 79%) compared with those who attend nearly every week (46.7%). The point is that claiming weekly attendance is an important signifier for a person, particularly for evangelicals, even if very few actually attend every single week in a given year. That is why in this book we focus on weekly attendance.

THE DATA: CANADIAN EVANGELICAL CHURCHES STUDY

For the Canadian Evangelical Churches Study (CECS) the lead pastors (the senior pastor or only pastor) of 478 evangelical congregations were interviewed by telephone in 2009.[7] The response rate for these interviews was roughly 40 per cent. In addition, 100 telephone interviews with youth and children's pastors were conducted in these same congregations; these are discussed in more detail in chapter 7. Prior to the telephone interviews, we (with the help of some colleagues) conducted face-to-face interviews with fifty other lead pastors in major regions across Canada (the Maritimes, Toronto area, Calgary area, and Vancouver area). Finally, we interviewed the national leaders of the denominations in our study. The data provided us with a rich portrait of evangelical congregational life including priorities, programs, finances, evangelism, social activism, children, and youth. The specific details about our methodology including response rates and representativeness can be found in the Appendix.

We ourselves personally completed roughly thirty of the fifty face-to-face interviews, as well as the telephone interviews with the denominational leaders. We also visited many evangelical congregations. In this way we gained first-hand knowledge of the churches themselves. We interviewed pastors of Chinese, Filipino, and other ethnic congregations who struggled to communicate in English; lay pastors in small, rural churches who could not afford pastoral salaries; pastors of mega-churches in major urban centres; pastors with doctorates and some with only high school education (and a few online theological courses); pastors from Vancouver to Halifax. Pastors told us about the history, vision, programs, outreach efforts, and demographics of their congregations. Our hope in this book is to accurately reflect what we heard from them.

The congregations were from five major evangelical denominations in Canada – Pentecostal Assemblies of Canada (PAOC), the Christian Reformed Church (CRC), the Mennonite Brethren (MB), the Christian and Missionary Alliance (CMA), and the four Baptist conventions – the Convention of Atlantic Baptist Churches (CABC), Canadian Baptists of Ontario and Quebec (CBOQ), the Canadian Baptists of Western Canada (CBWC), and the French Baptist Union / Union d'Églises baptistes françaises au Canada (FBU). These are the largest denominations in the Pentecostal, Reformed, Mennonite, Holiness, and Baptist traditions within Canadian evangelicalism. These denominations represent about 3,100 congregations, or about one-third of all the evangelical congregations in Canada. They are evangelical in the sense that they are all conservative Protestant denominations, and they are also all members of the Evangelical Fellowship of Canada. Nearly three in four of the pastors interviewed for the CECS (72.6%) stated that the term "evangelical" describes their congregation very well, and nearly all the rest said "somewhat well" (24.7%).[8] Of course, the data gathered do not represent all of the hundred or more evangelical Protestant denominations in Canada, not to mention the independent congregations.[9] However, we compare our data with other data sources, giving us more confidence in the generalizability of our findings.

The data in our study rely on pastors telling us about their congregations. Research in the United States involving interviews of key informants, particularly key informants in leadership positions like the clergy, was found to be very accurate on directly observable features of the congregations and their people. This includes congregational size, programs, and the age, sex, and race compositions of the people who participate. McPherson and Rotolo (1995) report that key informant estimates are as good as asking the people themselves, in these specific areas. Other areas, like clergy estimates of parishioner income and education show some mixed results (Schwadel and Dougherty, 2010; Frenk, Anderson, and Martin, 2011). In comparison, key informants are less likely to accurately report the goals or beliefs (attitudes) of people in the congregation (Chaves, 2004). For this reason, we ask about directly observable features of the congregations and congregants, and use broad categories to increase reporting accuracy. When we do look at priorities and purposes, we ask about the congregation as a whole, not about the individuals within it.

Thus, key informant or pastor interviews fit our purpose, which is to analyze the characteristics of churches – or to study churches as *organizations*. Our focus was not on the *individuals* who attend them. The key informant method has been used in congregational research by scholars like Chaves (2004), Carroll (2006), and Ammerman (2005). Other researchers have focused on the individuals in the pew (Woolever and Bruce, 2002),[10] or on the community around the congregation (Ammerman, 1997). Still others select churches as case studies and use ethnographic methods (Ammerman, 1997; Warner, 1988; Edgell, 2006). The advantage of such studies is more detailed information on a smaller number of churches, but they do not use representative samples. Our strategy allowed us to study a representative sample of over 500 congregations within five large evangelical denominations. Using this strategy, we captured more of the diversity of evangelical congregations from across Canada.

THE PLAN OF THIS BOOK

Chapter 1 looks at the decline of congregational participation and shows that evangelicals are still institutionally strong. For example, while evangelical Protestants only make up about 10 per cent of the population, they account for approximately one-third of the nearly 30,000 congregations in Canada. Why do evangelical Protestants make up a disproportionate number of congregations? Why are evangelical Protestants maintaining institutional vitality when the Canadian trend is toward declining religious participation in congregations? What we argue is that congregations are central to evangelical Protestantism and understanding congregations provides an important optic for making sense of the evangelical subculture.

In chapter 2 we discuss the cultural aspects of evangelical congregations and what makes them unique. Each congregation is somewhat unique culturally. However, each one is also shaped by the larger evangelical subculture, which is increasingly interconnected with an evangelical global culture (Hutchinson and Wolffe, 2012). In this chapter we show how evangelical congregations are contextualized in Canada, how they respond to culture, and why evangelical congregations continue to be vital organizations in spite of an overall decline in religious participation.

Chapter 3 offers a demographic overview of evangelical congregations. Attention is given to the growth patterns found in the denominations represented in our study. We also look in detail at the size, age, ethnicity, class, and location of evangelical congregations. While evangelical congregations appear to be doing well when compared with mainline Protestants, there are some demographic factors that show growth is slowing, or has stopped completely.

Church growth or organizational consultants will tell you that congregations need a compelling vision. Chapter 4 focuses on the purposes and priorities of evangelical congregations. We discuss questions regarding the mission and purpose of evangelical congregations, their goals and objectives, and their corporate vision. We pay attention to both internal and external purposes and priorities, reviewing congregational responses to administrative and theological issues and social and political aspirations.

Successful organizations adapt to change, and evangelical congregations have to do the same if they want to survive and thrive. Canadians are not going to the churches, unless they are relocating regular attendees, so the churches are coming to them. Evangelicals are leaving their religious buildings and going into the community to try to show their relevance. As a result, many evangelical congregations have shifted (at least in rhetoric) from a program-based orientation that reached its peak in the 1980s. The "missional church" paradigm, frequently mentioned by the evangelical leaders and pastors we interviewed, is based on the assumption that Canada is a post-Christian society and evangelicals need to find new ways to evangelize and missionize Canadians. Chapter 5 reviews this shift and examines the internal and external programs of evangelical congregations, including transdenominational cooperation and evangelical identity.

In the view of the denominational leaders we interviewed, congregations rise and fall on the quality of their pastoral leadership. In chapter 6, we examine leadership and pastoral well-being. We look at leadership qualifications, women in ministry, lay leadership, and concerns over aging leaders with fewer young pastors to take their place. We then move to our survey findings that focus on pastoral well-being, how pastors view ministry, personal issues, time management, stress, family issues, and other matters related to personal health.

While leaders seek to redirect their congregations toward being missional, or externally focused, they still realize that they must tend to the young already in the fold if they want to keep their doors open. In chapter 7 we focus on the findings from our 100 youth and children's pastor interviews. James Penner, a youth researcher and fellow sociologist, brings his considerable expertise as a co-author of this chapter. Evangelicals place a high priority on youth and children, and we ask how well they are doing at retaining their youth into young adulthood.

Chapter 8 examines how evangelical congregations are resourced financially. Nearly all congregations are dependent on the generosity of time and money of devoted volunteers. Here we review overall income and expenses based on congregational budgets. We draw upon Canada Revenue Agency data from charitable organizations. These T3010 data are publically available, and have been coded and cleaned by our colleague Rick Hiemstra, who co-authored this chapter. The data allow for assessing congregational financial records across denominations and Christian traditions.

In sum, congregations, at least thriving ones, need a clear understanding of their cultural and demographic context, compelling vision and purpose, healthy leaders, focused outreach, ways to keep their youth in the fold, ways to attract and integrate immigrant populations, and sufficient financial resources. In the conclusion, we summarize our findings showing that in spite of fragmentation and decline in Christian religious organizations in Canada, evangelical Protestants still value congregations with evangelicalism largely remaining institutionally based. We speculate about their future growth or decline.

I

Evangelicalism in Canada

The crumbling state of the churches is a physical embodiment of
the state of religious observance – and the phenomenon is hardly
limited to Quebec. From British Columbia to Newfoundland,
places of worship of all mainstream denominations are falling
victim to dwindling attendance, rising land values and maintenance
costs too onerous for congregations to bear.

Ingrid Peritz[1]

We have known for some time now that Canadians are not going to
church as regularly as they used to. In 1957, some 53 per cent of
Canadians claimed to attend church weekly (Bibby, 2011, 29). Six
decades later, by 2008, this proportion was below 20 per cent.[2] In
Quebec, the decline has been even faster. In 1957, nearly 90 per cent
of people in Quebec said they were attending weekly, compared with
14 per cent in 2005 (ibid. 29). Attendance will continue to drop as
the younger cohorts replace the more religious older cohorts. Young
Canadians are less likely to attend than older Canadians (Eagle,
2011, 197), which means that many "greying" churches face an
uncertain future.

Lower church attendance is a symptom of a larger trend away
from participation in religious groups. Institutional forms of religion
have less influence and authority in people's lives. Canadians increasingly ignore the orthodoxy and orthopraxy prescribed by organized
religion. They are losing confidence in religious leadership, disaffiliation (the growth of religious "nones") is increasing, and being spiritual, not religious, is all the rage.

The Roman Catholic Church is a case in point. An April 1993
Maclean's magazine cover story reported that "God Is Alive" in Canada,
but that significant numbers of Canadian Catholics do not follow

the teachings of their church. Against the official doctrine of the Vatican, 91 per cent approve of contraceptive use, 84 per cent think priests should be allowed to marry, and 82 per cent think it is okay for unmarried people to have sex (49). There is also a growing loss of confidence in religious leadership. In 1985, 50.7 per cent of Canadians said they had a "great deal" or "quite a bit" of confidence in people in charge of "the church." In 2005, only 32.6 per cent said they had similar levels of confidence in those in charge of "religious organizations."[3] No doubt, the sexual scandals involving priests, residential schools, and prominent televangelists south of the border did not help people's confidence (Bibby, 1993).

When it comes to religious belonging and identity, Canadians are increasingly likely to claim that they have no religious affiliation: 24 per cent said they had no religion in 2011, compared with 21 per cent in 2008, 11 per cent in 1986, and 4 per cent in 1971 (Eagle, 2011, 195; Census Canada[4]). Among Canadian teens aged 15–19 years, 32 per cent said they had no religion in 2008, compared with 12 per cent in 1984 (Bibby, 2011, 32). That is not good news for congregations, as non-affiliates rarely, if ever, go to church (see Thiessen and Dawson, 2008; Thiessen, 2012).

Finally, spirituality seems to have a privileged status in Canada. People, who claim to be spiritual, but not religious, tend to avoid congregations. Reginald Bibby, the leading researcher of religious trends in Canada says, "While religion has been scorned and stigmatized and rejected by many, spirituality has known something of celebrity status" (2011, 118). It is not that most are angry at the church, it is more that Canadians do not "feel compelled to worship in an established church any more" and their beliefs tend to be "private ones" (*Maclean's*, April 1993, 32). So, are institutional forms of religion dying in Canada?

No, institutional forms of religion are not dying – not yet, at least not for all Canadians. In fact, immigrant religions – Buddhism, Islam, Hinduism, Sikhism, etc. – are growing exponentially in Canada, and we know that recent immigrants are more likely to go to church than non-immigrant Canadians. However, while there is a "remnant" of active church participants in all Christian traditions, Roman Catholics in Quebec and mainline Protestants have shown the most rapid declines. By comparison, Catholics outside Quebec in Canada are faring better (Bibby, 2006). Yet, there is one major Christian

tradition in Canada that remains comparatively strong institutionally: the evangelical Protestants.[5] Bibby (2006) reports that evangelicals have held their own, at about 8 per cent of the population,
a figure that has been stable since the 1871 census. Larger polls with
more thorough denominational data estimate that about 10 per cent
of Canadians affiliate with evangelical Protestant denominations,
and some estimates are even higher (see Hiemstra, 2007; Reimer, 2003).
Evangelicals are still going to church, and the majority still hold to
their churches' teaching. The beliefs of the majority of affiliates
seem fairly well matched to the official doctrine of their tradition.

Evangelicals hold that the Bible's teaching is the final authority
on issues of doctrine, and they are well known for their traditional
views on things moral and theological. They are particularly staunch
on sexual moral values; at least, this is the area that gets all the
media attention (Reimer, 2003). In Table 1.1 we present 2005 data
for evangelical Protestants, mainline Protestants, Catholics in Quebec,
Catholics outside Quebec, and all Canadians. Evangelicals are much
more likely than other Christian traditions (especially mainline
Protestants and Quebec Catholics) to hold traditional Christian
beliefs, like the divinity of Jesus, life after death, and conservative
sexual mores. The overall pattern regarding sexual mores among
evangelicals in Canada is one of stability over the past thirty years
(Reimer, 2011). At the bottom of the table, we include data that
show roughly half of evangelicals attend church weekly or more
often, compared with about 1 in 5 of all Canadians on average.
Data indicate that evangelicals are attending church at least as often
as they did twenty years earlier (Bibby, 2006).

Furthermore, things are looking good for the future of evangelical congregations, because they seem to hold on to their youth and
mobile members (Bibby, 2004). Bowen (2004, 50) notes that there
has been a rapid decline in church participation for mainline
Protestants and Catholics, but not for evangelical Protestants; in
fact, Bowen expects evangelical Protestants to become an "ever more
dominant force" within Canadian Protestantism, because they are
younger and more committed, and they have more people in the
pews on any given Sunday than do mainline Protestant congregations
(see also Rawlyk, 1996). In other words, evangelical Protestantism
is a uniquely congregational style of Canadian religion, and its institutional form remains relatively strong.

Table 1.1 Beliefs and weekly (or more often) attendance of Canadians across Christian traditions, 2005 (%)

	Evangelical Protestants	Mainline Protestants	Catholics in Quebec	Catholics outside Quebec	All
Jesus is divine Son of God (definitely)	77.2	33.3	32.5	53.6	37.4
Life after death (definitely)	63.8	29.0	29.1	44.2	34.1
Experienced God's presence (definitely)	62.7	19.1	19.4	31.8	24.2
Homosexual sex (always wrong)	66.5	28.0	22.7	40.0	31.2
Premarital sex (always wrong)	49.7	5.2	5.8	12.7	12.2
No abortion for any reason	81.7	47.5	70.0	66.6	57.0
Attend weekly or more often	53.1	11.7	11.6	31.9	18.8

Source: Reginald Bibby, Project Canada 2005 dataset.

If evangelicals are more likely to attend church and hold to their churches' teachings, how are the congregations themselves doing? Although some evangelical congregations are struggling, overall, they are doing well in comparison with other Christian traditions. Based on Rick Hiemstra's estimates, there are over 11,000 evangelical churches in Canada, which closely matches the total given by Outreach Canada (10,500).[6] The number of congregations remained stable (or up slightly) over the past five years (Hiemstra, 2010). Even though evangelicals make up only about 10 per cent of the Canadian population, they account for about one-third of the roughly 30,000 congregations in Canada. This is about one congregation for every 300 evangelicals. If we compare this with Catholics, the difference is stark. There are nearly thirteen million Catholic affiliates in Canada, and with some 6,000 churches that is roughly one church for every 2,100 Catholics. This is partly because Catholic churches tend to be larger, but also because Catholic attendance has declined, particularly in Quebec. If we compare the ratio of declared affiliates to reported attendees – those who affiliate with a denomination on the 2001 census compared with average attendance that congregations report to their denominations – then only about 1 in 10 United Church of

Canada affiliates attend church in a typical week. For the Lutherans, the ratio is about 1 in 9, while it is 1 in 7 for Anglicans and 1 in 4 for Presbyterians. The Catholic ratio is 1 in 3.7. Evangelical congregations report roughly a 1 to 1 ratio, with some denominations claiming more attendees than affiliates (Hiemstra, 2009).

Even more telling is actual attendance. In Table 1.2 we look at the average weekly attendance of select mainline Protestant and evangelical Protestant denominations, based on data from the denomination's website or on estimates derived from statistics supplied to us by the denomination. With roughly 175,000 attendees and 3,200 congregations, the United Church of Canada averages about 55 attendees per congregation. Comparatively, the Pentecostal Assemblies of Canada claim almost as many attendees (154,134) but only about one-third as many congregations (1,069), with an average of 144 per congregation. Overall, the limited data available show more attendees per congregation in the evangelical denominations on the lower half of the table.

The combination of declining membership and declining attendance is hard on mainline Protestant churches. The United Church of Canada declined from over one million members in 1965 to 494,791 in 2010.[7] Similarly, the Anglican Church of Canada had over one million members in the 1960s, and in 2008 its membership numbered 532,731.[8] The United Church members and Anglican each now represent less than 2 per cent of the population of Canada. The United and Anglican churches are also concerned about disparity between the growing costs of maintaining old buildings with the declining revenues from membership. According to retired United Church of Canada minister and blogger David Ewart, "I believe we are at a tipping point. That is, we currently have the strength and resources to repair and operate our properties, but continuing to do so will create a burden that within a short time (perhaps 10 or 15 years), will be too great for those who are part of the congregation to cope with."[9]

Of course, not all news is good news for evangelical congregations. There are many evangelical congregations, particularly in rural areas, that are struggling to make ends meet. Some are greying rapidly and others are closing. Many evangelical denominations are no longer growing, even after years of reported growth. Evangelicals, no doubt, exaggerate their church attendance, too. Yet overall, there

20   A CULTURE OF FAITH

Table 1.2 Number of congregations and average number of weekly attendees for selected Christian denominations in Canada

Denomination	Year	Congregations (n)	Attendees (n)
United Church	2010	3,196	174,660[a]
Presbyterian	2011	899	64,250[a]
Lutheran	2010	594	N/A
Pentecostal (PAOC)	2010	1,069	154,134[a]
Mennonite (MB)	2009	246	44,500[b]
CRC	2009	251	55,000[b]
CMA	2010	430	85,855[a]
Baptist	2010	1,065	N/A

[a] From the denomination's website.
[b] Estimates are derived from a list of congregations and attendance figures from the denomination.
CMA = Christian and Missionary Alliance
CRC = Christian Reformed Church
MB = Mennonite Brethren
N/A = no data available
PAOC = Pentecostal Assemblies of Canada

are a disproportionate number of congregations for the size of the evangelical population in Canada. Why is this? Part of the answer is resources. In addition to their higher rates of attendance, evangelicals also volunteer time and give money to their congregations at rates that are much higher than the national average, as we show in chapter 8. This allows evangelicals to have many viable small congregations.[10] But this answer only scratches the surface. The larger question is why evangelicals are more likely to hold to institutional forms of religion, when the larger trends are toward declining congregational participation.

WHY CONGREGATIONS MATTER TO EVANGELICALISM, SOCIETY, AND INDIVIDUALS

In this book, we argue that congregations are at the heart of the evangelical subculture. This is because the congregations are where evangelicals interact most regularly and where the emergent social reality stemming from this interaction is largely produced. This social reality goes out from the congregations (not only, but primarily) and shapes both individuals and the larger subculture, just as individuals and the broader subculture influence the churches. The point is this: to understand evangelicals or the evangelical subculture, we should look at their congregations, as we do in this book. The congregations provide an institutional foundation for a thriving subculture. They link the individual and the subculture. Without the congregations, the subculture would not hold together.

If evangelicalism has been relatively successful in Canada, the reason for its vitality is partly, if not primarily, found in the congregations themselves. To state it another way, we think the key causal mechanisms that explain evangelicalism's institutional success are supplied by the congregations themselves (and to a lesser extent, other evangelical institutions), and they do not originate primarily from the characteristics of individual evangelicals or the larger religious economy. This is because congregations form the vital institutional link between the individual's institutional commitment (on the micro level) and the strength of the evangelical subculture (on the macro level). Evangelicalism rises or falls on the strength of its congregations. The purpose of this book is to understand these congregations. We examine them from the point of view of those who lead them, the pastors. Throughout, we look at the characteristics of evangelical congregations themselves to help us understand their vitality relative to other Christian traditions in Canada.

If the congregations are the key conduit through which evangelical subculture norms get internalized in individuals, then the congregations themselves merit careful study. This book, then, is not primarily about evangelical persons, even those in the pew. Nor is it about the evangelical subculture, although we will address both the micro (individual) and the macro (subculture) levels. This book focuses on the mezzo level: the congregations. We look at congregational goals and mission statements, diversity and demographics, programs and procedures, internal ministries and external outreach, and their finances. Our claim is that we cannot really understand evangelicalism unless we understand the congregations. The central questions of this research, therefore, are the following: What are these congregations like? What is it about evangelical congregations that promotes this brand of organizationally committed religiosity? What are their weaknesses and liabilities? How do they engage culture? How well do they keep their young and attract non-evangelicals? Where do they allocate their finances? Underlying all the discussions in this book is the recognition that evangelical congregations are the hub that links evangelical persons and the evangelical subculture, and thus congregations are centrally important.

Why study congregations at all? We suspect that few readers will debate the importance of congregations to evangelicals, but for those interested in religion in Canada more broadly, there is much to say about why institutional religion is important to both society and to the individuals within it. This discussion is not limited to evangelical congregations, but includes all kinds of congregations, Christian and non-Christian alike. There is ample research that shows that congregations matter, even beyond the people that attend them. First, we look at evidence for the significance of congregations at the macro level of civil society, and second, at the micro level of the individual.

Alexis de Tocqueville, the famous French visitor to the United States in the 1830s, argued that religious values were important to society, for they moved people away from self-interest and toward community concerns, providing the impetus for civic involvement (1945 [1863]). Since Tocqueville, several American social scientists have decried the weakening community bonds in America, most famously in *Habits of the Heart* (Bellah et al., 1985) and *Bowling Alone* (Putnam, 2000). In these books, one major concern was the individualism that was undermining civic and religious involvement. Institutional forms of religion, the authors argue, are important for a strong civic society, since those involved in congregations are involved in charitable giving, volunteering, and public life. In *Bowling Alone* (2000), Putnam estimates that "nearly half of all associational memberships in America are church related, half of all personal philanthropy is religious in character, and half of all volunteering occurs in a religious context. So how involved we are in religion today matters a lot" (66). Possibly the most recent and thorough case for the importance of congregations to civil society is from Putnam and Campbell's tome, *American Grace* (2010), in which they argue that those actively involved in congregations are more generous with their time and money to both religious and secular organizations, are more civically active (e.g., memberships, involvement in neighbourhoods, voting), and are more likely to do acts of kindness. They argue that church attendees are better neighbours, not because of denomination or certain religious beliefs, but because of religious networks. Thus, it matters less which religious group people attend, and matters more that they are actively involved in religious institutions and religious networks at all. Non-religious relational networks and (individual) private religiosity do not do it. Putnam and Campbell conclude, "Good neighborliness (by all our measures) and involvement in religiously based social networks are, in short, highly correlated in every survey we have examined, even when we hold constant everything from demographic and ideological factors to general religiosity and general sociability" (476).[11]

Why do religious networks support civic involvement and philanthropy? Religious relationships reinforce a sense of moral responsibility for others, not just one's self (Hodgkinson and Weitzman, 1992; Wilson and Musick, 1997, 708–9; Wuthnow, 1991, 51). Church involvement promotes the kind of skills – like public speaking, leadership, and group mobilization – that easily translate into social action (Verba, Schlozman, and Brady, 1995). The combination of moral responsibility and empowerment, and possibly a captive audience that takes seriously the views of religious leaders, make churches fertile ground for mobilization.

In addition, recent work in the sociology of culture and social psychology has argued that beliefs are not the key drivers of behaviour (e.g., Swidler, 2001; Chaves, 2010). That is, believing it is important to care for other people is only weakly correlated with caring behaviour, such as volunteering or giving to help the poor. What matters more are habits and practices that are accumulated over time and then activated by circumstances that cue a caring response. In other words, routine activities develop habits and skills that become "cultural toolkits" or "strategies of action" that are employed in certain situations. Of course, values and attitudes do matter, as they often influence which "tools" are employed in a given situation (Vaisey, 2008). However, people often cannot articulate the values or attitudes to explain their behaviour. Instead, they seem to operate based on a "default" or implicit response learned through practice. If this theory is correct, then it is important for children and youth to be placed in situations where they develop habits and skills through practice that can drive implicit behavioural responses. Such habits are more important than acceptance of propositional beliefs. Congregations are places where habits of giving and volunteering are observed in others and developed over time into "schemas" of action. Congregations make people aware of needs in the community, involve people in charitable activities, and provide relational networks that support and emulate pro-social behaviour. Skills are learned that make the move from belief or feeling to action relatively seamless. Thus, for example, research consistently shows that congregational participation drives philanthropic behaviours like financial giving and volunteering (e.g., Vaidyanathan, Hill, and Smith, 2011).

It would be incorrect to assume that mainline Protestant congregations do the lion's share of social compassion and justice work, while evangelical Protestants focus internally on caring for each other or evangelizing those outside. In fact, in 1998 researchers in the United States showed that it was the evangelical Protestants, not the mainline Protestants, who had resisted individual privatization and had remained publicly engaged, both politically and in voluntarism. While church attendance increases civic engagement across the board, it is the evangelicals, particularly the educated evangelicals, who lead other groups in the "deprivatization" of their religion (Regnerus and Smith, 1998).

The reader will note that all the above evidence comes from the United States. While it is often not true that American religious research accurately portrays realities in Canada, there are many similarities between the two religious milieus. Reimer (2003) found that a singular evangelical subculture spanned the 49th parallel, meaning that American and Canadian evangelicals resemble each other more than they resemble non-evangelical Americans or Canadians – at least religiously. Nonetheless, there is also research in Canada that supports the contention that religious participation promotes certain pro-social behaviours. Bibby (2011) states,

> These findings point to a fairly consistent pattern in both Canada and around the world: people who are religious are more likely than those who are not to endorse positive interpersonal values and exhibit positive interpersonal behaviour ... [O]n balance, religion appears to be making a noteworthy contribution to social well-being. Yet, religion typically has a positive influence to the extent that it also is associated with other institutions that have a positive impact on interpersonal life. (160)

Similarly, Acadia University sociologist Kurt Bowen (2004) argues that religiously committed Christians, who he defines, in part, as those actively involved in a congregation, are more likely to volunteer time and give to charitable causes. Evangelical Protestants lead all other Christian groups in donating time and money. Hiemstra (2009) found that evangelicals "volunteer and give to charitable causes, both religious and non-religious, at higher rates and higher levels than other Canadians" (1).

Another positive outcome of institutional religion is personal well-being, according to Bowen (2004): "Compared to other Canadians ... the very committed are more likely to say they are satisfied with life, happy, and confident they will carry out their plans" (99). Bowen's argument is that institutionally committed religiosity is qualitatively different from non-institutional forms, because the former involves higher levels of both private devotional behaviour and public action. The implication of Bowen's research is that Christian institutional forms of religiosity are good for Canada, and for Canadians themselves. More surprisingly, evangelicals actively volunteer in non-religious organizations as well. To quote Uslaner (2002), whose research included a representative sample of roughly 3,000 Canadians and 3,000 Americans,

> Let me reiterate that I have not simply demonstrated that more religious people spend more time volunteering for their faiths. That should be obvious and we know that religious people (who attend services frequently, who pray a lot, etc.) are more likely to give their time to faith-based causes. My analysis here shows something very different: Christians who hold conservative religious values, who see themselves as apart from people with different traditions and ideals, are much more likely to give their time to their churches than people whose values are more mainline (or even secular). Religious conservatives were as likely to volunteer for secular causes as liberals. (246)

Finally, congregations matter for civil society because of their cultural production and extensive social services. As Chaves (2004) has argued, congregations are primarily about worship and religious education. This means that a sizeable proportion of the "arts," including music and dance that is produced and viewed comes via congregations. While social services are not their primary function, nonetheless, there are many congregations who run or support soup kitchens, educational programs, shelters, after-school programs, and the like. Cnaan and colleagues (2002) have estimated that the average congregation in the United States provides $184,000 worth of social services annually. While they found that congregations in Canada provide a somewhat lower dollar amount of social services (based on a small number of congregations in Ontario), their contribution was still substantial.

Of course, some would argue that not all that congregations do or produce is good for Canadian society. Congregations can exacerbate differences as much as bridge them. The religiously devout can insulate themselves from those who do not share their views or lifestyle, leading to more tension. Furthermore, churches mobilize and often empower in ways that not all appreciate. Evangelicals proselytize, and a few do so in pushy ways. Evangelicals carry their faith with them into the public sphere, where many Canadians wish they would leave it at home or at church. Political activism (particularly conservative politics) is not appreciated by all.

Still, congregations are one of the two most common forms of association in Canada (similar to athletics), even if participation is rapidly declining (Bibby, 2006). If congregational participation ultimately fails in Canada, alternate means of promoting the generosity, civic involvement, meaning and belonging, and sense of well-being will need to be explored.

FIVE EVANGELICAL CONGREGATIONS

These congregational profiles are based on data from our face-to-face interviews with some fifty lead pastors from all across Canada. We selected one congregation from each denomination that we studied, although the profiles better represent the overall diversity of evangelical congregations than all the congregations in that denomination. Each story shows how evangelical congregations vary demographically, in their vision and programs, and in their vitality. However, evangelical congregations also share much in common. For each story, we changed the names of the pastor and congregations to maintain anonymity.

African Baptist Church, Maritimes

There is a long history of African or Black congregations in the Maritimes. The Atlantic Baptist Convention has about twenty congregations comprised of people of African descent with eight of them pastored by women. There are comparatively few women leading the nearly 500 predominately white congregations in the convention. Reverend Paula is energetic and speaks expressively about her congregation. Trained at Princeton Seminary, Paula is actively involved in the community, sitting on a number of boards and teaching a course in Canadian African history at the local community college. Originally from the United States, she came to Canada to accept an invitation less than two years ago, as the first woman pastor of this congregation. She thinks there were probably some who wondered about a woman pastor, but she says the relationship since she arrived is excellent: "I won't say that nobody sweated it. I wasn't here for the discussion. But, I think it would be hard for me to believe that nobody in the Baptist church raised some question about it. But, I think that all of their concerns were addressed and they felt comfortable that they were perfectly in keeping with the Word and that God calls women too."

The congregation has about 200 members and 150 regular attenders who participate in the two services each Sunday. Those who attend are young and old, professionals and working class. The morning worship time is about two hours in length with lots of music, singing, a choir, and a call-and-response sermon typically observed in Black churches. "Oh, it's a long service," she says laughing, "lots of music, lots of laughter, and sometimes I talk to the congregation and they talk back." Following the morning service, people will linger, enjoy a cup of coffee and a cookie with one another. Trying to get someone to regularly organize the coffee time is a challenge, she says, but everyone wants to stay and be together. Once a month they have "Communion Sunday" followed by a meal: "People seem to like that. Sometimes it's potluck. Sometimes the church just buys and prepares the meal. But you still have to have people who are willing to heat the food, serve the food, and clean up afterwards. So even that gets to be a little difficult. The same women are like, 'We're tired now.'"

This downtown congregation was founded 180 years ago and has a long history with the Black community. People feel a certain connection with the congregation. Pastor Paula says, "People have a certain loyalty to the church. Their family have always been in this church. Even people who don't come to church on a regular basis feel like this is their church. If there is ever any event in their family, a funeral or a wedding, it's going to be here." While the congregation has a strong connection with the Black community, they also believe the church can be diverse and reach out to all people. On occasion First Nations or Asian people will visit the congregation. About 5 per cent of those who attend are white or from European descent. Pastor Paula says, "Our vision statement says we are culturally diverse because we recognize that even though we are historically a Black church, the Kingdom of God is made up of all people and so we kind of want to be a true reflection of the Kingdom." The congregation has a strong community focus with outreach programs, youth work, volunteering at local nursing homes, and programs for international students at the local university, especially those from Africa.

The congregation is also growing. In the past year, they baptized thirty-five new members. Still, the pastor believes they could do better and wants people to be more committed to the congregation's ministry: "I think we have to have many more people who are committed to the church. We have people who fill our pews on Sunday mornings, but are not necessarily working in any sustained capacity in the church, on an ongoing basis." About one-third of the members are active volunteers, teaching Sunday School, leading programs, and offering time to direct the ministry through participation on one of its boards. A building campaign is now underway with funds being raised to expand and renovate the building through special offerings, pledges, and events. The current building was built in 1925 and is showing its age. In spite of the challenges of recruiting more volunteers and serving, people are optimistic about the congregation's future, believing God has called them to serve the people in their city.

Multicultural Pentecostal Church, Toronto

Toronto is the largest urban multicultural centre in Canada, and this cultural diversity is often reflected in evangelical congregations. In the 1980s the Pentecostal Assemblies of Canada planted a new congregation in the Toronto area. While it may not be a large congregation, like the ones many people associate with Pentecostals, it is one that reflects the make-up of the city. Beginning in the 1980s many Pentecostals were outgrowing their current buildings and, after selling their property, moved further out to the suburbs. There were those who stayed in the city, but not many. Starting a new congregation in the city has its challenges, especially with the value of land. When this congregation began, it rented space in a school for almost a decade. From there it shared a facility with another group and finally, after another decade, took possession of the building. About ninety people meet regularly for Sunday worship, with people mostly of European descent, but also a substantial number of people from Bermuda, Trinidad and Tobago, Jamaica, the Philippines, India, and other countries of the world. With roughly two-thirds of new immigrants to Canada eventually settling in Canada's three largest cities – Toronto, Montreal, and Vancouver – these cities are becoming increasingly diverse ethnically. As a result, evangelical congregations are becoming increasingly diverse and the majority of new congregations are ethnic.

Attendance has been stable over the past decade, but Pastor John is hoping for more growth by refocusing his congregation to be more community oriented while building relationships with those around them. John says, "I think we need to break out of the walls. Like any church, any established church, they tend to think the building is the church, let the people come to us. Well, that is not the modus operandi in the gospels. We need to be more outward focused." The theme of getting outside the building and meeting the felt needs of the un-churched in the community was common. Evangelicals are finding that Canadians are not coming to worship services, so they are taking the congregation and its mission to them. They are also finding that they must earn the trust and respect of the non-churched through long-term relationships and community care. They call this "missional" or "incarnational" ministry, as discussed in chapter 5. Refocusing means trying things they have not done before. The congregation is holding a new midweek program where people can come and eat together followed by specialized programs to help parents develop stronger families. The pastor wants to be more focused on offering programs that are holistic, intentionally addressing relevant local issues such as how to strengthen your marriage or biblical principles for economic hard times. It also means they are trying to be more casual on Sunday, making the congregation more open to people who have never attended. The congregation also supports other programs that allow volunteers to work with the homeless, troubled youth, and single parents. They have started an "Adopt a Street" program encouraging, as the pastor says, "One-on-one evangelism as opposed to a massive evangelism [event] ... So, it's a relational evangelism I like to model and promote in the church." Evangelism also means partnering with other organizations to help others, and not necessarily other Christian organizations: "Just a social organization that deals with a women's centre, immigrants. So we're trying to partner with them and whatever initiatives we can help." Believing the congregation should have a global focus, members are encouraged to support ministry in the countries from which many of them have come: "We're sending a team to Guatemala for ten days. They are going to build a church but in Guatemala it will be used for church, schooling, community events. So, we're sending ten people." Short-term mission work is very important to evangelicals with many reaching out across cultures, locally and globally, believing it is central to their mission and vision.

Still, Pastor John is afraid of "being stuck" doing the same things over and over again just because that's the way it has always been done. In his previous congregation he faced some who opposed him when he attempted to incorporate new technologies like PowerPoint for his sermons or during the singing of worship songs. "Being stuck" restricts evangelicals from reaching out and growing, he believes. The attitude of some, he says, was "if this worked in the 50s and if flannel boards were good enough for my grandparents, they're good enough for me." He goes on to say, "I made a point to make sure I did stuff that was not churchy at all. I'd play hockey with a bunch of guys and I made a point of telling people, you have a lot of church friends, but you don't have friends that are not from the church." This new relaxed and relational approach, which attempts to connect with non-church people, is characterized by pragmatism and a sense of being culturally relevant. The approach has not translated into a whole lot of new members. Time will tell how effective refocusing will be for the congregation.

Social Concerns and the Mennonite Brethren Church, Toronto

In the centre of one of the poorest areas of Toronto, and also one of the densest, is a new congregation that began in 2005. Originally a shared venture of the Salvation Army and the Mennonite Brethren Church, this congregation reaches out to the poor. While the relationship with the Salvation Army no longer exists formally, the congregation still partners with other congregations and social service organizations (government and faith-based), which reflects its ministry mission and vision. Ministry is directly oriented around the poor and needy. "Much of what we do," says Pastor Tim, "would fall under the loose heading of community development because we're there to work with people that are in the community, building capacity, strength, investing in their lives both with our time and with the resources that we do have. It's really a ground up kind of philosophy."

About fifty people meet for a regular service on a Saturday night. Thirty people call the congregation their regular home for worship. More people show up when they serve a meal: "One of the challenges we have in our community is that it is very transient. It is a bit of a revolving door kind of ministry." When Pastor Tim talks about growth he shifts back and forth between more regular attendance and personal development: "So we have not seen tremendous growth in numbers. I think we see growth in other areas like acceptance in the community, growth in the kinds of hands-on things that we are doing in the community, impacting lives. We are not really a church that gets too bent out of shape about numbers." Yet, Pastor Tim is developing a model that will attract other evangelicals to move into the city, living in the high rises, and developing smaller congregations: "We would rather see five, six, or ten groups of congregations of twenty or thirty people in the community. I think that's a more viable model." The cooperative nature of the Mennonite Brethren church may be greater than most, but it is not uncommon among the congregations we studied. Many congregations partner with both secular and religious organizations in their communities, and members are as likely to volunteer outside the congregation as in it.

The members are involved in programs that help clean up local parks, serve food, hold arts festivals in the summer, offer leadership training, assist new Canadians, and partner with community programs. The pastor explains that their ministry reflects their values of being incarnational or living like Jesus, being relational, missional, and transformational. He says they take a "not for profit" approach to ministry: "It is incredibly painful and slow, but we really want to build credibility in the community so that they trust us because they've heard all the promises before." His ministry journey has taken him to a place where he is learning to be content with who they are and not trying to be something they are not. Many people (he calls "religious tourists") will visit them thinking that serving the poor and needy is very attractive. However, it is not very long before they discover this type of work is demanding and they rethink whether this is the type of ministry they want to be involved with. There are many challenges, says Pastor Tim, working with the poor, those who are learning English, at-risk youth, and others in need. However, he is very optimistic about his work and envisions a long-term sustainable congregation that is multicultural, caring, and financially stable. Nurturing his own spiritual life is one way he attempts to keep some balance: "I try and maintain a daily devotional time. It's not a huge chunk of time. But I do try to spend time every day."

Christian and Missionary Alliance Mega-Church in the Prairies

In one of the fastest-growing cities on the Prairies is a large Christian and Missionary Alliance Church. About 1,500 people regularly meet to worship on a weekend. The congregation is located in the suburbs and reflects the largely white middle-class population of families that live in the area. The congregation is self-described as a family-oriented one with programs for everyone from newborns to adults. About 900 people called the congregation home in the 1990s. "Growth," says Pastor Luke, "is probably attributed to the energetic staff." They attract a lot of new people moving into the city but lots of people also slip away.

"We are trying to be more intentional," he said, "about connecting with newcomers and helping them fit into the life of the church." Welcome cards and small gifts are handed out to visitors. They are also invited to attend a video presentation that introduces them to the congregation and its many staff and programs. If people continue to come, they are asked to attend a class that provides a more detailed introduction to the congregation. All members are encouraged to join small groups for prayer, Bible study, and mutual support. About 30 per cent of the regular attendees participate in small groups. The congregation readily embraces the use of new technology in worship, teaching, and marketing.

Programs are designed to meet the needs of suburban families. The children's program has about 200 volunteers. The youth program is also well attended. The pastor emphasizes discipleship or the development of every person into being like Jesus, which means regular worship, conservative lifestyle choices, supporting local programs, and global mission work. Still, the Christian and Missionary Alliance Church has wrestled over the role of women in ministry and specifically whether or not women can serve as elders. At a national meeting in 2012, the denomination voted to allow women to be ordained. The congregation is also in the midst of a multi-million dollar campaign for developing and renovating the facility. Believing they can impact the city and the world, followers regularly give time and money as a sign of commitment to the congregation and its goals. As we discuss in chapter 8, evangelicals generously support their churches with time and money, which is part of the reason for their relative vitality. Another reason for their vitality is the priority they place on training and retaining their youth and children. Congregations in our sample were more likely to consider youth and children's ministry a top priority over any other priority, as discussed in chapter 7.

The congregation is also focused on outreach. Pastor Luke says, "Knowing God, loving others, and serving the world" is our mission. The congregation places a high value on discipleship, which means teaching everyone to be like Jesus, pray regularly, read the Bible, and serve others. Pastor Luke says, "This church gives a ridiculous amount of money to a benevolent fund that really enables us to do a lot of significant things in the community." Recently they hired a parish nurse and a social worker who work part-time out of the congregation: "Our parish nurse has been a good thing. She's done a lot of community events where she'll have seminars on things like depression or on caring for elderly parents or just different kinds of ways to make a difference." The congregation believes these types of ministries allow them to be generous in the city and to be, says Pastor Luke, an "incarnational presence in the community." About $150,000 is raised annually for the benevolent fund. Other ministries include English as a second language (ESL) classes for immigrants in the city. The spirit of serving is also expressed through their mission work in other countries either through supporting full-time workers or sending short-term volunteers from the congregation.

When asked to talk about what attracts people to the congregation, Pastor Luke says, with a little laugh, "We've been asking that question. I think that initially, we have a relatively attractive facility ... I think most people would say our services are relatively pleasant experiences, the seats are padded and the preacher, he's okay ... And the music is not bad. There are probably worse shows in town." Pastor Tim goes on to talk about the children's program as one of the more important ministries for people: "We're a nice respectable church that needs to become not less nice or less respectable. But, I'd love for us to become more impassioned, a little more dangerous, a little more involved in our community. We hear that the church is the hope of the world and I think Jesus is the hope of the world. He promised he'd build his church and his plan to change the world is through the church. While there's much to be cynical about the church, it's still God's plan and I love the church and I think if you love Jesus you love his church."

Christian Reformed Church, Vancouver

In the eastern suburbs of Metro Vancouver and into the Fraser Valley there are many Christian Reformed congregations. Originally founded by Dutch immigrants, these congregations built Christian schools as well as alternative sports programs, like the popular Church Hockey League for their members. One congregation, in particular, is about twenty years old and offers a stability appreciated by its members. The current pastor, Pastor Dave, only the third in its history, says, "I don't think the church has ever experienced a decline and my analysis of that has to do with healthy leadership in the sense that the board or the consistory has had fairly mature, wise, leadership for the better amount of time." The congregation has a strong sense of being hospitable, caring, welcoming, and outreach focused. Pastor Dave's emphasis is on strong leadership as important to vital congregations and is something we heard repeatedly from denominational leaders.

Pastor Dave says, "The hospitality factor is significant. We have a number of individuals who are gifted in finding new faces and making a point of meeting them, greeting them, having them over for coffee." The congregation established care groups to help integrate new people. Over 50 per cent are involved in a care group where new people can make friends. Pastor Dave also tries to visit new people at least once: "Integrating people into the church is fairly intentional." The congregation has twelve elders who meet with every family or every individual over a two-year period: "It's a fairly aggressive visitation program." Yet, for a large congregation, says Pastor

Dave, "We have a small church feel, where members of the church feel like they have access to the pastor." Caring and hospitality reflect Pastor Dave's view of the nature of the congregation: "The church is a hub of kingdom relationships within our community. It becomes a focal point of relationship with God as community. It becomes a resourcing and encouragement centre for those who are going out as light into their everyday lives. It becomes an equipping centre."

Over the years they have helped construct new buildings for congregations in Mexico, allowing members an opportunity to use their gifts to help others. The youth are active in short-term mission trips and other activities that help to demonstrate practical love and care around the city. Members in the congregation actively mentor the youth where they learn to serve others. But that has also impacted the whole congregation: "I would say our youth Mexico mission has profoundly influenced our congregation." The value of modelling Christian faith in action or in some sort of service is said to encourage and motivate others to do good things. A strong youth program, says Pastor Dave, is highly attractive for people looking for a congregation.

The pastor also describes the congregation as intentional about biblical-centred worship and preaching: "We are a Reformed Church with a reformed history, with hymns, and we have blended that with contemporary Christian music, and we are intentionally reformed and liturgical. We have a definite liturgy where there's a confession and assurance, and we are very intentional at helping people understand why we do what we do in terms of the order of worship." Pastor Dave also confessed he plays the guitar during worship. "But I don't sing," he says, "or people would start leaving." Approximately 500 people attend one of the two weekly services on a regular basis. The pastor claims the membership has grown by about 25 per cent over the past six years. The average weekly attendance, however, only increased by about 10 per cent. "Life is very busy for people with work and other commitments," he said, "and it is hard for people to come to church regularly." The church operates the Alpha program, a course for new Christians or for people who want to learn about Christianity. A women's group meets each week for Bible study and coffee. Care groups and strong leadership give people a sense of stability.

While the cultural heritage of the members is Dutch, the pastor and congregation recognize the need to become more diverse, reaching out to people around them. The pastor said a Korean congregation is now sharing the facility. On occasion some of the Koreans will attend their worship service. It may be a challenge for this congregation to connect with other ethnic groups. Yet, the congregation is trying to change so it can minister to the people around it. In Vancouver, this means that previous waves of immigrants, like the Dutch, are declining, as larger waves of immigrants arrive from China, South Asia, and Korea. "I think part of our ministry," says Pastor Dave, "is opening our church" to new immigrants.

These snapshots of specific churches show something of the unique congregational cultures that we found across the country. They are big and small, white and non-white, growing and shrinking, traditional and emergent, urban and rural. The similarities hint at the evolving evangelical subculture, which remains pervasive, even if it does not breed uniform congregations. These congregational and evangelical cultural elements are the focus of the next chapter.

2

On Cultures and Subcultures

Evangelical congregations are producers of a distinctive culture. It is this distinctiveness that helps explain why evangelicalism remains an institutionally centred religious tradition in a cultural climate of declining (Christian) religious participation. This chapter begins by explaining congregational culture, and then explains how congregational cultures interact with the larger evangelical subculture and the (even larger) Canadian culture. This lays the foundation for understanding why institutional religion is declining in Canada, and why evangelicalism is the Christian exception.

DISTINCTIVE CONGREGATIONS

The distinctive orthodoxy and orthopraxy evangelical congregations promote is often not supported by the norms of society. The natural result is a degree of tension with non-evangelicals and the broader Canadian culture. This tension does not stem primarily from aggressive opposition or open ridicule (Reimer, 2003; Smith, 2000). After all, Canadians tend to be civil and irenic. When evangelicals invite others to church, they are more likely to get a "No thanks, but I am glad church works for you" kind of response than mocking scorn. In a cultural climate that celebrates diversity, tensions with society tend to be much more subtle.

Of course, evangelical tension with the larger society runs both ways. Evangelicals sense that they are not always well liked, and that certain (exclusivist) views and attitudes they hold are not appreciated. Reginald Bibby's Project Canada 2005 data show that non-evangelical Canadians are often uneasy meeting "born again Christians." In fact, they are more uncomfortable meeting them, on average, than meeting "homosexual males" or "lesbians."[1] Evangelicals also perceive that the media portray them negatively, and research suggests there is support for this conclusion (Haskell, 2007). Conversely, evangelicals (in Canada and the United States) do not feel warmly toward groups that they think undermine their values, and they are concerned that societal values are sliding into secularism. Yet, in true Canadian fashion, evangelicals show high tolerance and civility toward individuals – including homosexuals and atheists – even if they oppose their views. They distinguish between *individuals* and *issues*, showing more compassion to the former while remaining staunch on the latter (Reimer, 2011). Nonetheless, tensions over issues do exist, and they are related to the distinctiveness of evangelicalism in Canada.

Pastors and lay leaders teach nonconformity in belief and practice, but they often find their efforts undermined by the subtle influences of the broader culture. In modern society, the faithful are not allured by foreign idols made of wood, stone, or precious metal. The "invisible idols" of consumerism, narcissism, secularism, and even individualism are bigger threats. As a result, those in the pew are often unaware of influences that undermine their religious distinctiveness. Evangelical pastors promote evangelization, when most Canadians think religious views should stay private and religious groups should peaceably coexist. Discussing religion with others is awkward in such a climate, and so evangelicals show declining commitment to evangelism (Reimer, 2003). Clergy urge congregants to find ways to show "love for your neighbour," both in the community and in the church, in a culture where voluntarism is declining and leisure time is entertainment-focused. They encourage prayer and meditation on Scripture even when the broader society rewards productivity. Youth exposure to the Internet and movies undermines their efforts to promote sexual chastity. Some stand firm. Others go with the larger cultural flow in ways they may not realize. Some mix influences from the "world" with those of the "church," sometimes in incoherent and eclectic ways.[2] Whether the Canadian evangelical behaves and thinks more like a devoted evangelical or more like a typical Canadian has a lot to do with how well enmeshed they are in an evangelical congregation.

The distinctive religiosity that evangelical congregations seek to promote is analogous to a minority language, suggests evangelical ecclesiologist Jonathan Wilson (2006). Of course, a language comes easiest to those who grow up speaking it. Native speakers, who were taught the language from a young age, are most fluent. Those who were introduced to the language later in life must first learn the grammatical rules (and exceptions to the rules), and this may be why the language seems particularly rule bound to outsiders or new speakers. However, once someone is comfortable with the language, that someone forgets the rules and its use becomes second nature. In addition, there is more to learning languages than memorizing vocabulary and the rules of grammar, because languages are part of larger cultures. To learn Korean, for example, a language learner must know something about Korean cultural norms and values. It is necessary to know that age differences are important and that one does not address an older person the same way one addresses a younger person. One must learn to "think" Korean. In the words of eminent sociologist Peter Berger (1969), religious devotees are "cognitive minorities ... a group of people whose view of the world differs significantly from the one generally taken for granted in their society" (6). Similarly, congregations must teach fledgling evangelicals not only how to act, but also how to think.

One problem with a minority language is that it is rarely used in daily life. It is easy to lose fluency. Or, you can pick up poor grammar when people around you use the language improperly. From an evangelical viewpoint, many in the broader society claim to be (religiously) fluent, but in reality they are not. False teachers of the language encourage people to express their language intuitively and creatively, ignoring proper grammar (as historically defined). Thus, evangelicals must frequently gather with and learn from those who are truly fluent – especially those more fluent than they themselves are. They must be taught to emulate great historical figures who used the language beautifully – those whose words are recorded in (sacred) texts. Clergy patiently correct vocabulary, grammar, and diction, pointing out those areas where correct usage has been undermined by day-to-day "worldly" interaction. For this reason, clergy must be thoroughly "bilingual." They should be well trained in the minority language, but also fully aware of the broader societal influences that undermine fluency.

If two strangers meet, it often does not take long for them to realize they share a common minority language. One can pick up cues from the words and actions of another. Once this realization is made, a deeper relational bond can be formed, as if an alternate, shared reality has been opened up to them. They share a love for and experiences of the "homeland." This reality can be more significant than the world of their day-to-day experience, since it represents ultimate reality. Naturally, people like to interact with others who share this deeper bond. Those fluent in the language can also evaluate the language skills of those they meet. Among evangelicals, subcultural boundaries are like grammar rules, which set limits around acceptable belief and behaviour. Watching another's behaviour is one way to tell if that person is "authentic." One can also discern fellow native speakers by whether or not they have an evangelical "vocabulary." Do they talk about being "saved" and having a "personal quiet time"? Do they know of popular evangelical music artists and authors? This is what Tanya Luhrmann demonstrated in her study of evangelical converts who later in life had to learn a new language including what is meant when one talks to God or how to talk about a God who speaks to them (2012).

The language metaphor illustrates congregational culture. According to leading sociologist Nancy Ammerman, "congregations ... are subcultures within a larger culture" (1998, 78). Any group of people that gathers together regularly, for religious reasons or otherwise, will develop symbols, stories, conventions, and identity unique to the group (Hopewell, 1987). Becker (1999) submits that "congregations develop distinct cultures that comprise local understandings of identity and mission and that can be understood analytically as bundles of core tasks and legitimate ways of doing things" (7). These "bundles" of tasks and ways of doing include rituals, worship styles, programs, and the beliefs, values, and mission statements that motivate them.

Congregational cultures, like all subcultures, are emergent realities that are greater than the sum of their parts. That is, the interaction between congregants – who gather, serve, teach, sing, evangelize, pray, study, and eat together – creates a social reality that is bigger than any one person involved in it. To continue the language metaphor, these emergent realities are like the intonation with which a statement is made, that often connotes more than the sum of the words that make it up. When people say, "That is a welcoming church" or "Church is boring," they are referring to a reality that is larger than any one person, including the pastor, even if he or she has the greatest influence. An organization like a congregation is greater than the sum of its parts because congregational cultures form not primarily from individual congregants themselves (as separate entities), but from the interaction between them. This is true to the degree that individuals are not atomistic, but interact to form a shared culture.[3]

Culture is often implicit. Just as a fluent speaker of a language uses the language with little thought, certain ways of doing or thinking in a congregation become the "default" that is followed without thinking. Few wonder why Communion is held the first Sunday of each month or why the sermon comes after the offering and special music. "That is the way we do it around here" may be the answer when these ways of doing are questioned. Since the combination of history, size, location, and people that form a congregation is unique, all congregations have unique cultures.

Congregational uniqueness, however, does not mean congregational cultures are formed from scratch, or that they have no similarities. Rather, congregations are "carriers" of religious traditions (Ammerman 1998). Evangelical congregations tend to be similar because they all draw from the norms within the evangelical subculture and their denominational culture. Congregations are also shaped by their local context and Canadian culture. Just as some modern languages draw from the same root languages (e.g., Latin), limiting the language variation in the world, so congregations draw from a storehouse of cultural ingredients that are available to them (Becker, 1999). They may intentionally or unintentionally select these ingredients, avoiding some broader cultural influences while embracing others. In this way, the subcultural boundaries of congregations are always permeable, regardless of their degree of tension or distinctiveness. The influences of the broader culture seep in, particularly in those areas that are not perceived to be a threat to orthodoxy and orthopraxy.

Although congregations use available cultural repertoires, we should not view congregational culture as simply the sum of cultural pieces taken from external sources. In reality, congregants create "culture in interaction" (Eliasoph and Lichterman, 2003). Similar organizations, for example, churches of the same denomination in close geographical proximity (Becker, 1999) can be very different because they create unique cultures through the interaction process. To mix metaphors, consider a bebop artist creating a Christmas album. The singer will apply his or her "style" to a musical piece originally from a different genre (consider, e.g., "White Christmas"). It may be true that no one else sings "White Christmas" quite that way, yet the innovations will be somewhat predictable, in that there will still be a recognizable genre (bebop) and lyrics ("White Christmas"); see Eliasoph and Lichterman, (2003). In the same way, congregants have considerable room to innovate in their use of culturally available repertoires, blending and bending them as they interact to create a new congregational culture. Yet the congregation will still have a "family resemblance" to its denomination or national culture, as cultural elements are borrowed from what "styles" are available to it (Brubaker, Loveman, and Stamatov, 2004).

CONGREGATIONS AND THE EVANGELICAL SUBCULTURE

Just as interaction forms a congregational culture, so evangelical congregations are the building blocks of the larger evangelical subculture. In *Evangelicals and the Continental Divide* (2003), Reimer argues that "there exists a transdenominational transnational evangelical subculture in North America. This subculture is distinctive, and those active in it have a clear sense of identity, a clear understanding of the subcultural boundaries, and knowledge of the norms and values associated with it" (21). When evangelicals on both sides of the 49th parallel described their faith, they consistently emphasized the centrality of a conversion experience (often called being "born again"), the centrality of Jesus Christ as the only way to salvation, the authority of the Bible, and the importance of orthopraxy, including regular church attendance, evangelism, and social action. The ways evangelicals talked about their faith matched Bebbington's well-known quadrilateral (1989) of (1) conversionism, (2) crucicentrism, (3) biblicism, and (4) activism, mentioned in the introduction. These are the four defining characteristics of evangelicalism. It was clear that these characteristics were central to the shared identity of both Canadian and American evangelicals.

Active evangelicals from diverse locales and denominational traditions also showed agreement on subcultural boundaries. They agreed on who is an evangelical and who is not (based on orthodox beliefs and a conversion experience), which groups they were close to (like Pro-Life groups, or other evangelicals), and which groups they were far from (like Hollywood movie producers and secular humanists). They have matching behavioural expectations, which include congregational participation and devotional practices like reading the Bible and praying. They shared very similar moral boundaries, particularly in areas of sexuality. Of course, there were some national and regional differences, including political alignment and tolerance (Reimer, 2003). However, the strength of the evangelical subculture leads to a fair bit of similarity between congregations, even across denominational and national divides. Believers can go to evangelical congregations in various places in North America and find a familiar message; this message emphasizes such things as religious conversion, the importance and protection of the traditional family (coupled with traditional sexual mores), the authority of the Bible, loving one's neighbour, and the like. This isomorphism increases the legitimacy of the evangelical congregation, and adds to its appeal.

Of course, congregations are not the only organizations that contribute to the evangelical subculture. Para-church organizations like Focus on the Family, Intervarsity Christian Fellowship, or World Vision also contribute to it. Para-church organizations produce evangelical music, books, teaching videos, conferences, and Sunday School curricula; they offer outlets for philanthropic giving and volunteering, educational opportunities, pastoral training, and a fair bit of evangelical kitsch that is marketed in Christian bookstores throughout North America and elsewhere. Educational institutions – including Tyndale University College and Seminary (formerly the Ontario Bible College and Seminary), Briercrest College and Seminary, and many evangelical private elementary schools, high schools, and colleges – train future leaders across denominations (Stackhouse, 1993). Sharing the same educational environment breeds similarities between pastors and other congregational leaders, both theological and otherwise, which in turn lead to similarities in the congregations. While these para-church organizations are important, they regularly reach their constituents through the congregations, which again form the link between cultural creators and the person in the pew.

If strong religious subcultures require regular interactions between co-religionists, normally accomplished in congregations,

44   A CULTURE OF FAITH

and if they are the conduit through which subcultural forces shape
individual adherents just as individuals shape the subculture, then
institutional religion is necessary for religious vitality. That is, institutional religion is needed to maintain religious commitment. This
position is as old as Emile Durkheim (1995 [1912]), a founder of sociology, who stated, "The idea of religion is inseparable from the idea
of a Church" and "religion must be an eminently collective thing" (44).
While we do not advocate conflating all religion with its institutional
forms (Luckmann, 1967), we do think that collective ritual, relational
bonding with co-religionists, collective identity, and shared beliefs
and boundaries – in short, collective religion which is normally institutionalized – are necessary for vigorous religion. Canadian evidence
supports this assertion. Bowen (2004), based on data from multiple
Canadian surveys, found that those Canadians who say religion is
important to them but do not participate in religious institutions are
not very distinct from those with no religion, and their religiosity
has few consequences for their daily life. By comparison, the institutionally committed are distinct in many areas, including claimed quality of relationships, greater concern for the welfare of others, much
higher levels of voluntarism and charitable giving, and distinctive
beliefs. Bowen argues that this should not be surprising: "Without
the shared rituals, joint projects, and reinforcements of communal
life, commitment to any cause is surely weakened" (281).

We think that the key social mechanisms that explain evangelical
institutional religiosity and relative vitality stem from the congregations themselves. Whatever else happens in these congregations, we
know that somehow they support the distinct set of beliefs, values,
and/or behaviours that keep people in congregations, as the larger
society does not seem to provide the props that hold up religious
participation.

CANADA'S RELIGIOUS CLIMATE

The "language" of the evangelical minority was the language of the
majority in Canada a century ago. Historian Michael Gauvreau
(1991) aptly called the nineteenth century in Canada the "Evangelical
Century." Even the (now comparatively liberal) United Church of
Canada – which brought together Methodists, Presbyterians, and

Congregationalists in 1925 – formed because of a broad and moderate evangelical consensus (Plaxton, 1997). Evangelical Protestant religiosity held sway in English-speaking Canada throughout the nineteenth century until about the middle of the twentieth century. The Protestants shaped the politics, economy, health care, and education of English-speaking Canadians. The cultural power of the Catholic Church was even stronger in Quebec. Even up to sixty years ago, American historian Mark Noll (2006) felt that Canada had "a much stronger claim as a 'Christian nation'" than did its southern neighbour (251).

We should not assume that the "evangelical century" prior to the Second World War indicated widespread religious commitment. Many attended church (at least partly) to socialize with friends, to find an eligible spouse, to gain social status (pew rents demarcated the rich from the poor in many congregations), or for other impious reasons. Clergy have long complained about the lack of piety and devotion, even in the Victorian era (see, e.g., Murphy, 1996). Societal norms supported congregational participation. Since the 1960s, however, Canadian culture has done little to buttress congregational participation. Many accepted the Enlightenment conviction that religion was nearing extinction, replaced by modern, scientific ways of knowing. As a result, fewer people were interested in what congregations had to offer. Going to church was like learning a dead (or dying) language.

In his important article, "What Happened to Christian Canada?" (2006), Mark Noll outlines the major changes that precipitated the post-war growth and then rapid decline of institutional religion in Canada. After the Second World War, the optimism fuelled by economic boom and a desire to "get back to normal" among Canadians also fuelled religious attendance. Capitalizing on the opportunity, the United Church alone built 1,500 congregations between 1945 and 1965 (Grant, 1988). However, the attendance boom of the late 1940s and 1950s "owed more to the cohesive nationalism of the war effort and the search for normalcy during the postwar economic expansion than to the religious dynamism of the churches themselves" (Noll, 2006, 256). It "evoked few signs of spiritual awakening among civilians" (162), and had more to do with the desire for moral training for the children of the baby boom. Added to this was anxiety over atomic war (from the Cold War) and job security (a residue from the Great Depression).

Even in these anxious times, the appeal of the churches was not ubiquitous. Growth came from the suburban and middle class more than the urban, rural, or lower-class Canadians (Grant, 1988).

The anti-establishment ethos of the 1960s eroded the authority of Canadian Christianity, particularly the more established mainline Protestants and Catholics. By the 1960s, the churches seemed irrelevant to many. Pierre Berton, in *The Comfortable Pew* (1965), may have best captured the public sentiment. His personal drift from Anglicanism corresponded to a time when a lot of Canadians were leaving the church, not out of anger as much as boredom. "In the great issues of our time," he wrote, "the voice of the Church, when it has been heard at all, has been weak, tardy, equivocal, and irrelevant" (30). Its irrelevance, he thought, was related to its lost distinctiveness: "The institution of religion, which once generated its own values, now merely gives its blessing to the majority held values of the community around it" (94). Once the churches were sidelined in society, attendance was not a priority.

A decade or so later, Canada began to move away from its historic Christian identity toward a vision of a multicultural country, a vision promoted by Prime Minister Pierre Trudeau. Multiculturalism meant that no religious ideology was given precedence; instead, mutual toleration and respect were to mark Canada's cultural ethos. Aiding the transition was the decoupling of religious traditions from political parties, education, and provision of other services. Concerns over regional politics (including Quebec's near separation on two different occasions), restitution for a history of abuse of Aboriginals (and other minorities), economic recession, and other factors captured Canadian attention. The Charter of Rights and Freedoms of 1982 fed these preoccupations, focusing attention on individual rights and away from religion. The result, argues Noll (2006), was that "the social cohesion that the churches once provided is now offered by political and economic loyalties or by ideologies of toleration, personal growth, and multiculturalism" (261). The change may be seen most compellingly in Quebec, where the Catholic/Protestant identities and tensions were replaced by political and linguistic alliances.

Other factors that contributed to the loss of Protestant hegemony outside Quebec were related to increased non-European and non-Christian immigrants, theological disagreements within Protestantism (Clarke, 1996), urbanization coupled with increased pluralism, and consumerism. Like the Catholic *aggiornamento* of Vatican II, the Protestant churches realized their need to update to align themselves with rapid societal changes. A spirit of reform gripped Christian churches in the 1960s and 1970s. Reforms included moving toward more democratic governance, lay participation, modernizing music and worship styles, and encouraging interfaith dialogue. However, even the most forward-thinking efforts to modernize could not keep up with cultural change. They did as much to reinforce the outmoded nature of church as make it relevant, and showed that the churches had lost their authority in society (Murphy, 1996).

The attendance boom of the 1950s and the decline of the 1960s affected evangelical congregations less than other Christian denominations, and their reaction to these social changes was unique. Instead of trying to update and accommodate, evangelical congregations tried to hold unflinchingly to their traditional beliefs. To them, the changes in society were evidence of a growing apostasy among both the mainstream denominations and mainstream culture. Their reaction included an effort to provide an alternate set of values for Canada, adding to their long-existing emphasis on evangelization. They began to organize, hoping to provide a prophetic voice in society, a role they felt the other Christian groups had abandoned through compromise (Grant, 1988). In 1964, cooperation between evangelical denominations resulted in the formation of the Evangelical Fellowship of Canada (EFC). The conspicuousness of evangelicals in Canadian society has grown with the EFC and other evangelical educational, philanthropic, and political organizations. This does not necessarily mean that evangelicals in Canada have grown in political or social influence. Rather, they are just one voice among a growing cacophony of diverse groups seeking to influence political and social outcomes.

Today, evangelicals and other Christian groups have lost most of their former cultural privilege. As Bramadat and Seljak (2005) argue, religious groups in Canada are trying to negotiate a new public relationship in a pluralistic state. On the one hand, evangelicals struggle to adapt to Canadian pluralism. Especially since the 1990s many immigrants coming to Canada are Muslims, Hindus, and Sikhs. Many are also Christians. Diversity for evangelicals in Canada means wrestling with their identity in relation to non-Christian groups and to non-European Christians arriving in Canada, and even coming to their congregations (Beyer, 2008; Bramadat and Seljak, 2005, 2008;

48   A CULTURE OF FAITH

Wilkinson, 2006). The impact on evangelical congregations is still to be determined.

On the other hand, Canada has struggled with religious pluralism. Bramadat and Seljak (2005) argue that the general population is ignorant when it comes to understanding the different religious traditions. As a result, they are often misunderstood and feel misrepresented by the media. Managing religious and ethnic diversity in public institutions like those for education and health care has also been difficult.[4] The net result of these Canadian cultural and demographic changes is declining institutional Christianity in Canada. First, we look at the numbers. Then we look at the cultural mechanisms that influenced these changes.

Gallup polls showed that weekly attendance in Canada at religious services was somewhere between 54 per cent and 61 per cent in the 1950s (Bowen, 2004), which is higher than attendance figures in the United States at the same time (Bibby 2011, 5). As seen in Table 2.1, weekly attendance had dropped to 30.3 per cent in 1985, and 16.3 per cent in 2010. While Bibby (2002) submits that there has been a slight upward trend in church attendance since the mid-1990s, these data and others suggest continued decline, at least among those who attend weekly or more often. The decline does seem to be slowing in the past decade, however.

David Eagle (2011) observes that church attendance has continued to decline in the past twenty to twenty-five years. This is largely because Catholic attendance (in both Quebec and outside Quebec) continues to decline, whereas Protestant attendance is relatively flat, or even increasing. Eagle also shows that the move away from the churches is much greater than seen in just attendance figures. Those with no religious affiliation are growing rapidly, and this increase adds to declining attendance, as "nones" rarely attend. He also shows that women, those with children at home, the foreign-born, and those with university degrees are more likely to attend. Older cohorts of Protestants (and much less so Catholics) are more likely to attend religious services than younger cohorts (cohort effect), and Protestants attend more frequently as they age (aging effect). Bibby (2006) maintains that much of the decline in congregational attendance can be attributed to the "boomer factor," as recent cohorts have inherited a tendency toward selective or no attendance from their baby boomer parents. Hiemstra (2012)[5] also shows that the largest decline in church attendance is among the boomer cohort.

Table 2.1 Canadians' church attendance, 1985–2010 (%)

Attendance	1985	1990	1995	2000	2005	2010
Weekly or more often	30.3	27.8	26.5	25.3	21.1	16.3
Never	21.5	26.5	31.9	26.1	32.8	N/A

Source: Lindsay (2008) and Statistics Canada (2012).
N/A = not available

Statistics Canada data do not allow Eagle to distinguish between mainline and evangelical Protestants; however, when all Protestants are combined, they seem to be doing better than Catholics in terms of congregational participation.[6] Fortunately for our purposes, Bibby's and Angus Reid's data do distinguish between the two traditions, because they ask respondents to give their denominational affiliation. In Table 2.2 we present attendance rates of those who claim affiliation with each tradition and claim to attend religious services "weekly" or "several times a week," based on Bibby's Project Canada data, over a thirty-year period. Note that the percentages are lower than what Bibby reports as he included the "nearly every week" category in his weekly attendance figures.

It is more important to look at overall trends in the table, as the minor fluctuations can be attributed to sampling error. For example, the subsamples of evangelicals are not large (normally between 75 and 100 respondents), and so minor blips are expected. The trend seems to be that evangelical attendance is going up, and possibly mainline Protestant attendance as well. Are the surprisingly high attendance rates among evangelicals due to sampling error? We think not. Recent data from other sources support this conclusion. Based on Angus Reid's 2011 panel data of over 30,000 Canadians, 56 per cent of evangelical affiliates attend services weekly or more often compared with 18.3 per cent of Catholics, 13.3 per cent of United Church affiliates, 18.6 per cent of Presbyterians, 16.1 per cent of Anglicans, and 21.5 per cent of Lutherans.[7] Ipsos Reid's 2006 election poll of the same size put evangelical weekly or more often attendance at 48.7 per cent, compared with 12.5 per cent and 14.1 per cent for mainline Protestants and Catholics, respectively. These data with large evangelical subsamples (around 3,000 each) confirm that roughly 50 per cent of evangelical Canadians claim to attend religious services weekly or more often. It is likely that weekly or more often

Table 2.2 Canadians who claimed to attend church weekly or more often, by religious tradition, 1975–2005 (%)

	1975	1980	1985	1990	1995	2000	2005
Evangelicals	31.2	42.0	44.3	41.8	50.6	45.7	53.1
Mainline Protestants	9.4	8.6	6.2	7.6	10.7	10.2	11.7
Catholics outside Quebec	34.0	34.4	22.5	22.5	26.4	22.4	31.9
Quebec Catholics	30.2	30.2	22.1	21.3	19.0	16.4	11.6
Other	10.9	16.3	15.9	13.5	11	19.9	17.7
None	0	0	0	1	0	0	0
All Canadians	19.3	19.6	15.5	15.8	16.9	15.6	18.8

Source: Reginald Bibby's Project Canada datasets.

attendance is propped up in some traditions because those who rarely attend drop their affiliation over time, thus removing rarely attending affiliates into the "none" category. We suspect this is part of the reason that Catholic weekly attendance appears to be declining while Protestant attendance is steady. Mainline Protestants have experienced mass disaffiliation, likely at a much higher rate than Catholics (particularly Catholics in Quebec). Between 1961 and 2001, Protestant affiliation fell from 41 per cent to 20 per cent of Canadians, while the Catholic population share remained fairly stable, near 45 per cent (census data cited in Bibby, 2006; 2011). However, the proportion of evangelical affiliates in Canada has been steady at between 8 per cent and 10 per cent over time (Bibby, 2006), so disaffiliation does not inflate their attendance numbers much.[8]

If we combine all these factors – disaffiliation and rapidly growing "nones," younger cohorts attending less than older cohorts, declining percentages of Christian immigrants, and falling attendance rates – the future of institutional Christian religion in Canada does not look promising.

EXPLAINING THE DECLINE OF INSTITUTIONAL RELIGION

There are two common answers to the question of why institutional religiosity is declining in Canada. The first is that there are problems with demand. In other words, people are not looking for churches anymore, because they are not interested in what churches have to offer. Churches, it is said, used to be able to build a building, hang up a sign, and people would come. By the 1960s, the flow of people who "dropped in" to churches started to dry up, and now it is more likely that people will drop out than drop in. Who or what is to blame for this lack of interest? Researchers usually say it is related to changes in Canadian society. Modernization and pluralism breed secularization, some argue, and religion loses its authority in the private lives of individuals as well as in the public sphere (e.g., Bruce, 2011). Others point to an expanding life-stage called "emerging adulthood," where the lifestyle of the "twenty-something" is not conducive to institutional religion (e.g., Arnett, 2004). While some young adults return to religious institutions once they get married and have children, the fact that they start families later in life means that they are away from churches longer, which diminishes the likelihood of returning. Still others point to time pressures, increased by the growing number of dual-earner and single-parent households (Bibby, 2011; Edgell, 2006).

The other common answer is that there are problems with supply. The churches just are not trying very hard to attract people, and they are not offering the kind of religious "products" that appeal to (particularly younger) Canadians. This is why institutional religion is shrinking, in spite of the fact that there is a fair bit of interest in spiritual things. In other words, there is a demand for the very things that religion is supposed to supply – like a sense of community and belonging, answers to life's big questions, or a relationship with God – yet churches are simply not meeting the demand (Bibby, 1993). Proponents of a supply-side problem argue that demand for religious/spiritual goods is fairly stable over time; it is the quality of the supply side that varies over time and place (Stark and Bainbridge, 1985).

Some supply-side scholars say that congregations and denominations have vitality if they are strict. Originating with Dean Kelley in the 1970s (see *Why Conservative Churches Are Growing*, 1972), this theory has been developed by Stark, Finke, Iannaccone, and others. Strict congregations, or those that are in tension with the society, are more likely to grow because they offer higher rewards (like rewards from a highly responsive, personal God) but at high cost (a God that requires devotion and separation from the world). High-cost religion results in a committed laity, because its adherents maintain tension with the world, which makes "heavenly" rewards more appealing than "earthly" ones. Strict congregations also screen out "free riders" or those who attend but do not contribute. Free riders compromise the overall value of the rewards enjoyed by committed members. Since growing congregations need resources like volunteer time and money from their congregants, those that are demanding are more likely to grow because of the sacrificial giving of its more committed laity (Iannaccone, Olson, and Stark, 1995; Stark and Finke, 2000).

We think both supply and demand problems contribute to the downturn in congregational participation (see Beyer, 1997).[9] Larger societal trends are not supportive of institutional religiosity. However, some congregations and traditions are doing better than others, so it is not simply reduced demand. Evangelical congregations are buffeted by many of the same unfriendly societal forces as other Christian congregations yet manage to have higher levels of participation and institutional commitment. Since our research focuses on congregations, we focus on the supply-side factors here.

Yet, to answer the question, "Why does evangelicalism remain an institutional form of religion in Canada?" we need more than theories of supply and demand. These theories focus more on the societal level of religious vitality and speak also to denominational growth. We know that the key mechanisms for growth are birth rates and immigration patterns and, to a much lesser extent, denominational switching or conversions (Bibby, 2011; Hadaway and Roozen, 1993; Scheitle, Kane, and Van Hook, 2011). Here, however, we are interested more in issues of retention. Why do evangelicals continue to participate in congregations, when most cultural supports for participation are long gone? The question is not about attributes of Canadian society as a whole, like secularization or the lack thereof.[10] We are interested in the mechanisms that distinguish evangelical congregational religious participation from those of other Canadian Christian traditions. In sum, we focus on those subcultural and congregational factors that promote congregational commitment and are distinct or more prevalent in evangelical congregations in Canada. This is what we think offers the best answers from a sociological perspective.

SUBCULTURAL FACTORS

Congregations thrive partly because of the supra-organizational norms and beliefs within their denomination or religious tradition (Roozen and Hadaway, 1993). The evangelical subculture promotes shared characteristics across evangelical denominations and beyond. The characteristics of this subculture also lend to its vitality, argues Christian Smith, in his book *American Evangelicalism* (1998). In pluralistic societies, religious groups that distinguish themselves from the broader society (through tension with the "world" and with certain "outgroups"), while remaining engaged with the broader culture, will be relatively stronger. The strongest religious groups are not those that separate from society and become countercultural, like certain fundamentalist groups. Rather, it is the process of "rubbing shoulders" with those who are different that strengthens subcultural boundaries and religious identities. Religious groups that maintain their central orthodoxies while adjusting their emphases and boundaries to (or in reaction to) the push and pull of larger cultural trends do better in the long run. However, clear boundaries are not enough. Religious groups must provide meaning, through which the person makes sense of the world and his or her purpose in it. Smith suggests that the sterility of modern materialism and secularism does not provide the normative answers people seek, thus increasing the appeal of identity-forming religion. Finally, the group must provide a sense of belonging that is salient. He suggests that for evangelicals, their religious identity remains primary partly because it involves personal choice; it is not something that is simply ascribed or inherited. Smith concludes that a "subcultural identity theory of religious persistence is this: Religion survives and can thrive in pluralistic, modern society by embedding itself in subcultures that offer satisfying morally orienting collective identities which provide adherents meaning and belonging" (118). Smith notes that evangelicalism is an engaged subculture that maintains a degree of tension with society, while providing religious meaning and identity to its adherents, and that is why it retains members and thrives.

Joseph Tamney's study of evangelical Protestant congregations in "Middletown, USA" led him to conclude that these groups succeed in late modernity, not because they have remained unflinchingly traditional in an ever-changing society, but because they accommodated

54   A CULTURE OF FAITH

in some ways while maintaining distinctiveness in others. In his book, *The Resilience of Conservative Religion* (2002), Tamney calls evangelical congregations neither modern nor traditional, but submits that these combine in a "modernized traditionalism" (230). By this he means that evangelicalism has accommodated to a modern "affluence ethic" and "self-realization ethos" (230–1) while remaining traditional in certain theological and moral ways. The affluence ethic has undermined the traditionalist emphasis on asceticism and sacrifice, and replaced it with a religion that is fun and entertaining. Long gone is the spirituality of the monastery, where detachment from worldly pleasures of wealth and sex was esteemed. Evangelical congregations rarely speak against wealth and pleasure, and they try to make participation entertaining. The self-realization ethos promotes individual choice, self-expression (e.g, in fashion), and therapeutic relationships. Evangelical congregations are supportive, or at least accepting of individualism that has replaced the authority of the group. Technology is also fully implemented in congregations with little critical reflection. Alan Wolfe sees similar trends in *The Transformation of American Religion* (2003). American religion in general has been "Americanized" in that,

> Old-time religion is no longer good enough for [the faithful]. Talk of hell, damnation, and even sin has been replaced by a nonjudgmental language of understanding and empathy ... More Americans than ever proclaim themselves born again in Christ, but the lord to whom they turn rarely gets angry and frequently strengthens self-esteem. Traditional forms of worship, from reliance on organ music to the mysteries of the liturgy, have given way to audience participation and contemporary tastes. Some believers are anxious to witness their faith to others, but they tend to avoid methods that would make them seem unfriendly or invasive. If Jonathan Edwards were alive and well, he would likely be appalled; far from living in a world elsewhere, the faithful in the United States are remarkably like everyone else. (3)

Not surprisingly, the affluent, self-actualized, individualistic ethos of modern society has made its way into Canadian evangelicalism as well. The Pentecostal Assemblies of Canada congregations studied by Adam Stewart revealed a move toward "therapeutic expressive individualism" which transformed the way Pentecostals understand God and religious experience (2012).[11] Evangelical subcultural boundaries are porous, and their congregations absorb certain cultural influences.

In spite of some accommodation, evangelical congregations remain distinctive, and in fact, compensate for problems in late modernity, argues Tamney (2002): "I suggest that the relative success of modernized traditionalist Protestantism results from accommodating, compensating for and struggling against late-modern society" (247). For example, they compensate for the relativism in society with "authoritative congregations" that affirm traditional values and religious experiences. These congregations argue for unchanging "Truth" based on the authority of the Bible. They struggle against society particularly in areas of sexual ethics, like abortion and homosexuality. In the United States sexual issues have provided clear us-versus-them boundaries.[12] In Canada sexual issues are important to evangelicals as well, but as discussed later, congregations are not focused on these issues, and they seek to be distinctive in less politicized ways (see Simpson, 2000). It is this mix of tension and accommodation that seems to work for evangelicals and their congregations.

We think that the kind of religiosity promoted by the evangelical subculture strengthens its institutions. That is, there are certain beliefs and practices within evangelical congregations that push individuals toward institutional participation. These factors, articulated below, do not help us answer why some evangelical congregations are doing well and others are not, but they do help us understand why evangelical congregations are doing well because of their evangelicalism. However, these factors are applicable to other traditions as well. This short list is not intended to be exhaustive.

Most importantly for maintaining religious institutions, we suggest, is that the subculture (and its congregations) endorses an *external locus of authority* among its constituents. Authority, according to Max Weber (1968) is legitimate power, involving voluntary compliance because the power is accepted. The authority is external to the individual and constrains his or her behaviour. To maintain institutional allegiance in a post-institutional religious climate, this authority normally must be strong enough to be a "master status" or "primary identity." It must trump individual authority. Evangelicals will often

point to the Bible as their source of authority, which they view as
their standard for doctrine and morality. Ultimately, obeying what
the Bible says is deference to God's authority. Biblical authority is
not simply individualistic. It is mediated through the congregations.
Pastors, Sunday School teachers, and small group leaders wield considerable authority because they interpret the Bible and show how it
should be applied to modern living. Without a doubt, "evangelical
pastors exert a high degree of moral authority over their congregants"
(Welch et al., 1993, 249).

The last statement may surprise readers. Are not evangelicals
known for congregational polity, where lay members, not the hierarchy, have the power, even to hire and fire pastors? Do they not
embrace the doctrine of the "priesthood of all believers," where
adherents have an unmediated relationship with God? Is not the
Bible to be read privately and interpreted even by the untrained? Do
they not hold to personal salvation and sanctification, where each
believer is responsible for her or his own spiritual well-being? The
answer is often "yes" to all these questions, at least in theory; but
this does not necessarily result in an internal locus of authority. Nor
is there a zero-sum, either-or relationship between institutional
authority and a personal faith. Instead, there is a dynamic tension.
Evangelicals believe that the Holy Spirit of God guides an individual
privately, but also speaks corporately through the group and its leadership. Biblical truth can be understood through private reading and
through expository preaching. Most evangelicals do not hold to a
word-for-word literalist view of the Bible (at least not in practice);
the meaning of biblical texts requires interpretation. Thus, the proper
interpretation and application often come through preachers and
spiritual leaders, and evangelicals submit to their spiritual authority
partly because they hold to the authority of the Bible. That is, the
Bible itself teaches believers that they are to submit to spiritual
authority, as part of their deference to the authority of God. The
writer of the letter to the Hebrews tells believers to "have confidence
in your leaders and submit to their authority, because they keep
watch over you as those who must give an account" (Hebrews 13:17,
NIV). The Bible also admonishes the faithful to spur one another
toward good deeds, including "not giving up meeting together, as
some are in the habit of doing, but encouraging one another – and
all the more as you see the Day approaching" (Hebrews 10:25, NIV).

When people become their own religious authorities, congregationalism is undermined.

Is there evidence that an external locus of authority is key to congregational participation? The answer is "yes." Joel Thiessen (2011) interviewed marginal Christian affiliates (those who attend rarely, often at Christmas, Easter, or special events like baptisms, weddings, and funerals) and active affiliates (those who attend regularly) in Canada. He concluded that there is a "defining feature of the marginal affiliates that I interviewed, relative to the active affiliates that I spoke with ... They believe that religion is primarily an individual phenomenon" (48; see also Thiessen, 2012). For most marginal affiliates, the locus of authority was themselves, which means that they understand religious attendance to be a personal choice and that it is good as far as the individual finds it fulfilling or helpful. Alternatively, Thiessen found that the active affiliates had their religious identity as their "master status," that their faith influenced all parts of their lives. Their locus of authority was external to themselves. One active affiliate (a mainline Protestant in this instance) said, "Sometimes God asks you to do stuff that doesn't make any sense. You know, you give up control of your life" (32). This locus of authority means that believers do not get to select religious beliefs or practices that appeal to them, but must submit to God. As a result, evangelicals are less likely to "pick and choose" their religious beliefs, accepting some from a religious tradition and rejecting others, famously called "religion à la carte" by Bibby (1987). Instead, they hold to the central evangelical tenets, with little variation over time (even if there is greater selectiveness as we move from devotees to less committed affiliates). External loci of authority also means attending worship services because God commands it, or believing that Jesus is the only way to heaven even if that does not sit well with a pluralistic culture.

Unlike active affiliates, marginal affiliates attend religious services rarely, and when they do, it is often for relational reasons, like for reasons of custom or tradition. Quoting Thiessen (2011), who asked one marginal affiliate why he attended at Christmas (and very rarely otherwise):

"Custom," he replied. Each Christmas his family goes out for
Chinese food, they attend a Christmas service, and they watch

A Christmas Carol, and the Chinese food is as important as the church service. Denying that he gains any religious significance when attending, he stresses that Christmas services are an opportunity for his family to spend time together. Not unlike sitting around the fireplace and talking, the Christmas service is another social event. He even leaves money in the offering plate, comparing the church service to watching a live show. He pays for the services that others offer for his enjoyment. In terms of the benefits of attending, he says that he feels good when he leaves; "it's nice to be there." It also helps remind his family that Christmas is not just about exchanging gifts. (47)

Thiessen notes that nearly half of his marginal affiliates stopped actively attending because of some form of individualism where they determined that attendance was an individual choice. In Britain sociologist David Voas (2010) found that children attend less because parents are more focused on inculcating independence and tolerance in their children than loyalty and congregational adherence. In the United States moral autonomous individualism seems to be the modus operandi, where moral views are made up by the individual (Smith and Emerson, 2008; Smith et al., 2011). Clearly the internal locus of authority, often called individualism, is widespread, and when people select their own beliefs and behaviours, congregational attendance declines.

More evidence comes from the United States. Froese and Bader's book, *America's Four Gods* (2010), states that American views of God vary depending on whether or not God is engaged in our lives and whether God is judgmental. Evangelicals, they note, tend to have an "authoritative" (engaged and judgmental) or "benevolent" (engaged but not judgmental) God. An engaged God tends to mean that there is a transcendent moral authority that one must adhere to, as compared with a "distant" God (unengaged and not judgmental) where the individual makes choices based on individual moral authority. An engaged God provides an external locus of authority. Froese and Bader argue that "church attendance and participation are closely connected to belief in an engaged God" (152).[13]

To be clear, those active affiliates with religious master statuses are not simply blindly following their leaders. Evangelicals know that individuals are responsible for their own beliefs and actions.

And there are obviously some within the evangelical fold who have individual loci of authority, just as there are many non-evangelicals with external loci of authority. It is just that evangelicals seem to have a disproportionate number of externalized-authority, congregationally committed affiliates. What is it about their congregations that facilitates this external locus of authority?

Distinctiveness

First, evangelical congregations promote distinctiveness. An external locus of authority naturally leads, at times, to tension with the broader society. If the Bible says – or is understood to say – that premarital sex or abortion is wrong, for example, then it is wrong regardless of popular opinion or personal preference. Evangelicals are concerned about the liberalization or secularization of society, and the negative influence it can have, particularly on children and youth. Thus, Stark and Finke (2000) consider evangelicals to have a relatively high level of tension with society, something that bodes well, in their view, for their growth potential. Religious groups that are in tension with society have greater distinctiveness from society, which strengthens religious identity and commitment (Smith, 1998).

Evangelical congregations reinforce this distinctiveness. The congregations provide programs where people can mingle with co-religionists and form relationships with those who share their beliefs and identities. Congregations provide Friday night youth groups, concerts, movie nights, etc. that offer youth an alternative from what evangelicals perceive to be less wholesome social and entertainment choices. Pastors and religious teachers remind attendees of the allure of sinful vices in the "world" that can erode religious commitment. Such warnings are rarely intended to produce withdrawal from society, for evangelicals tend to actively engage with society. In fact, this engagement means that in some areas, such as use of technology or consumerism, for example (Sider, 2005), there is little distinctiveness at all. However, in areas such as sexual mores, the exclusive belief in the salvific work of Jesus Christ on the Cross, and the authority of the Bible, evangelicals remain distinctive (Reimer, 2003). Over time, some areas may become more distinctive and others less so, but the important thing for subcultural strength is that at least some salient distinctions remain.

Relational Embeddedness

Second, an institutional-friendly religiosity will be a communal religiosity. Once a constituency's religiosity becomes atomized, or "a congregation of one" (Arnett and Jensen, 2002), it is in trouble. Evangelical congregations strengthen relational embeddedness. Much research supports the contention that relationships are key to retention (and recruitment for that matter). The congregational participation of *parents* and the religious ethos they provide at home – discussing religious ideas, praying with children, etc. – are among the most powerful predictors of an adult's future congregational participation (Hoge et al., 1994; Vaidyanathan, 2011; Smith with Snell, 2009). However, the parents' efforts at religious socialization alone are not enough to maintain youth. *Other adults*, often from the congregation, form relational ties with youth and reinforce the religious values, beliefs, and behaviours of the parents, strengthening religious socialization. For all ages, *peers* that are co-religionists and co-congregants are very important for congregational participation (Cornwall, 1988). Congregations provide opportunities for *religious education* and relationship building through Sunday schools, youth groups, Bible studies, small groups, camps, and some congregations (usually larger) even run Christian schools. In sum, congregations provide institutional "space" for this relational embeddedness.

Are evangelicals in their congregations more relationally embedded than other Christian traditions? The research again says "yes." Olson (1993) found that evangelical Protestant congregations had stronger relational ties than mainline Protestant congregations, which in turn strengthens religious commitment; he argues that distinctive religious subcultures promote closer network ties and stronger religious identities. Scheitle and Smith (2011) also found that conservative Protestants are less likely to have interreligious ties. Evangelicals are well known to promote close (and traditional) family bonds, and to provide separate educational institutions for their children, youth, and young adults.

Religious Experience

Third, evangelical congregations promote personal religious experience. Much research has pointed to the modern trend toward individualistic spirituality of baby boomers and generation Xers (e.g., Roof, 1993). Moderns tend to reject the institutional religion and traditions of their parents, and they embrace personal experience as their central authority (Bellah et al., 1985). This pattern is particularly true among young adults, who pick and choose religious options that fit their personal beliefs and experiences, drawing their religious beliefs from such eclectic sources as movies, music, friends, and their knowledge of various religious traditions (Arnett and Jensen, 2002). However, the tendency toward religious atomization or individualism is curtailed if the congregations themselves sanction and promote religious experiences. Evangelical congregations are well known for promoting conversion experiences. They also promote worship experiences with emotive, modern worship styles. They get their youth and adults involved in service events, conferences, camps, and mission trips where they experience their faith in action. They promote private Bible study, prayer, and other devotional practices. All these activities spawn religious experiences that are deeply personal and yet consonant with evangelical doctrine and practice. In this way, private experiences need not trump religious socialization for ultimate authority.

Such personal religious experiences help young people make their religion their "own," not something that is simply inherited from their parents. Young evangelicals, like most young people, see the default acceptance of ascribed religious views "as a kind of failure, an abdication of their responsibility to think for themselves, become independent from their parents, and decide on their own beliefs" (Arnett and Jensen, 2002, 464). Evangelicalism has long been about personal conversion, where a personal choice to commit oneself to Christ is the first step in becoming an evangelical. Religions that promote personal choice and conviction have affinity with an individualistic and consumerist culture, argues sociologist Christian Smith (1998). They emphasize the importance of a personal relationship with God. Congregations help individuals "own" their religion by making it intensely personal, which makes it real.

Youth and Children

Finally, vital religious subcultures prioritize youth and children and their faith development. For long-term sustainability, religious groups can gain affiliates by having children (fertility) and keeping them devoted. With the prevailing culture, that is difficult to do. Evangelical authors have spilled a lot of ink on parenting advice, and researchers study children and youth, because there is a lot of parental concern about wholesome entertainment, sexual purity, and the influences of secular education. As we shall see later, evangelical congregations prioritize their youth and children. They provide children's programs, Sunday School, youth groups, mission trips, and camps. They employ children and youth pastors, all at considerable expense. Evangelicals have historically had slightly larger families than other religious groups, so they have a growth edge because of higher fertility rates.[14] However, the family size differences are quickly disappearing.

In sum, churches will have relative success in individualistic, pluralistic societies like Canada if they facilitate an external locus of authority in their constituents; supply a religiosity that is distinctive and communal, yet personally experiential; and prioritize the faith development of youth and children. We think that part of the success of evangelical congregations, and evangelicalism more broadly, then, is the type of religiosity they promote.

ORGANIZATIONAL FACTORS

But this is not the whole story. Not all congregations with the right ingredients in their religiosity are thriving. This is because congregations are more than just suppliers of a certain brand of religiosity; they are also voluntary organizations. Organizations must attract constituents, hopefully those who voluntarily give time and money. They often compete with other organizations – including other congregations, philanthropic organizations, and volunteer opportunities – for the commitment of time-pressed individuals. Congregations must also mobilize whatever volunteer force they can muster to realize their organizational goals. Since not all congregations attract and mobilize resources equally well, some evangelical congregations are not faring as well as others. The resource limitations faced by a congregation can be both internal and external.

Internal factors are those that are specific to the inner workings of the congregation itself, like its programs, musical styles, sermons, vision statements, and leadership. These internal factors relate to research on congregational health or vitality. Much of this work is from the religiously committed, including church growth consultants. The focus on internal factors began in the 1960s with the "church growth" movement, stemming from the work of Donald McGavran and Peter Wagner of Fuller Seminary. This movement gave way to an emphasis on "church health" with the likes of Christian Schwarz (Natural Church Development), Lyle Schaller, and the Alban Institute. In turn, this was replaced with an emphasis on "missional church." The move to an emphasis on "missional" thinking was very clear in our interviews, and is the focus of chapter 5.

In addition to religiously committed researchers who seek the success of congregations, there are social scientists who research church vitality (Inskeep, 1993). Faith Communities Today research out of Hartford Seminary in Connecticut and the National Church Life Surveys (originating in Sydney, Australia) are leading sources here. Their research and that of others show that the attributes that contribute to congregational vitality are related to factors like high levels of commitment and involvement, and having a clear mission and purpose statement (see McMullen, 2011). While a detailed discussion of congregational vitality is published elsewhere,[15] the key area of leadership and pastoral health is examined here in chapter 6. Denominational leaders consistently pointed to the centrality of capable pastoral leadership as the most important ingredient to congregational success, and the steady supply of quality leadership is among their greatest concerns. In spite of these concerns, evangelicals are leader-rich when compared with the shortages of priests and pastoral staff experienced by other Christian denominations in Canada (Bibby, 2004). Furthermore, evangelicalism seems to be fertile ground for the emergence of entrepreneurial pastoral leaders, who often have big churches that account for much of the evangelical institutional growth. A minority of such congregations account for the majority of denominational growth.

While congregational consultants and church growth gurus tend to emphasize the importance of internal factors, sociologists view external factors as more important (Roozen and Hadaway, 1993). External factors include, first, *national trends* like cultural attitudes toward institutional religion, or demographic trends like immigration patterns and birth rates (Bibby, 2011). Second, they look into *local contextual factors*, like whether or not the community around the congregation is growing or shrinking.

One such externally focused theoretical framework is "organizational ecology" theories, which draw attention to supra-organizational factors like the number of similar organizations in the area. Congregations, like all voluntary organizations, compete for the time and money of people in their "market niche." If there are many similar congregations nearby, and a congregation fails to establish a unique niche, it is less likely to survive. Congregations, then, are more likely to grow if they are in an area where there is an ample population of potential affiliates in their "niche" without too much "niche overlap" with competing congregations (Baum and Singh, 1994; Hannan, Carroll, and Polos, 2003; Hannan and Freeman, 1977; Scheitle, 2007).

Organizational ecology postulates that congregations will tend to have a curvilinear growth pattern, as they balance the tensions between legitimacy and competition. As they start, they lack legitimacy because they are relatively unknown, so growth is slow. In midlife, growth is faster because of increased legitimacy and low competition. Then, as other congregations recognize the opportunities in the area, competition increases, and thus growth slows. Ultimately, some congregations die off and are replaced by congregations that are better fit for the changing environment (Scheitle and Dougherty, 2008).

Evangelical congregations have an edge, according to this theory, partly because their buildings are younger, and thus they are more likely to be located in areas of growing population, as we show in chapter 3. In addition, evangelical congregations have a fair bit of flexibility in presentation. While the central tenets of the faith are not to be tampered with, the worship style, programs, and sermon style, for example, can vary greatly, allowing congregations to find a "niche" and lessen competition with nearby congregations. Last, the small size of the average congregation has some advantages. Smaller congregations allow for more institutional diversity within a geographical area, a positive for consumer-minded Canadians. If you do not like the sermons, worship, or theological emphases at one church, there is probably another evangelical congregation within driving distance (maybe even within the same denomination). Several researchers in the United States have noted that diversifying religious options increases the market share of a religious group in the area, because it can appeal to different people of different age, race, or economic status (e.g., Stark and Finke, 2000; Scheitle and Dougherty, 2008).

Related to their evangelistic ethos, the evangelical denominations we studied plant new congregations as a key part of their evangelistic strategy. Evangelical denominations encourage established congregations to start another congregation and to support it financially, at least in the beginning. Some congregations are establishing satellite campuses, especially in urban areas, with the "home" or "mother" congregation providing administrative oversight. In some cases, the same "live" sermon is delivered to all the campuses through technology. This has obvious ramifications for the success of their religious institutions. They also invest resources in locating and training new entrepreneurial leaders and church planters.

To this point, we have situated evangelical congregations within the evangelical subculture and the larger Canadian culture. We suggest that congregations are integral to evangelicalism because of their culture-producing role, and their role of linking individuals with the larger evangelical subculture. We also suggest that congregations are the key to evangelical Protestant strength. To answer the question of why these congregations are doing comparatively well in a less-than supportive milieu, we look at macro subcultural factors, including their distinctive, relationally embedded and personally experiential religiosity, which helps keep evangelicals committed to an institutional religiosity. We have also looked at organizational-level factors, including those that are both internal and external to the congregation.

There are other reasons for their relative institutional success, which are related to the subcultural and institutional reasons discussed above. Evangelical congregations do not shy away from using technology and contemporary media within the church during worship and outside the congregation for promotion. Of the congregations in our study, 74 per cent have websites and 76 per cent said they "always" show PowerPoint or video in the worship service, and all but 3 per cent do so "sometimes." The point is that evangelical churches present themselves as more relevant and seeker-friendly when they embrace the new technologies to communicate their message.[16] In addition, the Canadian population is being sustained largely by immigration, as our current domestic birth rates are not keeping up. Much of the new congregations and new growth within Canadian evangelicalism is through immigrants. Evangelicals are attracting new immigrants and claim to be working hard to incorporate them within their congregations and denominations (see Wilkinson, 2006).

In conclusion, evangelical congregational resiliency in retaining members is partly explained through an understanding of evangelical subculture and organizational factors. Growth and vitality are also related to external factors, including demography. In chapter 3 we continue our discussion of demographic trends as they relate to religion in Canada. We also provide an extensive analysis of the demographics of evangelical congregations that partly explains their relative vitality.

3

The Demographics of
Evangelical Congregations

All religious subcultures are influenced by their cultural context. Subcultural walls are always permeable, although not equally permeable. Evangelicalism is an "engaged" subculture (Smith, 1998), meaning that evangelicals participate in nearly all aspects of Canadian life with non-evangelicals. They go to school, work, and shop like other Canadians. They go to movies, parties, sporting events, restaurants, and some even go to bars. They watch television, surf the Web, and send text messages. The broader culture also shapes them. Individualism, consumerism, and pluralism shape them, too, challenging subcultural distinctiveness and an external locus of authority. They are also influenced by demographic trends. Evangelicals are having fewer children, are less likely to be married, are more educated and more transient than they used to be, just like other Canadians. Among evangelical leaders, there is a fair bit of collective hand wringing about whether evangelicals are becoming too much like the world (e.g., Sider, 2005; MacArthur, 2010). For our purposes, we wonder if the anti-institutional nature of religiosity in Canada is making inroads into the evangelical subculture.

In the previous chapters, we noted that evangelical congregations are doing well relative to other Christian traditions and that evangelicalism has remained an institutional form of religion. We noted that evangelicals have more congregations, that the number of congregations is not declining, that they tend to do better holding on to their children and youth, and that they give money and volunteer at higher rates. To say they are doing comparatively well, however, does not necessarily indicate future growth and congregational vitality. In fact, there are signs that the future is not so bright. In this chapter, we look carefully at the demographics of evangelical congregations. We start at the denominational level, looking at their growth trajectories. We then look at the characteristics of the congregations – when they were founded, where they are located, and whether they are growing. Finally, we peek inside the congregations to examine the demographics of the people in the pews. Some demographics give reason for optimism; some do not.

IS EVANGELICALISM GROWING?

Throughout his three decades of polling, Bibby praised evangelicals for maintaining vital congregations, partly because they did a good job of holding on to their youth and mobile members. Yet his praise is qualified because, by his measures, they are not growing past 8 per cent of the Canadian population. In his report *Evangeltrends* (1995a), Bibby complemented evangelicals on the value they place on evangelism, the vitality of ministry, and their numerical success. Then he levels his critique:

> You have to do better. For years now – dating back to the early 1970s, my research on Conservative Protestant congregations in Calgary has been coming up with a consistent finding: most new additions have come from within the evangelical community. About 70% of new members and new attendees have come from other evangelical congregations, 20% are the children of evangelicals and only about 10% have come in "from the outside." To the extent they have, the key "bridges" have been friendship and marriage ... Let me be blunt: it's hard to imagine how these congregations could fail so badly at a task to which they seemed to be so collectively committed. (52)

Bibby refers to his "circulation of the saints" thesis in this quote (see also Bibby and Brinkerhoff, 1973; Bibby, 1983, 1994), whereby he found that the average evangelical congregation gained only 2.3 outsiders per year. All other additions were either transient evangelicals or children of evangelicals. Elsewhere, Bibby (1993) wonders if his "circulation" thesis is really a sign of ineffective congregations, since it indicates that evangelical congregations do a good job of holding on to their youth and mobile affiliates. Like Bibby, we have had good things to say about evangelicalism's relative institutional strength in Canada to this point. But there is evidence that it is facing some challenges.

To start, evangelism is not the main reason for evangelical growth. Other research supports Bibby's conclusions: the majority of denominational growth comes from birth rates and immigration, not evangelism.[1] William Closson James (2011) studied congregations in Kingston, Ontario, and he found that evangelistic efforts – including the door-to-door method – were not very effective. A study in the United States found that the majority of the relative growth of evangelical Protestant denominations vis-à-vis mainline Protestant denominations could be attributed to differential fertility rates (Hout et al., 2001). Evangelicals have grown partly because they have grown their own, and kept them. Statistics Canada does not distinguish between evangelical and mainline Protestant denominations, but the birth rate of those in the Protestant and "other Christian" category is close to the national average (Bélanger, 2006).[2] This is not good news, not only because evangelical collective identity is closely tied to evangelism, but also because evangelical Protestants are having fewer children. In addition, research (see, e.g., Eagle, 2011; Bowen, 2004; Bibby, 2009; Clark and Schellenberg, 2006) shows that the younger cohorts of Canadians are less likely to attend worship services than older cohorts. Evangelical youth also drop out and disaffiliate in significant numbers, as we show later. Evangelicals should not count on immigration, either. The religious groups that are growing the fastest due to immigration are Muslims, Hindus, Buddhists, and Sikhs (Statistics Canada, 2003). Immigration is increasingly non-Christian over time, and Canada is becoming increasingly more non-Christian over time (Beyer, 2005).

To quickly recap, the negative demographic news for evangelicals is that evangelism accounts for relatively few new converts. To the extent that evangelism is bearing fruit, it does not seem to be among the Canadian-born. Birth rates and immigration will not bolster evangelical numbers like they used to do in the past century. Even though evangelicalism is doing well in gloomy times for institutional religion in Canada, these demographics suggest that its long history

70   A CULTURE OF FAITH

Table 3.1 Evangelical congregations reporting increased (and decreased) church attendance (%) and other membership changes since 2007, by denomination

	Baptist	CMA	CRC	MB	PAOC	All
Attendance increase (decrease)	46.7 (11.1)	47.4 (20.6)	35.2 (19.4)	44.8 (20.7)	55.2 (20.8)	45.6 (18.6)
Median no. of new members	5	8	10	8	6.5	7
Median no. of new attendees	8	18	6.5	12	11.5	10
Median no. of new converts	2	4	1	2	4	2
Median no. left/died	5	10	10	10	8	8
Median net gain (n)	7	11	6.5	11.5	12	9

Source: CECS (2009).
CMA = Christian and Missionary Alliance; CRC = Christian Reformed Church;
MB = Mennonite Brethren; PAOC = Pentecostal Assemblies of Canada.

of growth – which has been at least equal to population growth in Canada – has come, or will soon come, to an end.

Our Canadian Evangelical Churches Study (CECS) data largely confirm the "circulation of the saints" thesis put forth by Bibby and his co-authors. Table 3.1 examines attendance rates for each denomination. In the first row, we see for which groups average weekly attendance increased or decreased in 2008 compared with 2007, based on reports from the congregations' pastors. The subsequent rows report median changes in membership and attendance, by denomination. The median represents the midpoint in the data and gives a more accurate picture of the typical congregation. The mathematical average (mean) is easily skewed by very large congregations in the sample, which make the average too large. If anything, we expect pastors to be optimistic about the growth of their congregations, which may inflate numbers slightly. Looking at the right-most column, almost half of the pastors said attendance in their congregations (45.6%) increased over that year, while 18.6 per cent said it decreased (the remaining 35.8% said it remained the same). The rest of the table shows the sources of growth. The typical congregation reported that 7 people officially joined the congregation, while 10 more started attending but did not officially join as members. This is not surprising. Evangelical denominations often report average attendance rates that are higher than their membership, with many who are not officially members participating in their congregations. In comparison, the typical congregation only welcomed 2 new converts, which is 11.8 per cent (2 of 17) of the total newcomers. This is nearly identical to Bibby's finding that 10 per cent of growth is due to conversions, and that 2.3 outsiders join per year. The typical congregation lost 8 members (due to moving away, death, dropout, etc.), so the median net gain was about 9 people. The differences between denominations are partly due to the size of the congregations. If we account for median congregational size, the congregations of the Pentecostal Assemblies of Canada (PAOC) are doing the best in terms of net gain and converts, since their congregations are relatively small (14% median gain in 2008). The Christian Reformed Church (CRC) is doing least well, since it has large congregations, with few converts and smaller gains (2.9%). The other denominations are all showing about a 7.8 per cent gain in 2008. One way to verify congregational growth that is not dependent on pastors' accounts is to look at the reports submitted to the Canada Revenue Agency. We will look more thoroughly at these data in the last chapter. For now it will suffice to say that the sample of congregations is much larger (over 6,000 evangelical congregations) than the CECS dataset, and congregations are required by law to report their financial information. In Table 3.2 we look at the percentage increase (and decrease) of total receipted gifts for each denomination from 2000 to 2009. Although imperfect, total giving is one indicator of congregational growth. The first column of figures shows the percentage increase or decrease in constant 2000 dollars (controlling for inflation)[3] and the far right column shows the percentage increase in actual dollar amounts. The cost of living increased roughly 21 per cent between 2000 and 2009. Subsequent years do not have all congregations reporting, so 2009 is the last year reported.

The first column in Table 3.2 shows that the Mennonite Brethren (MB) and the Canadian Baptists of Ontario and Quebec (CBOQ) fell slightly behind in giving, while the Convention of Atlantic Baptist Churches (CABC) basically broke even. The other denominations, particularly the Christian and Missionary Alliance (CMA) made gains during the decade, but these gains are relatively small. Of course, giving money and number of participants are not perfectly correlated, as some participants can give more, and others (particularly younger people) can participate with no or little financial support. What we

Table 3.2 Increase or decrease in total (median) receipted gifts, by denomination, from 2000 to 2009 (%)

Denomination	In 2000 dollars	In reported dollars
Mennonite Brethren	-3.0	17.5
Convention of Atlantic Baptist Churches	1.3	22.7
Canadian Baptists of Ontario and Quebec	-3.1	17.5
Canadian Baptists of Western Canada	8.0	30.8
Christian and Missionary Alliance	14.5	38.8
Christian Reformed Church	6.7	29.3
Pentecostal Assemblies of Canada	8.8	31.8

Source: CRA dataset (2011).

are claiming here is that giving is evidence of growth, and based on this evidence, the growth of the congregations is slight. This largely confirms the CECS data, which show a small net gain in attendees in 2008 based on pastors' reports. Of course, these data do not show the long-term trajectory of evangelical congregations. Below we contrast the growth/decline of mainline Protestant congregations – particularly the two largest, the Anglican and United churches – with the evangelical denominations in our study since the 1970s.

The 1940s and 1950s were boom years for mainline Protestants. In the 1950s the number of Anglicans in Canada grew by 37 per cent, members of the United Church of Canada (UCC) by 24 per cent, Lutherans (collectively) by 42 per cent, and Presbyterians by 13.6 per cent according to census data (Clarke and Macdonald, 2011). In 1961 the Anglican Church of Canada (ACC) claimed 3,635 congregations and an inclusive membership of 1,358,459. By 2001 the ACC reported 2,884 congregations and 641,845 members.[4] ACC confirmation and Sunday School attendance fell to one-sixth of what they had been in their peak years (1958 and 1961, respectively). Easter Communion and giving rates, however, show more favourable trends (Clarke and Macdonald, 2010). Overall, the decline since the 1960s is stark. Census data show a decline from 2,409,068 affiliates in 1961 when they accounted for 13.2 percent of the population, to 2,035,500 in 2001, accounting for 6.9 per cent of Canadians. The census numbers count all who identify themselves as Anglican, which is higher than the inclusive membership reported by the ACC.

Similarly, the United Church of Canada shows declines since 1961. Clarke and Macdonald (2011) observe that 1961 was the high water mark for UCC membership (1,016,879), which declined to 494,791 in 2010, roughly half of the 1961 figure. In 1971, UCC yearbook data report 4,442 congregations, compared with 3,196 in 2010.[5] Using 1951 as a baseline, Clarke and Macdonald report a "77% decline in Sunday School membership, 68% decline in baptisms and 73% decline in confirmations" (18). They further note that the decline accelerates over time. According to Canada census data, the UCC fell from 3,664,008 affiliates to 2,839,125 between 1961 and 2001, a fall from 20.1 per cent of the population to 9.6 per cent. The UCC website gives an average weekly attendance in 2010 of 174,660 in their 3,196 congregations, representing an average of 55 attendees per congregation.

Unlike the Anglicans and UCC, the evangelical denominations we examined maintained growth well after the 1950s.[6] However, that growth seems to have levelled off in the past decade or two. Unfortunately, the Canada census data do not give accurate enough information to track individual evangelical denominations, so we use the annual *Yearbook of American and Canadian Churches* (Lindner, 2012), which is based on reports from the denominations. The data have their limitations (Mentzer, 1991), but are the best available.[7]

Figure 3.1 shows the denominations in order of size in 1971. The convention Baptists, comprising four separate conventions, have shown little growth or decline in the number of their congregations, moving from 1,110 in 1971 to 1,065 in 2010. In the past decade, all three large conventions (excluding the French Baptists of roughly thirty congregations) have experienced decline in the number of congregations they reported. The Pentecostal Assemblies of Canada (PAOC) grew from 734 to 1,124 congregations over the same period. Similarly, the Christian and Missionary Alliance (CMA) grew from 188 to 430 congregations over the same four decades. However, both of these fast-growing denominations show slower growth over the past decade, as is the case for all five denominations. Between 1971 and 2010, yearbook data from the MB (125 to 246) and CRC (152 to 250) show increases in number of congregations as well, with slowed growth (or no growth) in the past decade.[8]

While the yearbook data[9] suggest that growth is levelling off, they are still more optimistic than the information we receive from

74 A CULTURE OF FAITH

Figure 3.1 Number of churches in evangelical denominations, 1971–2010

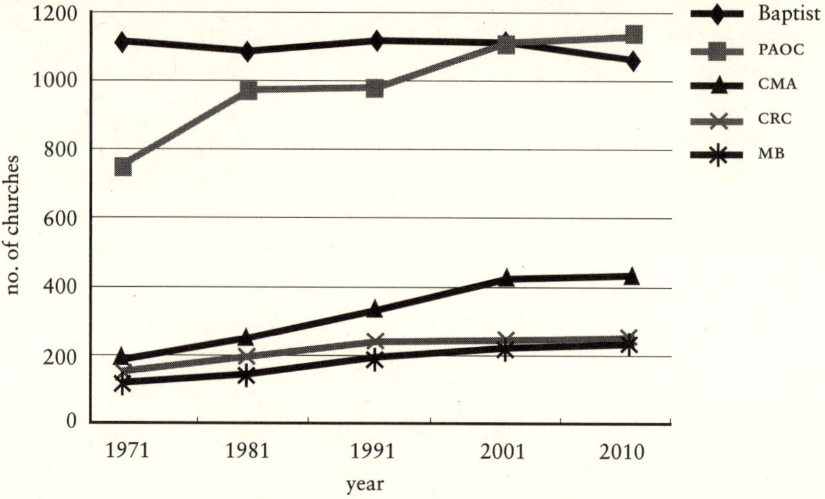

Source: 1971 to 2012 yearbooks for each denomination. The Baptist data combine all four Baptist conventions. In some cases, data are not available for the year given, so data from the closest year available is substituted, or data from denominational websites are used. CMA = Christian and Missionary Alliance; CRC = Christian Reformed Church; MB = Mennonite Brethren; PAOC = Pentecostal Assemblies of Canada.

denominational leaders. Specifically, the two denominations that show continued growth, the PAOC and CMA, were clearly not growing according to their leaders or their statistics. For example, the PAOC website shows no growth in attendance or number of congregations in the past five years. Data from a PAOC representative show that growth levelled off as far back as the 1990s.

Across all the denominations in our study, official leaders told us they are facing some difficult challenges that have implications for congregational vitality. When we asked them questions about the sources of church growth we consistently heard that growth primarily occurred because of immigration and new immigrant congregations. This growth was among a wide range of new immigrants and included Korean, Chinese, Spanish-speaking, and African members among many more. "The churches that are growing the quickest," said one leader, "are ethnic churches." However, we also heard that new immigrant growth has slowed down or plateaued. As one leader said, "Some ethnic churches were growing but are now plateauing."

Denominational leaders also told us that small rural congregations are struggling, with many closing or on the verge of closing. With the movement to urban areas in Canada, evangelical congregations that were established in small rural towns are experiencing the challenges of gaining new young mobile members. "Our rural congregations are aging," said one leader. "They are true to the demographics of the region and we need to come to peace with it." Another leader said it is true that rural congregations are facing issues, but also revealed "it is probably not true overall that urban churches are doing better than rural ones." If a rural congregation was growing, this was often attributed to the local leadership. "Rural churches are growing and shrinking," we were told. "Growth depends on leadership and the internal culture. Sometimes it is dysfunctional and not reflective of the context but the internal dynamics of the congregation." For some rural congregations, however, it may be the changing context of fewer people living in rural areas as well as the leadership challenges of keeping congregants' morale high when there are no young families and the youth and young adults have all moved to the city.

In sum, we conclude that the growth of evangelical congregations has plateaued in the past decade, at least for these five denominations. The growth rate has slowed considerably for all five denominations, and for all except the CMA, there has been no growth at all. There are, no doubt, some smaller and newer evangelical denominations that are growing. Yet, a widely travelled evangelical leader (who visits hundreds of evangelical congregations each year across many denominations) stated that he knows of no evangelical denominations that are growing. It is too early to say that evangelical denominations are declining in absolute numbers, even if some show signs of decline. Based on the limited data we have, all of the five evangelical denominations are falling behind the 11.3 per cent population growth from 2001 to 2011, so they are declining in comparison with the population.[10] All we can say is that the demographic and cultural realities in Canada indicate that future decline is probable.[11]

CONGREGATIONAL SIZE

Not all demographics point to a dim future. As mentioned previously, a good number of active participants are needed to maintain a vital

76 A CULTURE OF FAITH

Table 3.3 Number of evangelical congregations and weekly attendance, by denomination, 2008

Denomination	No. of congregations	Median no. of attendees	Average no. of attendees
Baptists – Atlantic Canada	524	48.0[a]	76.1[a]
Baptists – French	30	45.5	73.3
Baptists – Ontario and Quebec	354	55.5	91.3
Baptists – Western Canada	165	100.0	140.0
Christian and Missionary Alliance	427	116.0	211.3
Christian Reformed Church	251	197.5	229.3
Mennonite Brethren	246	130.0	230.0
Pentecostal Assemblies of Canada	1,102	75.0	148.0
All denominations combined	3,099	89.2	150.0

Source: Derived from statistics made available by denominational staff.
[a] 226 congregations that reported 0 weekly attendance were removed.

congregation. Evangelicals have a lot of congregations. Is the average weekly attendance (which we call congregational size) in these congregations sufficient for a vital ministry? Table 3.3 presents the number of congregations in each denomination, and the median and average numbers in attendance per congregation in each denomination. According to the denominational data, the median congregation has 89.2 regular attendees (typical weekly attendance, including adults and children).[12] The Baptist and Pentecostal congregation sizes tend to be smaller, partly because they are more likely to be rural. Those denominations with more congregations in Western Canada tend to have larger ones, with Christian Reformed congregations being the largest on average. Since we think the denominational estimates are a bit low, our best estimate of the median size of congregations in these denominations is about 100 (see Appendix). The denominational data also match well with our CECS data, lending validity to each dataset (see Appendix).

THE DEMOGRAPHICS OF EVANGELICAL CONGREGATIONS   77

Table 3.4 Attributes of small and large congregations

Attribute	Small congregations (< 75 N = 112)	Large congregations (≥ 250 N = 127)
Median annual congregational income	$80,842	$500,000
Adults with 4-year university degree or higher education (%)	26.2	36.9
Affluent families[a] (%)	5.8	20.2
Women who volunteer (%)	55.2	52.4
Men who volunteer (%)	46.0	39.9
Adults who give money faithfully (%)	73.3	62.9
Urban (%)	51.8	89.8
Unconverted members (%)	6.7	9.8

Source: CECS, 2009.
[a] With annual family income > $100,000.

Research on congregations in the United States by Mark Chaves (2004) of Duke University found that the median evangelical Protestant congregation has 74 regular attendees (counting adults and children), but the typical evangelical Protestant goes to a religious service of 230 regular participants.[13] The difference is important, and undoubtedly applies to evangelicals in Canada. Since large congregations skew the data on average congregational size, the average attendee goes to a congregation that is much larger than the median-sized congregation. Thus, there is a perception that the average congregation is much larger than it actually is.

Congregational size affects demographics and participation in a variety of ways. In Table 3.4 we present the data for roughly the smallest 25 per cent of the congregations and the largest 25 per cent. Obviously, bigger congregations have much bigger incomes, but their attendees are also more highly educated and more affluent, on average. Probably related to the fact that larger congregations are more likely to be urban (as opposed to rural),[14] they are slightly more likely to have a higher percentage of unconverted participants (based on the pastor's definition of conversion). However, the smaller congregations have the edge in terms of the percentage of the regular participating adults who actively volunteer and faithfully give money to the congregation.[15]

78   A CULTURE OF FAITH

Table 3.5 Number and age of evangelical congregations, by denomination

Denomination	Congregations (N)	Year founded (median)
Baptist	87	1901
Christian and Missionary Alliance	92	1975.5
Christian Reformed Church	108	1957
Mennonite Brethren	87	1980
Pentecostal Assemblies of Canada	94	1961
Total	468[a]	1962.5

Source: CECS, 2009.
[a] Total does not include all 478 churches in the sample due to missing data.

CONGREGATIONAL AGE

In Table 3.5 we look at the age of the congregations. The average evangelical congregation in Canada is about forty-five years old (in 2009) according to the CECS data. However, the age varies significantly by region and denomination. Regarding region, congregations in Atlantic Canada are the oldest, while those in Quebec and British Columbia are the youngest. Forty-three of the forty-five congregations that began before 1901 (in our data) are Baptist, and they are mostly in Ontario and the Maritimes. On average, congregations were founded in 1925 in Atlantic Canada and 1974 in British Columbia, with an overall median year of 1962. The oldest congregation began in 1763, while three congregations started in 2008. The average Baptist congregation is over 100 years old, while the average Mennonite congregation – the denomination with the youngest congregations on average – is only thirty years old.

Once again dividing the congregations into quartiles based on congregational age, we present data in Table 3.6 for the oldest and youngest 25 per cent of the congregations. Older congregations on average have older participants, who are less educated and somewhat less wealthy.[16] Like smaller congregations, older congregations have slightly higher rates of giving money. Younger congregations are more likely to be urban, and their participants are more likely to be immigrants, Asians, and small group attendees.

THE DEMOGRAPHICS OF EVANGELICAL CONGREGATIONS   79

Table 3.6 Attributes of old and young evangelical congregations (%)

Attribute	Old congregations (founded before 1947) N = 119	Young congregations (founded after 1987) N = 121
Members aged 18–29 years	11.0	20.4
Adults with 4-year university degree or higher education	26.7	43.8
Affluent families[a]	10.5	14.5
Adults who give money faithfully	70.2	66.7
Urban	58.8	86.8
Recent immigrants[b]	3.4	10.3
Asian	3.6	14.1
Adults who participate in a small group	33.0	43.9

Source: CECS, 2009.
[a] With annual family income > $100,000.
[b] Came to Canada within the past 5 years.

Possible explanations for higher levels of commitment in smaller, older congregations include a combination of demographics and generational effects. Younger affiliates are more likely to leave small, older (often rural) congregations and move to urban centres or other regions for economic and/or lifestyle reasons. This leaves a remnant of older participants with a strong commitment to the congregation, demonstrated over a long period of time. We are not suggesting that younger evangelicals are less religiously committed overall, but many students of modern religion would agree that younger cohorts lack some of the loyalty, perseverance, and sense of duty characteristic of older cohorts (e.g., Bibby, 2006). Thus, they have less commitment to any one congregation. Add to this the fact that older, smaller congregations lack programs for children, contemporary worship music, and often have an older pastor who may not relate as well to a younger generation. The older, small congregation does not attract casual attendees because it does not appeal to those who are "shopping" for a church. Another possible reason is related to the basic principles of organizational growth. As organizations grow, so does the diversity of commitment among its members/affiliates (Blau, 1970). Since it is easier for "free riders" to hide in big congregations than in small ones (Finke, 1994; Iannaccone, 1992), it is more difficult for larger congregations to maintain an ethos of high commitment among the majority. However, this should be understood within the larger point that evangelical congregations do relatively well at holding the allegiance of both young and old. Note that the differences in giving/participation levels between older/small congregations and younger/large congregations are relatively small.

Why does congregational size and age matter? First, congregations need to have enough participants to remain viable. Well-attended congregations are more stable because of their established giving and volunteer base. A substantial base not only helps the congregations, but since congregations and individuals give to the denomination, it helps the denominations run programs that strengthen local congregations. The denominations in our sample plant new congregations, and support those that are young or struggling. This increases their viability over time. The small size of the average congregation can have some advantages, too. Smaller congregations allow for more institutional diversity within a geographical area, a positive for consumer-minded Canadians. If you do not like the sermons, worship, or theological emphases at one congregation, there is probably another one within driving distance (maybe even within the same denomination). Several researchers in the United States have noted that diversifying religious options increases the market share of a religious group in the area, because they can appeal to different people of different age, race, or economic status (e.g., Stark and Finke, 2000; Scheitle and Dougherty, 2008). Second, age of congregation matters because younger congregations are more likely to be located in growing communities. Congregations founded long ago often find themselves in previously thriving but presently declining areas. Furthermore, newer buildings are assets and are usually less expensive to maintain. They are also better suited for modern ministry and technology. Since evangelicals tend toward greater austerity and less elaborate buildings, relocating a congregation is often less costly. Without the draining costs of maintaining old buildings, more congregational finances can be used to resource staff, ministries, and outreach, which has obvious advantages for institutional religion. Size (small, but not too small) and age (fairly recent) of congregations, then, is relatively good news for evangelical denominations.

CONGREGATIONAL LOCATION

Evangelicalism is an English-speaking phenomenon in Canada. There are few congregations in Quebec, where Catholics enjoyed a quasi-establishment status for many years prior to the Quiet Revolution (Beyer, 1993). Even after Catholic hegemony weakened in the 1960s, however, most francophone Quebecers still identify with Catholicism, and other denominations are viewed with suspicion. At present, the proportion of evangelicals in Quebec is likely less than one per cent, and of those who attend evangelical worship services it is in the range of 0.5 per cent.[17]

Table 3.7 uses the Canada Revenue Agency's Charitable Organizations sample (see Appendix), a sample of nearly 6,000 evangelical congregations, to show the number of evangelical congregations in each province. These data are better for our purposes because the CECS data have small sample sizes in some provinces. We will look at these data in greater detail in chapter 8. For now, we report the median annual congregational income to give a sense of the typical size of the congregations in each province. We also report the number of congregations listed in the Church Map Canada (CMC) dataset compiled by Outreach Canada.[18] The "population per evangelical congregation" column was computed by dividing the province's population by our best estimate of the number of evangelical congregations in that province.

There are several conclusions that can be made from these data. First, Quebec stands out. The number of evangelical congregations in each province roughly follows the population of the province, except in Quebec. Looking at the column showing population per evangelical congregation (EC), we see that Quebec has only one congregation per 16,295 residents, compared with roughly one congregation to 3,000 residents outside Quebec. Evangelical congregations have struggled to take root in this historically Catholic province (see Zuidema, 2011). Second, on a per capita basis, Manitoba and Saskatchewan in the Prairies and New Brunswick and Nova Scotia in the Maritimes have more evangelical congregations than the more populated provinces of British Columbia, Alberta, and Ontario. Third, based on congregational income, the congregations are larger in western Canada than in eastern Canada. In Nova Scotia and New Brunswick, Convention Baptist congregations dominate, and with

Table 3.7 Evangelical congregations (ECs), Canadian provinces and territories

Province / Territory	CMC data	CRA data estimate[a]	% of all ECs	Population per EC	Median Total 2010 Congregational income ($)
British Columbia	1,880	1831	15.9	2,402.60	171,443
Alberta	1,326	1525	13.3	2,390.60	191,754
Saskatchewan	739	741	6.4	1,394.40	106,967
Manitoba	595	683	5.9	1,769.40	151,582
Ontario	3,794	4,456	38.7	2,884.00	171,552
Quebec	765	485	4.2	16,294.80	85,168
New Brunswick	500	599	5.2	1,253.10	84,368
Nova Scotia	537	704	6.1	1,308.90	73,245
Prince Edward Island	92	70	0.6	2,007.50	103,668
Newfoundland and Labrador	311	357	3.1	1,441.40	139,984
Territories[b]	50	52	0.5	2,047.80	180,317
All	10,589	11,503	100	2,901.00	147,940

Source: Canada Revenue Agency's Charitable Organizations sample (see Appendix); ChurchMap Canada data, http://www.churchmapcanada.com/Default. aspx?tabid=1133, accessed 25 July 2012; and Canada Census 2011. CRA sample data are for congregations that were registered as of 29 June 2012.

[a] We think the best estimate of the number and distribution of the ECs is from the CRA data, but not all the congregations in these data have been categorized. Since roughly 6,000 congregations of the estimated 11,500 have been categorized, we multiplied each provincial CRA total by 1.94 to come up with the estimates in this column.
[b] Territories were combined because sample size for each territory is too small for accurate numbers.

THE DEMOGRAPHICS OF EVANGELICAL CONGREGATIONS   83

their long history in the region, they tend to be older, smaller, and more rural. The comparatively few congregations in Quebec also tend to be small. Congregations in the western provinces and Ontario tend to be younger, more urban, and are more likely to benefit from favourable migration patterns. With more Canadians moving to economically prosperous Alberta, and many immigrants moving to big cities like Toronto, Calgary, and Vancouver, evangelical congregations in these regions gain more from "circulating saints" moving into their area. In addition, the population to congregation ratio means that evangelical congregations in the West have less competition and a larger pool of Canadians to draw from. Hiemstra (2010) found that about half of the congregational size variation could be attributed to this population to congregation ratio.

CONGREGATIONAL SOCIAL CHARACTERISTICS

The demographics of regular participants in congregations have drawn interest in the United States, particularly concerning race, where it is often said, "Sunday morning remains the most racially segregated time in America" (e.g., Emerson and Smith, 2000). There has also been considerable interest in class and age differences (e.g., Reimer, 2007). In Canada research on the demographics of congregations has focused on new immigrant populations (e.g., Wilkinson, 2006). The demographics of congregations are important not only to researchers, but to congregational leaders as well, who are concerned about reaching racial/ethnic minorities or encouraging commitment among the younger generations. The demographics of congregants also influence a wide variety of congregational activities. Age often affects the worship style or programs of a congregation, just as the education and income of attendees influence a congregation's budget, or the credentials of the pastor they wish to hire.

In Table 3.8 we look at the demographic make-up of the regular participants in evangelical congregations based on denomination. Regarding the age of the participants, there are as many people under age 18 as there are over age 65 in the congregations, lending support to Bibby's (2006) and Bowen's (2004) claim that evangelicals do well at promoting youth participation.[19] Baptists, particularly Maritime Baptists, are older than the participants in other denominations.

84 A CULTURE OF FAITH

Table 3.8 Demographic attributes of evangelical congregations,
by denomination (%)

Attribute	Baptists	CMA	CRC	MB	PAOC	Average
Age (years)						
< 18	17.8	23.8	22.8	23	20.8	21.6
18–29	13.1	16.4	13.8	16.4	14.9	14.9
30–64	40.4	46.0	42.2	45.3	47.5	44.3
≥ 65	32.1	15.2	21.0	16.0	17.7	20.3
Female	60.5	56.4	54.2	55.0	56.6	56.4
Education						
High school or less	51.1	48.2	52.2	42.0	57.4	50.1
4-year university degree or more	33.4	36.9	34.5	41.0	28.6	34.7
Graduate degree or more	7.8	8.7	7.2	8.3	7.6	7.9
Annual family income						
< $25,000	19.4	15.7	8.7	12.7	21.2	15.4
>$100,000	8.1	14.9	18.3	15.2	10.8	13.5
Recent immigrant (came to Canada within past 5 years)	5.3	9.8	3.1	5.2	5.5	5.8

Source: CECS, 2009.
CMA = Christian and Missionary Alliance; CRC = Christian Reformed Church;
MB = Mennonite Brethren; PAOC = Pentecostal Assemblies of Canada.

Regression analysis (not shown) demonstrates that the strongest predictor of having a disproportionately large number of older participants (≥ 65 years) in a congregation is the year the congregation was founded. Older congregations on average have older attendees and pastors.

Regarding gender, women make up 56 per cent of regular attendees, according to pastors' estimates. Based on Chaves' (2004) data in the United States, an almost identical 57.4 per cent of participants in evangelical congregations were female. Bowen (2004), in his data, finds a similar gender gap (57% female, 43% male) among the religiously committed, which is fairly consistent across Christian traditions. Actually, the gender gap is nearly universal. Why women are more religious than men has led to interesting speculations on the part of researchers (see, e.g., Bradshaw and Ellison, 2009; Miller and Stark, 2002).

It is often assumed that evangelicals are less educated and less affluent than non-evangelicals, an impression likely gained from dated studies in the United States. Evangelicals, and particularly fundamentalists, have historically been disproportionately rural, poor, and uneducated (Hunter, 1983). However, it is hard to find evidence for this in recent decades (Rawlyk, 1996; Bowen, 2004). For example, using Bibby's 2005 Project Canada data, we find no statistically significant differences between evangelicals and the rest of the religious traditions (Quebec Catholics, Catholics outside Quebec, mainline Protestants, Other, None) in education or income: 38.5 per cent of evangelical respondents had a university degree or more formal education, compared with 39 per cent of non-evangelical Canadians. Evangelicals who regularly attend church are even more educated, with nearly half (49%) having first university degrees or higher. Bowen (2004), using the 1997 Canada Survey of Volunteering, Giving and Participation with a sample size of roughly 18,000 Canadians, also concludes that education and income differences between religious traditions are minimal, and stereotypes of uneducated evangelical Protestants are "not supported by these data" (62). In our data, pastors estimated that roughly one-third of attendees have a university degree or more. Recall that estimates of income and education are less precise than the more visible age, gender, and race/ethnicity estimates. Pentecostals are slightly less likely to have a university education, while Baptists and Pentecostals have lower incomes on average. Statistical analysis (not shown) indicates that more educated participants (those with university education) are more plentiful in urban, large, and old congregations.

One important source of social change for denominations and congregations is migration. Not only has Canada changed with new immigration patterns beginning in the 1970s, so too have congregations. Increasingly, immigrants are arriving in greater numbers from Africa, Asia, and Latin America. Moreover, while many Muslims, Hindus, and Sikhs are arriving, so too are Christians from these regions (Bramadat and Seljak, 2008). Evangelicalism has become far more culturally diverse in the past thirty years with far-ranging implications, including the de-Europeanization of Christianity (Wilkinson, 2006; Guenther, 2008b). The study of new immigrant congregations has exploded with numerous reports that have focused on the establishment of new immigrant congregations (Warner and Wittner,

1998), cultural adaptations (Ebaugh and Chafetz, 2000), transnational networks (Wilkinson, 2000; Ebaugh and Saltzman, 2002), and multicultural congregations (Marti, 2009).

Like other religious groups, evangelicals are attracting new immigrants, and they claim to be working hard to incorporate them within their denominations/congregations.[20] Importantly, the denominational leaders and spokespersons we talked to consistently affirmed that ethnic and immigrant congregations account for the majority of new congregations in their denomination. This is somewhat surprising, as a small minority (10.7%) of immigrants are Protestant Christians (up to 16% if we count the census "other Christian" category). Are large numbers of new immigrants converting to Christianity, so that converts are filling these new evangelical congregations? Unfortunately, we do not know. Research using Canada census data allows us to only track religious affiliation, and we know that many affiliates do not attend regularly. As Bibby notes (1993), affiliation often changes due to marriage, which may be more for convenience than commitment. Since Canada is still predominately Christian by affiliation, some second-generation immigrants will change their religious affiliation to Christian as part of acculturating to Canada. Using census data, Beyer (2005) did find a slight tendency toward Christian affiliation: "immigrant cohorts and second generation birth cohorts usually become more Christian and less identified with other religions over time" (192). However, Beyer notes that this tendency is not strong and may not continue as large immigrant populations in metropolitan areas allow for intra-religious (and intra-ethnic) marriages. These cities also have mosques, temples, etc. nearby to support non-Christian religiosity. Whatever the conversion rate of immigrants, we know that a significant minority of (particularly south Asian) immigrants come to Canada as committed Christians, and many find their way into evangelical congregations.

The CECS study asked pastors to estimate the ethnic/racial composition of their congregations. Regarding recent immigrants in congregations, shown in Table 3.8, the CMA has the largest percentage of immigrants while the CRC is the least diverse of the five denominations. Congregations in Atlantic Canada report that only 3 per cent of the congregants are immigrants, compared with 13 per cent in Quebec. Obviously, ethnic diversity is related to the number of congregations that are in Toronto, Montreal, and Vancouver, which

THE DEMOGRAPHICS OF EVANGELICAL CONGREGATIONS   87

Table 3.9 Number of minority congregations, by denomination[a]

Racial Group	No. of Congregations					
	Baptists	CMA	CRC	MB	PAOC	Total
Asian	0	16	1	3	1	21
Latin American	1	1	0	0	0	2
African/Black	4	0	0	0	1	5
Aboriginal	0	1	0	0	2	3
White	70	51	99	67	65	352
Multiracial (no race > 80%)	16	26	8	16	26	92
Total	91	95	108	86	95	475

Source: CECS, 2009.
[a] Number of congregations where ≥ 81% of regular participants/attendees belong to racial group.
CMA = Christian and Missionary Alliance; CRC = Christian Reformed Church;
MB = Mennonite Brethren; PAOC = Pentecostal Assemblies of Canada.

hold roughly two-thirds (63%) of Canada's immigrant population (Trovato, 2009).

The top five rows of Table 3.9 show the number of ethnic congregations in our data. In total, there are 31 ethnic congregations (6.5%) in our sample.[21]

We define ethnic congregations as those where more than 80 per cent of the congregation belongs to one ethnic grouping. The Christian and Missionary Alliance reported 16 Asian congregations (over 80% Asian) in our sample. Overall, CMA pastors report that 22.2 per cent of the attendees in all CMA churches in our sample are Asian (not shown). Baptists have the largest Black/African contingent. Some 20 African congregations are part of the Convention of Atlantic Baptist Churches. These are historic Black congregations from the eighteenth and nineteenth centuries. Pentecostals have a large number of Aboriginal/First Nations congregations. The PAOC claim 90 congregations that are First Nations on its website, along with 39 Spanish, 18 Korean, and 14 Chinese congregations, among others (out of 1,100 congregations total). The CMA is the most ethnically diverse overall in our data, and it claims 7 First Nations, 89 Chinese, 20 Vietnamese, 15 Filipino, and 12 Korean.

There has been much research south of the border on multiracial congregations partly because researchers consider them an important means toward racial reconciliation. Yancey (2003; see also DeYoung et al., 2004; Emerson and Smith, 2000) defines a multiracial congregation "as a congregation in which no one racial group makes up more than 80% of the attendees of at least one of the major worship services" (15). By this measure 8 per cent of congregations in the United States are multiracial. Emerson and Woo (2006) state that 4.5 per cent of evangelical congregations in the United States are multiracial. Emerson and Woo suggest that "the more successful a faith tradition is in terms of relative size [compared with other traditions] the less successful it will be in having racially mixed congregations" (39) because people will have a greater choice of congregations and thus are more likely to choose to attend a congregation that matches their ethnicity or race.

If we accept Emerson and Woo's (2006) theory, we would expect to find more multiracial congregations in Canada because there are fewer evangelical congregations to choose from. Furthermore, Emerson and Woo also found that Asians and Hispanics were more likely to be in multiracial congregations. The long history of denominational and congregational racial divisions (Niebuhr, 1929) between Black and white congregations in the United States does not exist to the same degree in Canada. We found that 92 of the 478 congregations or 19.2 per cent of the sample are multiracial congregations according to pastors' estimates (13.2% if we exclude the 80th percentile). The Pentecostals and the CMA lead in this area, with 26 multiracial congregations each in our data. Not surprisingly, multiracial congregations are five times more likely to be urban than rural and are very rare in Atlantic Canada.[22]

Like the old adage, we have good news and bad news for evangelical congregations. First, this is the good news. Evangelical congregations and denominations are doing *comparatively* well. The majority of evangelicals still participate in congregations, the denominations have been growing during the decades when mainline Protestants have been declining, and they are recruiting immigrants and keeping their young – comparatively well. No doubt, attracting and/or keeping immigrants will be key to the growth trajectory of evangelical congregations, just as it is for all Canadian religions. The good news is that evangelicalism (particularly its Pentecostal forms) is growing rapidly in many parts of the non-Western world (see

Anderson, 2013), and Canadian evangelical congregations benefit from their passionate religiosity because of immigration. The age and size of the congregations are also good news, as younger congregations are more likely to be located in growing areas, and buildings are less financially burdensome. Evangelical church buildings are, on average, forty-five years old (in 2009). We do not know the average age of Catholic and mainline Protestant buildings, but they are likely much older. Smaller congregations allow congregants to reach different niches and provide more choice. With a median of 100 regular attendees, these congregations are, on average, large enough to sustain the congregation and its ministry.

The bad news for evangelical denominations and congregations, at least those in our sample, is that they are not growing or their growth has slowed significantly over the past decade. Those congregations that are experiencing growth can attribute most of their attendance gains to favourable "circulation of the saints." It is hard to grow congregations when demographics are not on your side. Yet, as Adams (2006) says, "Demography is not destiny" (20). Evangelical congregations may still see a brighter day if effective means of evangelism are found, or if demographics change.

4

Priorities and Purposes

To understand the goals of evangelical congregations, we need to be attentive to the voices of evangelical leaders themselves. Popular opinion is likely to be misinformed if media and a few of the loudest (evangelical or otherwise) voices shape our perceptions. These voices are often not representative of the whole. In Canada, much attention is focused on the perceived right-wing politics and intolerance of evangelical Protestants, and many assume that congregations are the breeding grounds for these attitudes.[1] However, sexual issues or political mobilization are not the focus of evangelical congregations. When we talked to actual evangelical pastors and denominational leaders about their goals and vision, these issues are not even mentioned. When we look at the actual use of time and dollars in congregations, they too show that evangelical congregations are focused on worship, religious education, and serving their communities. The same is true of evangelical congregations in the United States.

In his book *Christian America? What Evangelicals Really Want* (2000), University of Notre Dame sociologist Christian Smith warns against believing that certain evangelical (often self-appointed) spokespersons are typical of the person in the pew, or that evangelicals are a unified, mobilized army for the political right. In fact, evangelicals are much too inconsistent, multi-vocal, and internally diverse. They are committed to promoting Christian values in society at the same time as they are committed to pluralism and diversity. They think that morality cannot be legislated but still hope for legislation on some sexual morals. These tensions lead Smith to conclude that ordinary American evangelicals "reveal not the triumphalism of the Christian Right, but the triumph of ambivalence" and that most people "who disparage evangelicals in general terms really don't know what they are talking about" (195). Whatever the cues they are receiving from their congregations, the message does not seem to be consistent or distinct enough (at least when mixed with all the other messages they receive) to create a unified force. If such cautions are warranted in the United States, we would be wise to heed them in Canada, too. Bean, Gonzalez, and Kaufmann (2008) show that Canadian evangelicals are less likely than American evangelicals to mobilize politically because of different subcultural identities. While both groups are morally conservative, Canadians recognize their minority status within a "post-Christian society," and see evangelism, not political action, as the way forward. Carleton University political scientist Jonathan Malloy (2011) cautions, "Observers need to be careful not to exaggerate the unity of the religious right," which is often internally divided.[2] Furthermore, the smaller number of evangelical Protestants in Canada means they have much less of an impact on the politics of Canada (Bibby, 2002). In contrast with what some in the popular media believe, there is no significant organized "religious right" in Canada, as in the United States, where a strong coalition of conservative Protestants support the Republican Party (see Grenville, 2000; Lyon and Van Die, 2000; Simpson, 2000; Stackhouse, 2000). Historically, in Canada evangelicals have not aligned with a single political party, and although recent polls show growing support among evangelicals for the Conservative Party, we doubt that a solid voting block will develop and be sustained or that we'll see the importation of US style politics into Canada.[3] Many evangelicals remain uninterested or uncommitted in such political battles. What about actual behaviour? Where do evangelicals invest their money and time? Studies of congregations and giving trends show that American congregations do not place high priority on political mobilization. In his leading study of American congregations, Duke University sociologist Mark Chaves (2004) found that congregations are primarily about "the cultural activity of expressing and transmitting religious meanings through worship and religious education" (8). If we look at time and money usage in congregations, says Chaves (2002), it points to producing worship services, music, and religious knowledge; comparatively little time is spent on political mobilization or service provision (ibid.; see also Wuthnow and Evans, 2002). Studies of giving show that politics is not a top priority. Hamilton

(2000) found that for every dollar evangelicals send to political organizations, they spend $12 on overseas missions/relief, $13 in bookstores, $25 on higher education, and $31 on elementary/secondary education. He estimates that less than one per cent of evangelical giving goes to political organizations. "If we follow the money," Hamilton notes, "it is clear that evangelicals have made but light investments in politics while making deep, heavy, sustained investment in social welfare causes. This suggests that the primary impact of evangelicalism on American culture is to be found outside of politics" (133). Certainly there are evangelical organizations on both sides of the border that have political mandates, but this is not the focus of the congregations, or the rank-and-file evangelical Protestant.

PASTORAL PRIORITIES

How do Canadian evangelical Protestant congregations compare with their American counterparts? It is reasonable to conclude that politics receives less attention in Canadian evangelical congregations than in the United States. For one, congregations with political agendas risk losing their tax-exempt status in Canada. Second, the political views of evangelicals in Canada have historically been more diverse than in the United States, and there is a stronger connection between partisan politics and religion among American evangelicals than there is in Canada (Bean, Gonzalez, and Kaufmann, 2008; Reimer 2003). We took an informal poll of researchers who have been in many evangelical congregations across the country to see if they could recall a pastor addressing partisan politics from the pulpit. Not one could. Even the politically active Evangelical Fellowship of Canada, which represents the majority of Canadian evangelicals, is non-partisan and moderate (Stackhouse, 1993; Patrick, 2011). Yet, some informal cues seem to be communicated largely through issue awareness. While congregations and most evangelical organizations do not support specific political candidates or parties,[4] they do flag certain issues related to religious freedoms, protecting the sanctity of life and the traditional family, but also some "left-wing" issues of poverty, the environment, and social justice which may cue voters toward certain parties (Malloy, 2011; Steensland and Goff, 2013; Wilkinson, 2010). Evangelical pastors we talked to have decidedly

Table 4.1 Number of times an evangelical pastor preached on the following topics in the previous six months

	Mean	Median
Devotional practices	7.56	5
Evangelizing	7.53	5
Caring for needs of others in the congregation	6.48	4
Evil and suffering	5.90	3
Caring for poor and needy outside the congregation	5.27	3
Participating in small groups	4.65	2
Sanctity of marriage or healthy marriage (not same-sex marriage)	3.54	2
Financial giving or tithing	3.46	2
Sexual moral issues like premarital sex and same-sex marriage	2.78	1.5
Negative effects of the media	2.17	1

Source: CECS, 2009.

non-political priorities, and the more mundane concerns of worship, religious education, and evangelism shape both their priorities and their programs. We look at the former in this chapter, focusing on the latter in chapter 5.

One way to find out what pastors prioritize is to ask about the topics of their sermons. Pastors told us the number of times that they had preached (for at least 2–3 minutes) on various specific topics in the previous six months. Table 4.1 gives the average (mean) number of times a topic was addressed from the pulpit, along with the median (the middle case). The median is the more helpful number, since a few pastors who claim to address certain issues very often can skew the mean. The table is ranked in order of most common to least common topics. The table clearly indicates that sexual morals and concerns about the media are addressed much less often than promoting religious practices, like devotionalism (e.g., reading the Bible and prayer), and evangelizing. On average, pastors addressed these issues about 7.5 times from the pulpit in the past six months, whereas the median was five times. Even when discussing marriage, pastors are likely to talk about its sanctity and health more often than premarital sex or same-sex marriage, which the typical pastor addressed only 1.5 times in the past six months of preaching. This indicates that religious practice is a much higher priority for these pastors than issues of sexual morality.

We asked evangelical pastors in our face-to-face interviews to tell us about their pastoral priorities. One way to establish these priorities is to ask them about the mission and vision of their congregation or its purpose. We also asked them to provide examples of how they see their purpose in practice. Overwhelmingly, the respondents from our face-to-face interviews expressed that their purpose revolved around worship, teaching, and serving. These three practices are expressed in a variety of ways theologically, biblically, and socially.

When evangelical pastors talk about their priorities, they usually reference the Bible and two texts in particular: the Great Commandment and the Great Commission. These two texts are found in the gospels and summarize for many pastors the focus of their ministry: to love God and others and to go into the world and make disciples. Loving God, for example, is often expressed through worship. Evangelical pastors spoke to us about the importance of gathering together to worship God through singing, preaching, and sharing Communion or the Lord's Supper. Worshipping God is celebrated in community where the people of God come together regularly to be encouraged, motivated, and sent back into the world to love others. A Mennonite Brethren pastor in Vancouver said, "We're a worshipping community, committed to showing love, sharing hope, strengthening the faith, showing love through practical kinds of deeds and kindness to anybody and everybody, anywhere and everywhere."

Loving others is the way in which evangelical pastors frame outreach activities like volunteering at a local soup kitchen, assisting in social services, and responding to family needs. A Baptist pastor in Calgary said, "We want to be a neighbourhood church" and talked about how that congregation opens its building for community groups to use. This too was thought of as an act of outreach. A Baptist pastor in the Maritimes shared how the congregation supported families in need through boxes or baskets with food and other goods. Another Baptist pastor in the Maritimes said, "We have this huge mission field, just one block from us ... and it's just wall-to-wall people. And we're also very close to the low-income public housing ... and we're reaching the kids, but also impacting their families."

Loving others is also about international mission work. Evangelical pastors encourage members to support mission work through giving and in many cases by travelling internationally for a short-term mission trip. A Pentecostal pastor in Toronto spoke about partnering with missionaries in India and how they supported the building of a hospital. Another Pentecostal pastor in Calgary shared how the congregation helped start a church in Ethiopia and how it financially supports ten missionaries in India. A Baptist pastor in the Maritimes said, "We had a mission tour which to me is always the place where God touches our youth. So we had an amazing mission tour this past summer and we had a good number of kids who wanted to go because it was to New York serving the homeless for ten days." Mission activity may involve building homes, churches, schools, medical missions, and relief work. Mission work is also about evangelism or sharing the gospel, the good news of Jesus.

Evangelism was identified as a priority in all of our interviews. Evangelical pastors place a high value on sharing their faith with others. The pastors see this as an authentic expression of their Christianity whereby they tell others about the love of God and extend an invitation for people to receive God's love. A Mennonite Brethren pastor in Vancouver spoke about evangelism as "inviting people to experience the life changing power of Jesus Christ." A Christian Reformed pastor in Vancouver said, "We are to be a witness to the truth of Christ to the rest of the world." The Great Commission – when Jesus commands his followers to "go and make disciples of all nations" (Matthew 28:19 NIV) – is often referenced when evangelical pastors speak about their priorities. Evangelical pastors believe the discipleship process or the making of disciples is about teaching Christians how to love God and others more effectively.

Discipleship programs are highly valued among evangelical pastors. Some of the programs we heard about included the Alpha program, which is a set of video-based messages intended to introduce non-Christians to the basics of Christianity. Nicky Gumbel, the Vicar of Holy Trinity Brompton Church in London, England, developed the program, which has been adopted by congregations all across Canada. The course covers basic questions like how does God lead us, who is Jesus, how does the Holy Spirit empower, and what is the role of the church, as well as other questions about the practice of faith like how to pray. The Alpha program is widely used among evangelical congregations in conjunction with other Alpha programs like preparing for marriage, programs for youth, campus ministry, and seniors.[5]

Many evangelical pastors adopt programs developed from evangelical leaders like *The Purpose Driven Life* by Rick Warren (1995). Warren's program focuses on discovering your purpose in life, which is to love God through worship, to enjoy fellowship with God and one another, to become more like Christ as a disciple, to serve God in ministry, and share your faith with others through evangelism. Warren's approach is not unlike most of the basic discipleship courses that evangelical pastors use to teach their members the basics of Christianity.

In some cases pastors develop their own curriculum. The curriculum covers basic Christian teaching that focuses on loving God and others through worship and service. The programs typically cover general questions about who God is, following Jesus, listening to the Holy Spirit, worshipping together in community, and reaching out to others. Those pastors who develop their own curriculum usually adapt the material from some of the more popular programs. They usually include extra modules that cover church membership, local congregational governance, spiritual gifts, and specific courses that train volunteers to serve in particular programs.

In some cases evangelical pastors speak about "incarnational ministry," referring to the theology of the Incarnation, when God became human in Jesus and lived among the people. Pastors referenced this idea to talk about how they wanted to be "incarnational" and live among the people in their neighbourhoods. A Christian Reformed pastor in Calgary said in reference to the congregation's purpose, "We reflect on who we are in Christ, be incarnational, like Jesus in our community." This idea was expressed by numerous pastors as "having a presence" among those who are in need. It captured the idea that they believed the people were to "live among" those God has called them to serve. Incarnational ministry is encouraged among evangelicals and illustrates how they desire to express ministry or evangelism in everyday life. As one Baptist pastor from Calgary said, "We're more interested in [being] incarnational ... and what I do with my neighbours." A Mennonite Brethren pastor in Toronto spoke about his congregation's values, including "the incarnational one, which is to be a people of presence."

A Christian and Missionary Alliance pastor in Vancouver expressed his priorities this way, which summarizes what the vast majority of our interviewees said:

> We are here to help people to know God personally and to share Christ's love with others, and that statement has four components to it: to know God, as basically our world does not know who God is. It's just the era in which we live in. So there is an element of teaching that is required. To know God personally means it's relational and that comes back [to] a sense of enjoying and worshiping God; to share Christ's love, that's within the body, caring for the body; and with others representing that we need to get outside of the church with that love in the sense of evangelism and mission. So that's the purpose statement broken down, leading to four core objectives which are celebrating the life in Christ which is worship, cultivating the word of Christ which is teaching, caring for the body of Christ which is mutual fellowship, and then communicating Christ to the world again which is evangelism and missions.

CONGREGATIONAL MISSION

Not all congregations, including evangelical congregations, prioritize numerical growth, but almost all want healthy congregations. Regardless of how congregational health is defined, all of them need sufficient and, it is hoped, growing, numbers to sustain that vitality. Research in both Australia and the United States shows that a clear purpose, with strong congregational buy-in, is central to congregational vitality. In Australia, some 400,000 attendees from 7,000 congregations and 22 denominations participated in the National Church Life Survey (NCLS) over three decades. Here is one of their major conclusions: "If there is one core quality that stands out as making a powerful difference in church vitality, it is the presence of a clear and compelling vision" (NCLS, 2006, 15). The report goes on to state that vital congregations take the time to create a vision that is owned and developed by the lay members. This vision inspires the congregation and sets a clear direction for the future. However, only 27 per cent of attendees say they are strongly committed to their congregation's vision, and this is a "significant challenge for congregational leaders" (Powell, Bellamy, and Kaldor, 2011, 4). In the United States, the FACT (Faith Communities Today) survey included some 10,000 congregations over the past decade, and it concludes:

> One of the stronger correlates of growth was the extent to which the congregation has a clear mission and purpose. For congregations that have such an orientation, growth is quite likely, but for those that do not, very few are growing. Not surprisingly, churches in conservative/evangelical denominations and "other Christian" groups are considerably more likely to "strongly agree" that their congregation has a clear mission and purpose than mainline congregations. So it would appear that at least part of the explanation for mainline decline is lack of a clear motivating purpose. (Hadaway, 2011, 8)

Since mission or vision statements are so important, we asked pastors several questions about them. There are, of course, a lot of congregations that have mission statements that are no more than a plaque on the wall from some long-forgotten visioning process. It may be true that Canadian evangelical congregations, like those in the United States, are more likely to have mission statements, but we wanted to know if the mission statement shaped current priorities and if people were accountable for reaching specific goals. So we asked:

Does this congregation have a mission or purpose statement?
In your view, does this mission or purpose statement shape the priorities and goals of this congregation at the present time, or not?
Has the leadership set specific goals for the next six months, year or two years for this congregation?
Has the leadership designed ways to measure these goals, so that one can determine whether or not the goals have been reached?
Are there set times or dates when the leadership will evaluate the extent to which these goals have been reached?
Are those responsible for implementing these goals held

accountable by someone or some group within the congregation?

We asked pastors if the laity were aware of the goals and if the leadership were committed to the mission. This is important because having a mission statement that generates clear and measureable goals is not sufficient. The lay volunteers must find the mission compelling and be committed to seeing it accomplished. Table 4.2 shows the pastors' perceptions of the lay leaders' awareness of the mission and goals of their congregation, broken down by rural and urban congregations, since this was the strongest demographic correlate of these measures (stronger than age of congregation, size, denomination, and numerical growth).[6] The table gives the percentages and in parentheses the number of congregations.

Table 4.2 shows that 89.3 per cent of the congregations have a mission statement (or 427 of 478 congregations in our sample). Of those with mission statements, 82.2 per cent said that their statement shapes the congregation's current priorities or about three out of four congregations polled (351 of the 478 congregations, 73.4%). Evangelical congregations in our sample have a mission statement that is current and influential. It is not surprising that the first question (whether the congregation has a mission statement) is not positively correlated with vitality, but if the mission statement is current and influential (second question), then it positively impacts vitality (Reimer, 2012). Yet, even current mission statements can be broad and difficult to implement unless they are broken down into specific, time-sensitive goals. Two-thirds of the congregations (65.3%) have set short-term goals. In general, we find that rural congregations are less likely to have current mission statements and short-term goals. Further analysis (not shown) found that having a current mission statement and goals is correlated with the presence of younger and more educated attendees, which are less common in rural congregations.

In the final questions, we looked at the percentage of pastors who disagreed with the statements, "The vast majority of laypeople are NOT aware of the goals and direction of this congregation" and "The lay leaders are committed to this congregation and fully endorse its mission." The results show that a majority (58.1%) of pastors disagreed or strongly disagreed with the first statement, but 150

Table 4.2 Pastors' perception of lay leaders' awareness of the congregation's mission and goals, rural and urban evangelical congregations

	Rural	Urban	All (N)
Has mission/purpose statement (% yes)	78.2	93.2	89.3 (478)
Mission statement shapes current priorities (% yes)	70.1	85.8	82.2 (427)
Leadership sets short-term goals (% yes)	50.0	70.6	65.3 (478)
Congregation has ways of measuring goals (% yes)	66.1	76.7	74.6 (311)
Dates to evaluate goals (% yes)	67.7	80.4	77.9 (312)
Someone is responsible to implement goals (% yes)	87.1	88.0	87.8 (311)
Majority of laity unaware of goals (% disagree)	48.4	61.6	58.1 (278)
Lay leaders are committed to and endorse congregation's mission (% agree)	91.9	92.7	92.4 (442)

Source: CECS, 2009.

congregations agreed with the statement (50 were neutral). In comparison, the pastors felt that the vast majority of lay leaders (92.4%) are committed to the congregation and endorse its mission. Overall, it seems that while the majority of congregations have mission statements, there is considerable slippage in how well they are communicated or implemented. If there is a problem with communication or commitment to the congregation's mission it is not among the lay leaders; instead, the issue seems to be that some of the people in the pew (or possibly those who are often not in the pew) are unaware of or less committed to the congregation's goals. As noted by the Australian researchers above, the challenge for congregational leaders is getting the laity on board with its goals and mission.

CONGREGATIONAL PRIORITIES

Of course, mission statements can reflect the priorities of the pastor more than the priorities of the laity. So we asked pastors about the priorities of their congregations, offering 16 statements to consider in our phone interview. We asked, "As you know, congregations operate according to certain values or priorities, even if they are not explicitly stated. In your view, what are the actual priorities of this congregation, based on how they function, even if they are different from your priorities?" These are listed in order from highest priority (percentage who consider it a "very high priority") to lowest in Table 4.3. The table gives denomination-specific information, as there were at least a few interesting denominational differences across the items; we highlight these in boldface in the table.

One would expect evangelical congregations to unanimously place very high priority on "Maintaining an active evangelism and outreach program, encouraging members to share their faith" (item 9, Active evangelism). Such "activism" is considered a defining characteristic of evangelicalism historically (Bebbington, 1989). However, this item ranked 9th among the 16 priorities, with less than half (44.2%) of all the congregations considering it a very high priority. This is only slightly higher than "promoting cooperation between the churches in the community" (item 10). While only 10 per cent of pastors said this was "not a priority" for their congregation, 45 per cent said it was a "somewhat high priority"; we suspect that some pastors were frustrated that they could not say that their congregation considered evangelism a "very high priority." Recall from Table 4.1 that pastors promoted evangelism from the pulpit very often (at least about once a month), indicating it was a high priority for them. Yet in actual congregational practice, it did not make the top of the list. One would wonder if the pastors are pushing the laity to evangelize when societal norms are pushing them the other way. "Protecting people in the congregation from the negative influences in the world" (item 13) was not a very high priority either, with only one in four congregations considering it a "very high priority" (not surprisingly, this item was highly correlated with a fundamentalist identity, as noted below). "Working to preserve traditional morals and family values" ranked quite high as the fifth item on the list, endorsed by half (49.9%) of the congregations as a top priority. Another 45 per cent considered it a "somewhat high priority." This places traditional morality fairly high; yet, there are four items that are rated higher. Furthermore, the item does not indicate whether "working to preserve traditional morals" is internal (among members) or external (in the society). Regardless, the level of endorsement does not indicate that evangelical congregations are primarily about equipping the faithful to transform the morality of Canadians.

Instead, the highest priority, across all the denominations, was "promoting the faith development of our children and youth." This

Table 4.3 Very high priorities reported by evangelical congregations, by denomination (%, in average rank order)

Very high priority	Baptist	CMA	CRC	MB	PAOC	All
1 Faith development of children and youth	76.7	76.3	85.2	84.9	80.2	80.7
2 Providing a welcoming worship service	61.1	60.8	56.5	62.8	67.7	61.6
3 Encouraging people to serve in their gifts	56.7	59.8	**47.2**	**74.4**	64.6	60.0
4 Strengthening marriages/families	42.2	57.7	43.5	53.5	66.7	52.6
5 Preserving traditional morals	60.0	55.7	36.1	40.7	58.3	49.9
6 Building volunteer leadership	45.6	50.5	38.9	54.7	54.2	48.4
7 Providing care for members	42.2	**32.0**	46.3	53.5	**58.3**	46.3
8 Promoting deeper spirituality/disciplines	42.2	46.4	**22.2**	43.0	**76.0**	45.5
9 Active evangelism	43.3	44.3	**22.2**	48.8	**65.6**	44.2
10 Promoting cooperation between churches	41.1	37.1	25.9	44.2	39.6	37.1
11 Serving the poor and needy	36.7	**19.6**	32.4	36.0	**45.8**	34.0
12 Teaching the theological distinctive features of our religious tradition	25.6	30.9	28.7	18.6	37.5	28.5
13 Protecting the congregation's people from the world	30.0	22.7	20.4	20.9	38.5	26.4
14 Enhancing beauty of the congregation's building and grounds	28.9	14.4	15.7	16.3	26.0	20.1
15 Preserving ethnic culture or language	12.2	11.3	2.8	5.8	8.3	8.0
16 Helping members get ahead financially	4.4	5.2	1.9	4.7	7.3	4.6

Source: CECS, 2009.
Note: Interesting denominational differences are highlighted in bold face.
CMA = Christian and Missionary Alliance; CRC = Christian Reformed Church;
MB = Mennonite Brethren; PAOC = Pentecostal Assemblies of Canada.

item was a "very high priority" for 80 per cent of the congregations, which is nearly 20 percentage points higher than all other priorities listed. It really stands out. This priority, of course, bodes well for institutional religion. As noted in chapter 2, keeping the children committed to the congregation is one of the best retention strategies, and is key to the long-term vitality of a congregation (also see Bibby, 1993). "Providing a worship service that is welcoming and comfortable to non-churched visitors," "encouraging people to serve according to their gifts," and "strengthening marriages and family relationships" round out the top four, and were all considered a "very high priority" by over half the congregations. Overall, the highest rated priorities seem focused on the goals of training, worship, and service. On the opposite end of the table, congregations do not prioritize the building and property, ethnic preservation, and financial success of their members. The final item suggests that the "health and wealth gospel" or "prosperity gospel" (see Bowler, 2013) is not widely endorsed by the congregations in our sample, as over two-thirds (67.5%) of the pastors stated that this was "not a priority" for their congregations.

Another conclusion from Table 4.3 is that there is general agreement on the priorities across denominations. This suggests that something supra-denominational, like the evangelical subculture, is shaping the priorities of the congregations. It is true that Christian Reformed pastors are less likely to consider these items "very high priorities" than the average, while the Pentecostal pastors were usually above the average. Yet, overall, the order of the priorities is similar across all the denominations. Note also that "teaching the theological distinctives of our religious tradition" was ranked near the bottom (12 of 16), and was considered a "very high priority" by less than one-third of the congregations. This suggests that congregations may be leaning more toward ecumenical cooperation, or are less interested in denominational differences. Note that cooperation between congregations (item 10) is ranked higher than this item. Our impression from the face-to-face interviews with pastors and the denominational staff is that some are concerned about whether denominational distinctive features are being swept away by the powerful current of generic evangelicalism.

In practice, evangelical congregations work together to reach their goals, requiring them to downplay differences. Interdenominational organizations bring congregations together, and pastors train in trans-denominational seminaries and universities. Since evangelicals are a small proportion of an already sparsely populated country, the institutions that support the subculture often do not have the luxury of offering denominationally specific services if they want to remain viable. They need to draw upon as many evangelicals as possible. The result is a tendency toward emphasizing evangelical boundaries instead of denominationally specific boundaries. Stewart (2012) found that PAOC congregations he studied have "transformed their religious self-identities, beliefs, and practice from a traditionally Pentecostal to generically evangelical forms" (139). The Mennonite Brethren have long had a dual evangelical and Anabaptist identity. Yet, they are concerned that they are losing their "Anabaptist" distinctiveness as their evangelicalism takes precedence (Dueck, Guenther, and Heidebrecht, 2011). Some denominational leaders expressed this loss of denominational identity as problematic and believed the best way forward was to develop a "franchise model" for their pastors to adopt. Other evangelical leaders specifically rejected the "franchise model" and opted for a more pluralistic approach to congregational forms and style, recognizing that because the society is diverse and people's needs are as well, the denomination needs a variety of congregational forms.

While general agreement is evident, there are some interesting differences between the denominations. "Encouraging people to serve in their gifts" (item 3) is strongly correlated with having a current mission statement, a missional identity, and a younger and more educated laity. Mennonite Brethren congregations are somewhat more likely to prioritize gift-based service, while Christian Reformed congregations are less likely to do so. The difference between the CRC and PAOC on item 9, "active evangelism," is also correlated with a missional identity. In general, CRC pastors rated their congregations lower than average on issues related to mobilization and activism, including cooperation between congregations. Possibly the strong ties to their ethnic (Dutch) heritage partly account for their insular tendencies. The same does not seem to be true for the MB, however, who are high on cooperation (item 10) and low on the priority of teaching their theological distinctives (item 12). The MB seems quite ecumenical and externally focused by comparison. The differences between the CMA and PAOC on "providing care for members" (item 7) and "serving the poor and needy" (item 11) is related to the demographics of these denominations. The PAOC congregations are more likely to be older and rural than the suburban and younger CMA congregations. The PAOC services a poorer clientele partly because of the location of their congregations, no doubt resulting in a higher emphasis on these caring ministries. Finally, the somewhat higher priority Baptists place on the building and property (item 14) is related to the fact that their facilities are much older on average (especially in Atlantic Canada), and thus require more care and upkeep.

PRIORITY ORIENTATIONS

Based on the 16 priorities in Table 4.3, we found that congregations tend to rate sets of priorities higher or lower, which is indicative of different basic types of congregations. Using a statistical technique called exploratory factor analysis, three factors emerged that could be considered general orientations of congregations. Put simply, factor analysis reduces a larger number of survey questions into fewer "factors" if the questions tap into the same underlying concept. In Table 4.4 we present the factor loading of each item, along with the percentage of congregations that considered the item a "very high priority" (as shown in Table 4.3). Factor loading simply indicates the strength of the connection between the item and the underlying factor. Note that there are a few factors not included in Table 4.4 that are either a "very high priority" for most congregations or "not a priority" for most congregations. These items were left out because they did not load onto any of these factors consistently.

The factors seem to approximate three orientations, which we call the activist orientation, the traditional orientation, and the moderate orientation. The first factor brings together five questions, which include prioritizing evangelism, developing volunteer leaders, encouraging service, promoting the spiritual disciplines, and strengthening relationships. Together, the questions point to an active and mobilized ethos. The congregations with a high activist orientation (Factor 1) tend to have certain correlates, as shown in Table 4.5. The correlations in Table 4.5 are easy enough to understand; they are simply a statistical measure of the strength of the relationship between two variables. The asterisks (***) after each correlation indicate statistical

Table 4.4 Factor analysis of priorities of evangelical congregations

	Factor loading	Very high priority (%)
Factor 1 – Activist Orientation		
9. Active evangelism	0.691	44.2
6. Building volunteer leadership	0.638	48.4
3. Encouraging people to serve in their gifts	0.625	60.0
8. Promoting deeper spirituality/disciplines	0.605	45.5
4. Strengthening marriages/families	0.577	52.6
Factor 2 – Traditional Orientation		
5. Preserving traditional morals	0.775	49.9
13. Protecting the congregation's people from the world	0.662	26.4
12. Teaching the theological distinctive features of our religious tradition	0.494	28.5
Factor 3 – Moderate Orientation		
10. Promoting cooperation between congregations	0.716	37.1
11. Serving the poor and needy	0.646	34.0
14. Enhancing beauty of the congregation's building and grounds	0.573	20.1

Source: CECS, 2009.
Note: The factor loadings in Table 4.4 are based on Varimax rotation, and these factors consistently loaded on the same factors using Oblimin, Quartimax, and Equimax rotations. There are a few items that did not load consistently on the factors, and were removed. There was also one more factor (made up of item 1 and item 15) that had an eigenvalue slightly above one, but was not included in the table because it provided no theoretical clarity.

significance. If it is statistically significant (as opposed to not significant, or NS) we can be sure that the correlation in the sample represents a real relationship in the population. Congregations high on the activist factor tend to be slightly larger (higher weekly attendance) ($r = .113^*$), growing in attendance ($r = .230^{***}$), and more likely to be urban ($r = .102^*$). The attendees are, on average, younger ($r = .244^{***}$) and more educated ($r = .244^{***}$). Pastors are much more likely to have a positive opinion ($r = .512^{***}$) about their congregations. These congregations are considerably more likely to have a mission statement that shapes their current priorities ($r = .336^{***}$). Although not shown in the table, activist-oriented congregations are described by their pastors as "missional" ($r = .397^{***}$) or "purpose driven"

(r = .351***). The CRC congregations are, on average, significantly lower than the other denominations on this factor (r = −274***). The PAOC is high on all three factors, because their pastors were more positive about their congregations in general, ranking more factors as very high priorities. In short, activist-oriented congregations tend to be evangelistic and vital. Since it is true that congregations high on this orientation also tend to be growing and receive higher reviews from their pastors, and since mission/vision is so important for congregational vitality, these priorities deserve a second look.

When we look at what researchers and congregational growth specialists have to say about healthy congregations, there is considerable overlap between the priorities in the activist orientation factor and the qualities of healthy or vital congregations that they promote. For example, Christian Schwarz's Natural Church Development research tools have been widely used by evangelical congregations in Canada, as well as by some 40,000 congregations in 70 countries (Schwarz, 2000).[7] Their eight essential qualities of healthy congregations include "gift-based ministry," "passionate spirituality," "need-oriented evangelism," and "loving relationships," among others. It is not hard to see the overlap with four of the priorities grouped in the activist orientation: encouraging people to serve in their gifts, promoting spirituality, active evangelism, and strengthening marriage/ families. To the degree that Schwarz and others are right, this orientation correlates with congregational vitality. Furthermore, 78 per cent of the pastors said that the items in this scale were either a "very high priority" or "somewhat high priority" for their congregations (compared with less than 50% for the other two orientations). The implication, not surprisingly, is that the priorities of evangelical congregations are part of their institutional strength.

Those congregations that are high on the traditional scale are on the opposite side of the spectrum. They prioritize preserving morals and values, protecting their people from the world, and maintaining their distinctive theology. This orientation is not correlated to the size or growth of the congregation, meaning that they are typical in the sample on these traits. Congregations high on this orientation tend to be rural with an older and less-educated laity, as the negative correlations in Table 4.5 show. This orientation is not correlated with a positive pastors' rating or a current mission statement. The Mennonite Brethren congregations are less likely to be high on

108   A CULTURE OF FAITH

Table 4.5 Correlations with priority orientations – activist, traditional, and moderate – of evangelical congregations

	Activist	Traditional	Moderate	All (%)
Total weekly attendance	.113*	NS	NS	
Increase in attendance	.230***	NS	NS	45.6
Urban	.102*	-.157***	NS	25.9
Age 18–29 years	.244***	-.112*	NS	14.9
With university degree+	.244***	-.105*	NS	34.7
Pastor opinion score	.512***	NS	.244***	74.9
Current mission statement	.336***	NS	NS	82.2
Denomination				
Baptist	NS	NS	.108*	
CMA	NS	NS	-.152***	
CRC	-.274***	NS	NS	
MB	.091*	-.121**	NS	
PAOC	.232***	.165***	.146***	

Source: CECS, 2009.
CMA = Christian and Missionary Alliance; CRC = Christian Reformed Church;
MB = Mennonite Brethren; PAOC = Pentecostal Assemblies of Canada.
NS = not significant; * $p < .05$; **$p < .01$; ***$p < .001$.

this factor than are the other evangelical denominations. Not surprisingly, congregations high on a traditional orientation are much more likely to be labelled as "fundamentalist" by their pastors ($r = .274***$, not shown). They seem to be more encapsulated and protectionist, avoiding worldly influences. As a result, growth is not correlated with this orientation.

The third factor, the moderate orientation, groups items on cooperation between congregations, helping the poor and needy, and enhancing buildings and grounds. These priorities are not unique to evangelicalism, and they seem more typical of some historic mainline denominations. Congregations high on this factor tend to be demographically average, as this factor is not significantly correlated with size, growth, urban location, or the age and education levels of attendees. Their pastors do tend to have a positive opinion of their congregations ($r = .244***$), but this is not as strong a correlation as with the activist orientation.[8] The Christian and Missionary Alliance is less likely to have congregations in this category. Congregations that rate high on this factor are also more likely to be considered "missional" (r = .276[***]) and "purpose driven" (r = .229[***]), and we suspect that is because this orientation points to a community focus which is what a "missional" congregation is about.

So what are the priorities and goals of evangelical congregations and their pastors? They seem to prioritize passing the faith on to their children, providing welcoming worship services, encouraging gift-based service, and the like. Our interviews with denominational leaders, and over 500 evangelical pastors from across Canada indicate that political mobilization or changing our country's moral standards are not top priorities for them. The purpose and goals are more mundane, and focused on engaging worship services, deepening the faith of the laity, and evangelizing and caring for their community.

We remind readers of the obvious: priorities are not always put into action. In fact, as noted in the next chapter, there is often little relationship between stated priorities and actual organized efforts or programs to mobilize people toward a priority. Even when programs exist, this does not mean that the congregation is achieving outcomes. Yet, the value of a priority cannot simply be measured by quantitative results. One example is the importance of prioritizing evangelism.

As Reginald Bibby and his colleagues (1973; 1983) have repeatedly noted, the actual numbers of conversions achieved by the average evangelical congregation is not very impressive, in spite of the high priority placed on evangelism. This is an important critique, but does this mean that evangelistic priorities and programs are unimportant to congregational growth and vitality? We actually think they are important and that the importance of priorities cannot be fully captured in numbers (even if evangelical congregations and denominations value counting converts).

Vitality relates to our earlier discussion of subcultures. Evangelical congregations create an ethos of evangelism that bolsters the congregation's vitality. Even a rare convert energizes a congregation. New converts are often "fired up" about their newfound faith, and their eagerness to share it inspires others. Since a new convert often has a network of non-evangelical friends and family, a conversion can have a snowball effect, leading to more converts. Such conversions, however rare, legitimize the congregation and its programs for those attending. The convert's testimony reinforces the significance of a salvation experience to the congregants, as they "relive" their own conversions. Public baptism by immersion and the telling of one's story or testimony are often inspirational for those in attendance. The testimony ritual enhances the shared experience and distinctiveness of those in the congregation.[9]

Other examples exist. If a congregation prioritizes and offers programs for children and youth, it enhances vitality even if the young are not retained as adults and few children are evangelized. Why is this so? Evangelicals "expect" the spiritual formation of their children and youth to be a priority and programs to be offered for them. Youth programs legitimize the congregation. Even for lay members who have no children or youth, they are more likely to support a congregation that prioritizes ministries for the young. Priorities and mission statements, if communicated regularly and owned by those in the congregation, often have value in and of themselves because they add to the congregational culture. This is true even if the congregation cannot show results, or lacks any means of measuring results. This is not a new idea. Organizational research has argued that within an "organizational field," like all evangelical congregations, organizations are constrained by contextual factors to adopt similarities that legitimize those organizations. For this reason, we see considerable similarities, or isomorphism, within organizations in that field (Powell and Dimaggio, 1991). Such is the power of the evangelical subculture, which in some ways reinforces those norms that are good for institutional religion.

5

Programs and Identity

Religion, Thomas O'Dea said, paradoxically, needs and suffers from its organization and institutionalization (1961). New religious groups, including those that have sought to revitalize the tradition, have faced numerous tensions as they organized. How does an organization create rationalized structures, statuses, and roles, while maintaining flexibility and openness to the Holy Spirit? Balancing religious experience with liturgy and repetition and developing administration while remaining relevant and up-to-date have been identified as real challenges. Numerous studies have examined these institutional dilemmas for denominations (see, e.g., see Poloma, 1989; Poloma and Green, 2010; cf Weber, 1993 [1922]). Evangelical Protestants are especially aware of these tensions and wrestle with communicating a message of personal salvation, devotional Bible reading, evangelism, and social activism in ways relevant to twenty-first century listeners. A particular response to these dilemmas is often heard among evangelicals in comments like, "The gospel never changes, but our methods need to adjust." Notwithstanding these challenges of the twentieth century, evangelical Protestants have found ways to take the heart of their message and transform it into institutional patterns that are culturally and socially relevant.

In the twentieth century, evangelical Protestants organized their congregations with increasing bureaucracy and included multiple levels of staff with specialized functions like lead pastors, associate pastors, assistant pastors, youth pastors, campus pastors, children's pastors, preaching pastors, counselling pastors, and administrative pastors. Programs were also specialized and structured around age and gender and included a host of activities focused on serving the needs of members from infants to seniors, men's groups, women's groups, youth groups, children's groups, choirs, Sunday School, evangelism teams, service groups, prayer groups, Bible study groups, and many more.

By the 1990s questions were raised by theologians about Christianity's place in Western society, and what this meant for the churches. For evangelicals this was taken up in two sets of literature and included works by those like Brian McLaren (2004) and the "Emergent Church" movement and others like Darrel Guder and the "Missional Church" movement (1998). While these two groups represent nuanced differences in their theologies of church and society, they share something in common: Canada is a post-Christian society and the church in North America needs to rethink the way it engages culture. The "Emergent Church" movement is more controversial and is not embraced by evangelical Protestants as much as the "Missional Church" movement is. The essence of the emergent church, argues Bielo in his book *Emerging Evangelicals* (2011), is a critique of the (Western) evangelical subculture, which has been shaped by modernism. While diverse, Bielo sees the following five contours of the movement: (1) a theological critique of epistemological certainty and systematic theology; (2) a missiological critique of old evangelistic methods with a move toward being "missional" (see below); (3) an ecclessiological critique of mega-churches, and subsequent movement toward house churches; (4) an "ancient-future" style of worship that embraces liturgy and (monastic) spiritual disciplines; and (5) a political activism that embraces left-leaning or progressive issues. Above all, they seek authenticity in an age of simple answers and surface manipulation. Emergent writers like McLaren are associated with the so-called new evangelical left and have become the target of criticism from some evangelicals (Gushee, 2008). Guder, on the other hand, and the contributors to the pivotal book, *Missional Church: A Vision for the Sending of the Church in North America* (1998) represent another group of writers who have examined what the church would look like if it truly believed North America was a mission field. Guder states, "It has taken us decades to realize that mission is not just a program of the church. It defines the church as God's sent people. Either we are defined by mission, or we reduce the scope of the gospel and the mandate of the church. Thus our challenge today is to move from church with mission to missional church" (6). Working through a range of issues on culture, society, secularization, theology, and contextualization, the contributors have established an agenda for churches to rethink who they are and what they do. Advocates of the missional church seek to take the church back to Jesus' mission to reach their community and world. They focus on the needs external to the church by incarnating Christ to their neighbours, and are less focused on needs and program development inside the church. Key spokespersons include Alan Hirsch, Tim Keller, and others.

In this chapter we present our findings from a series of questions on internal programs, those aimed at participants within congregations, and external programs – those activities traditionally referred to as evangelism, mission work, or social action. We then show how these programmatic elements are shaped by congregational identity, like whether the congregation identifies as "missional" or "emergent." Generally, our findings show a level of consistency in the types of internal and external programs among evangelical churches. These similarities, we suggest are indicative of significant isomorphism in the field, due partly to the strength of the evangelical subculture. There is very little variation among evangelicals on internal programs where activities for children, youth, and small groups are prominent.

Second, there is a general pattern among evangelical Protestants to partner with local social service agencies and para-church mission organizations (see Steensland and Goff, 2013). In spite of stereotypes that evangelicals are insular and uncooperative, we found high levels of cooperation with evangelical and non-evangelical (and secular) organizations. Evangelical congregations also tend to support denominational efforts for international missionary programs. Moreover, some pastors questioned the role of programs, especially those that focus inwardly, in light of the shift toward being "missional." Others continue to promote traditional programs. What we argue is that in spite of the different identities and debates about "missional" and "emergent" church, there are very strong similarities among and across evangelical congregations when we examine internal and external programs.

INTERNAL PROGRAMS

As we have argued in this book, institutional forms of Christianity are important for evangelical Protestants. The culture and structure of evangelical congregations are organized in such a way that their mission and vision are expressed through numerous activities, including programs. An internal program refers to those activities that are primarily for the benefit of members and adherents. Evangelical congregations prioritize and resource these programs with staff, volunteers, and money. In our face-to-face interviews with pastors across Canada, we asked them to tell us about the most important internal programs, excluding the main worship service. Overall, the pastors often spoke first about programs for children (e.g., Sunday School, children's ministry, Vacation Bible School, boys' and girls' clubs), and then youth and young adult groups, and then small groups (e.g., Bible Study, support, fellowship). These programs primarily focus on providing for the needs of members and adherents but in some cases contain an "outreach" component like Vacation Bible School. Pastors typically spoke of these internal programs as having some "discipleship" component where children and youth would learn the basics of Christianity, illustrating what sociologists refer to as "socialization" and the learning of the subculture through "education" as an agent of socialization.

The importance of children's ministry was highlighted by one Christian Reformed Church pastor from Calgary who said, "It is by far the biggest one [program]." This church conveniently operates an adult mid-week Bible study at the same time as the children's programs, so, "a lot of parents just stick around because they have to bring their kids here and then an hour and a half later, pick them up." The mid-week boys' and girls' program runs with two primary volunteers and on occasion some parents when needed. However, their children's programs are underresourced, which is troubling for other pastors we interviewed. In response to the question about what percentage of the congregation's budget went to children's ministry, the Calgary pastor said, "I did some calculating on that and I was not happy to see that it was surprisingly low." Other congregations like a Christian and Missionary Alliance congregation in Vancouver or a Baptist congregation in the Maritimes offered a standardized program called Awana. Awana Canada is an evangelical organization that offers a range of resources for local congregations.[1] Some congregations offer Sunday School programs that traditionally operate during the Sunday morning service or before it.

Evangelical congregations provide summer community programs, like Vacation Bible School, for children in their communities. A Christian Reformed pastor in the Maritimes described how 150 children would come from the community for their program in the summer. A Mennonite Brethren congregation in Vancouver operated summer camps that competed with other community programs focused on sports and creative arts. While not called "Vacation Bible School" they generally followed a similar pattern. Typically, the programs operated by congregations are less expensive than those offered by local sports associations or publicly funded programs.

The pastors we interviewed talked about youth and young adult programs as being very important. One Baptist pastor in the Maritimes spoke very highly about the youth program in his church. He described how the youth were also trying to reach out to the community and began a soup kitchen for the needy. Once a month the youth provided a meal for about 180 people. A Pentecostal congregation in Vancouver mentioned their vibrant youth ministry, with about one hundred youth coming out on a Tuesday evening. Young people would attend from other congregations that did not operate youth programs. In some cases youth were evangelized and joined the church. Young people were increasingly given responsibilities including leading worship during the main worship meeting on Sunday. The lead pastor spoke of the importance of the youth ministry and how the congregation wanted to keep "the young" by "releasing people into ministry." Another Christian Reformed pastor in Vancouver spoke about the importance of youth ministry and youth serving in the church. He said, "There are significant numbers of youth lining the pews and activities for youth to be involved in. It becomes very attractive to new families."

Small groups were important to the pastors we interviewed. The small groups were diverse in purpose, and they included Bible study, support for the divorced, recovery from addictions, and fellowship. Fellowship groups where meals were shared were especially important for ethnic congregations. For example, a Chinese CMA congregation in Toronto hosted regular fellowship groups. A Filipino pastor in Toronto also spoke about the importance of small groups for fellowship and sharing meals together. Small groups in the Filipino congregation were described as "cell groups" – a model of small groups that also focuses on evangelism, growth, and "multiplying."[2] The Filipino congregation has about 200 people attending the main worship meeting on Sundays: "We have cell groups and we are able to reach approximately 30 to 40 per cent of the members during the

Table 5.1 Internal programs of evangelical congregations, by denomination (%)

	Baptist	CMA	CRC	MB	PAOC	Total
Bible studies	96.7	95.9	99.1	98.9	**91.7**	96.4
Children religious education classes (0–12 years)	95.6	91.8	98.1	95.4	93.8	95
Prayer meetings	90.0	95.9	88.0	93.1	**97.0**	92.7
Organized way to help members	80.0	88.7	**97.2**	88.5	**76.0**	86.4
Marriage classes, premarital counselling	**68.9**	71.1	**86.1**	80.5	80.2	77.6
Baptism classes	71.1	84.5	68.5	**90.1**	71.9	77.2
Purpose of church discussions	76.7	78.1	68.5	73.6	76.0	74.3
Organized way to follow up on newcomers	72.2	60.8	59.3	72.4	74.0	67.4
New member classes	64.4	67.0	82.4	71.3	45.8	66.5
Spirituality/spiritual disciplines groups	57.8	53.6	63.0	70.1	66.7	62.1
Youth religious education classes (13–18 years), not youth group	52.2	**75.3**	69.4	63.2	**47.9**	61.9
Organized way to reconnect past attendees	47.3	**42.3**	**68.5**	55.2	58.3	54.8
Music ministry / worship leader training	**42.2**	61.9	50.0	51.7	57.3	52.7
Missionary or mission teams	50.0	64.9	46.3	44.8	54.2	52.1
Religious education teacher training	46.7	58.8	43.5	49.4	52.1	50.0
Evangelism classes	45.6	49.5	33.3	39.1	43.8	42.1
Spiritual gifts classes	36.7	36.1	34.3	33.3	53.1	38.7
Parenting classes	33.3	37.1	25.9	34.5	38.5	33.7

Source: CECS, 2009.
Note: Interesting denominational differences are highlighted in bold face.
CMA = Christian and Missionary Alliance; CRC = Christian Reformed Church;
MB = Mennonite Brethren; PAOC = Pentecostal Assemblies of Canada.

week. They are spread throughout the city and usually they meet every other week. And that's where they get to know each other more personally ... So they get solid fellowship as well as knowing one another and being able to minister to each other."

A Christian Reformed Church pastor in Vancouver spoke about small groups as a network of people across the city. They meet for a variety of purposes including Bible study, support, and fellowship: "There is a network of small groups ... All these [groups] have to have a relational component. People need to belong to them because they want to and they see it as a holistic thing, not as an obligation to attend. So, the men's group has a very strong relational component, as does the women's group, as do all the home groups. Nobody goes unless they are genuinely interested in being authentic."

From this pastor's comments, several observations can be made about small groups. First, evangelical pastors see small groups as a way of gathering members and adherents throughout the week. Gathering together sustains support and commitment to the mission of the congregation. Second, evangelicals see small groups as important for developing close personal relationships where people can share openly and freely about their faith. Third, small groups vary and can be formed around affinity, geography, gender, age, and ethnicity. Finally, there is a value expressed among evangelicals that small groups are places where "authentic" Christianity can be experienced (see Wuthnow, 1994).

These qualitative interview findings were supported by the quantitative results. The surprising level of uniformity across the evangelical denominations in internal programs can be seen in Table 5.1. Overall, there are few statistically significant differences, and fewer yet seem important. For example, nearly all of the evangelical congregations have Bible studies, children's religious education classes, and prayer meetings, although the Pentecostals (PAOC) are slightly less likely to have Bible studies according to these data. Most congregations have an organized effort, committee, or designated individual whose purpose it is to provide help to members or regular participants, for example, by cooking meals for a new mother or someone who just got home from the hospital, or providing financial assistance to someone who needs it. Most also offer marriage/pre-marital counselling services.

There are a few denominational differences, in boldface, that are worth noting. Not surprisingly, the Christian Reformed Churches (CRC) are often highest on "teaching"-related programs (Bible studies, children's religious education classes, premarital/marriage classes, etc.), likely because of their historical emphasis on the "life of the mind." The Christian and Missionary Alliance (CMA) congregations are predictably high, given their emphasis on missions, in outreach activities like mission trips/missionary training, and evangelism classes.[3] The PAOC are predictably high on spiritual gifts classes, and are also highest on prayer meetings. The Mennonite Brethren (MB) are highest on classes related to spirituality/spiritual disciplines, and baptism classes (even higher than the Baptists). The Baptists are lower than expected on some programs, and this is related to the higher number of small, rural congregations, particularly in Atlantic Canada. Obviously, larger congregations have more internal programs, and urban congregations tend to have more programs, even when we control for size.[4]

EXTERNAL PROGRAMS

Evangelical congregations are also active in "mission" programs or social service provision toward the poor and needy, a form of outreach about meeting needs in the community and not just about traditional evangelism as a stand-alone approach. Research on evangelicals and social issues in Canada is not as extensive as in the United States (Schwartz, Warkentin, and Wilkinson, 2008), where researchers have explored the role of faith-based social services (Boddie and Cnaan, 2007; Cnaan et al., 1999; Cnaan et al., 2002; Pipes and Ebaugh, 2002; Segers, 2003; Solomon, 2003; Wood, 2003; Wuthnow, 2004). Research in Canada has shown that faith-based groups have contributed a valuable civic role especially when government services have declined (Hiemstra, 2002). Some research has focused on social action among specific groups like the Pentecostals or the Salvation Army (Warkentin, 1998; Wilkinson, 2007; Wilkinson and Studebaker, 2010). Still, little is known about the types of programs operated by evangelical churches aimed at those in need outside of their congregations.

When we asked pastors to tell us about the external programs of their congregation, we learned that local programs centre on service provision. That is, the long-held assumption that evangelicals evangelize and leave service provision to other faith traditions, no longer holds. In fact, we heard very little about stand-alone evangelism efforts, and a lot about meeting felt needs in the community. We also learned that evangelical congregations tend to cooperate with local service programs that offer a range of services like food banks, nursing homes, English as a second language (ESL) programs, addiction services, and thrift stores. This cooperation was not limited to other evangelical organizations. Churches often cooperated with non-religious service providers, and sometimes with non-evangelical churches. We found cooperative, service-focused outreach dominated the local external activity of evangelical congregations.

This service provision was diverse. In some cases, local congregations kept a small supply of canned food goods for emergency situations in their buildings. Some operated a daycare or ESL program out of their building with volunteers from the congregation. Most partnered with para-church organizations like the Yonge Street Mission in Toronto, Mustard Seed in Calgary, or Mission Possible in Vancouver.

Evangelical pastors gave numerous examples of outreach activities. A Christian Reformed pastor in Vancouver, for example, told us about a daycare they operated since the 1980s, mostly with Chinese families. "I think for most of its history [it was] really a connection to the Chinese community." The pastor attributes growth in his congregation to the daycare. The pastor spoke about how the church is trying to connect with the people that live near them. While those from a Dutch immigrant background initially populated the Christian Reformed Church, the congregation believes it needs to reach out to all people, especially the Chinese who now live in the area. The daycare is one way they see the congregation providing for the needs of people. The congregation is now trying to find other ways of serving the Chinese population through community dinners, Alpha courses, and Bible studies: "We have a Chinese ministry that is kind of official this year for the first time, and Chinese Bible study, which is not really something intentional we did, but the Chinese community needed that so we're trying to support and encourage that."

Congregations support food banks across the country. A Pentecostal pastor in Toronto serves as the chair for the local food bank society. Another PAOC congregation in Vancouver works with other evangelical congregations to operate the local food bank. When talking about the food bank, the pastor rhetorically asked,

> If it were to shut down today, how would it impact our church? To be honest, I think our church would just keep flying, because the food bank is one of those odd ones [programs] that sits on the side and it begins to spin its own life. So the church operates somewhat separately from it. We want to communicate to the community that this isn't about being preached at or anything. So we give it its own little identity. But it is a ministry of this church. We involve lots of people, dozens of volunteers and there we have a director for the food bank. They collect money. We do all of the administration of the finances.

Evangelical pastors view these kinds of partnerships as ministry and as examples of serving "the least of these."

Evangelical pastors spoke about English as a second language programs as opportunities to serve the local community. In some cases local congregations networked together to offer ESL, as a group of congregations do in Calgary. In some cases individual congregations offered a program. For example, a PAOC congregation in the Maritimes worked with international students from a local university, helping them develop English language skills. The congregation saw it as an opportunity to "reach out" to students and in that sense the program fulfils its mission and vision: "We have people involved [in ESL] and in the past we have had live in our home three different Chinese students. They've all graduated and gone on now. So that's an area of concern that we have, and so we have been working with international students."

A range of local social needs are met by evangelical congregations including volunteering in nursing homes, serving in soup kitchens, working with addicts, and breakfast programs in the Maritimes; cleaning up neighbourhoods, providing assistance to the poor through fundraising and volunteering in Toronto; and, in Vancouver, making quilts for the ill, providing shelter from inclement weather, and Christmas hampers. Service programs are primarily oriented toward the needs of people who live near the congregation. Table 5.2 presents the results from our national survey on the types of service activities among evangelical congregations. Again, significant differences between denominations are given in boldface. We also asked the pastor to estimate the number of volunteers involved in these different service areas in their congregation in an average week, and the median number of volunteers (for those congregations that have that service) is given in the right-most column of the table.

Although evangelical congregations are widely involved in service (only 4% of congregations said they did none of the activities shown in Table 5.2), there is not the ubiquity of certain activities seen in the internal programs. Bible studies, children's religious education classes, prayer meetings, and organized help for members were present in more than 80 per cent of the congregations. The top service activities, giving cash or vouchers to the needy and visitation, are the most common at 78 per cent and 63 per cent, respectively, but no other service was present in more than half of the congregations in the survey year. The services offered involved a large number of volunteers.

There are few interesting differences between denominations in Table 5.2. Baptists are more likely to give out cash and/or vouchers and visit the elderly and hospitalized, partly because this is more common among rural and small congregations. A stranger asking for money or requesting a minister for hospital visits often contacts congregations. This is a service that does not require a lot of volunteers and can be performed by smaller congregations. The Christian Reformed Church is lower than the other denominations on several types of services, but is much more likely to have people volunteering with other organizations. Language training is most common in the Christian and Missionary Alliance, and this is related to the CMA's high proportion of ethnic and multiracial congregations. The Mennonite Brethren are high on community workshops, substance abuse programs, and education programs. The Pentecostal Assemblies of Canada are most likely to offer a food pantry and substance abuse programs.

The pastors estimated that the total number of volunteers used to run these outreach programs is 10,700 (of course, the same volunteers could be involved in more than one program). Another 9,225 volunteers are involved in service programs run by other organizations. The total weekly attendance is 100,475 for all 478 congregations, which means that up to 20 per cent of attendees are involved

Table 5.2 Service activities for the benefit of people outside the congregation, by denomination (%)

	Baptist	CMA	CRC	MB	PAOC	All	Median no. of volunteers
Cash or vouchers for needy	**86.7**	72.2	82.4	74.7	75.0	78.2	3.0
Visiting elderly, hospitalized	**74.4**	60.8	50.9	56.3	**74.0**	63.0	5.0
Counselling	55.6	51.5	31.5	55.2	63.5	50.8	2.0
Food pantry/soup kitchen	46.7	42.3	35.2	47.1	**54.1**	44.8	8.0
Community workshops	30.0	29.9	19.4	**46.0**	29.2	30.3	3.0
Prison ministry	22.2	20.6	21.3	17.2	22.9	20.9	3.0
Daycare, preschool, or after school program	20.0	**12.4**	**11.1**	25.3	19.8	17.4	5.0
Substance abuse	**7.8**	14.4	11.1	**20.7**	**21.9**	15.1	3.0
Language training	13.3	**21.6**	**7.4**	**17.2**	11.5	14.0	3.0
Employment services	8.9	18.6	12.0	13.8	14.6	13.6	2.0
Volunteer in other organizations	76.7	66.0	**90.7**	78.2	78.1	78.2	8.0

Source: CECS, 2009.
Note: Interesting denominational differences are highlighted in bold face.
CMA = Christian and Missionary Alliance; CRC = Christian Reformed Church; MB = Mennonite Brethren; PAOC = Pentecostal Assemblies of Canada.

in outreach programs. The Mennonite Brethren are the only denomination where the total number of congregants serving with other organizations is higher than the number of volunteers serving church-based outreach programs – 2,260 church program volunteers compared with 2,762 affiliates (members) who volunteer for other organizations. Overall, volunteerism with other outreach organizations is high, as other denominations are not far behind the Mennonite Brethren in this regard.[5] While the median number of volunteers is 8 per congregation (as shown in the last row of Table 5.2), the average number is 19.3, partly because large churches skew the data upwards. Combining the number of volunteers in both church-based outreach programs and those serving with other local organizations, the median number of volunteers is 25.

Naturally, evangelical congregations are not only involved in service provision. They are also active in evangelism or outreach. In reality, the pastors we spoke to considered all external programs outreach, since for them, feeding the needy or cleaning up neighbourhood areas has an evangelistic element. That is, serving the community can lead to evangelistic opportunities, even if that is not their primary intent. Table 5.3 looks at those programs that are primarily for people who do not attend the church and that are evangelism and outreach focused. Aside from the most common program, foreign missions, the other programs are usually for those in the community around the congregation. Ads in the phonebook or newspaper, websites, flyer distribution, and other outreach efforts are typically about raising awareness of the church or its special events. Acts of kindness (often called "random acts of kindness"), such as handing out free water at a community event, giving free car washes, or raking leaves for free, can be viewed as service to the community, but often they do more to raise awareness of the church. They tend to be short term, fun events often performed by energetic youth groups. Barbecues, block parties, or carnivals are similar in this regard. Daily Vacation Bible School (DVBS), Alpha programs, Bible studies, or small groups for non-attendees are more overtly evangelistic. Evangelical congregations will also move their church service to a public location, like a local park (in good weather) or another public space to attract those who normally would not set foot in a church.

It is clear from these data that old methods of more pushy evangelism are being replaced with more relational and service-type events

Table 5.3 Common types of outreach or evangelistic activities, by denomination (%)

	Baptist	CMA	CRC	MB	PAOC	Total
Foreign missions program	84.4	80.4	83.3	81.6	87.5	83.5
Ad in phonebook or newspaper	78.9	82.5	76.9	73.6	70.8	76.6
Website	64.4	78.4	76.9	83.9	65.6	73.8
Acts of kindness	57.8	**54.6**	63.9	**69.0**	66.7	62.3
BBQs, block parties, carnivals	55.6	63.9	**50.9**	67.8	64.6	60.3
Daily Vacation Bible School	**66.7**	59.8	57.4	57.5	**51.0**	58.4
Distributing flyers	55.6	43.3	52.8	51.7	49	50.4
Service at another location	44.4	37.1	40.7	**56.3**	52.1	45.8
Bible studies, small groups	37.8	**50.5**	34.3	34.5	**47.9**	41.0
Alpha	**22.2**	38.1	35.2	37.9	30.2	32.8
Door to door	**30.0**	**17.5**	23.1	23.0	28.1	24.3
Street drama/singing	13.3	8.2	9.3	11.5	**26.0**	13.6

Source: CECS, 2009.
Note: Interesting denominational differences are highlighted in bold face.
CMA = Christian and Missionary Alliance; CRC = Christian Reformed Church;
MB = Mennonite Brethren; PAOC = Pentecostal Assemblies of Canada.

that present the congregation as a contributor to the neighbourhood. Door-to-door and street evangelism methods are among the least common. The Mennonite Brethren are significantly higher than at least one other denomination on service in another location (probably because they are least likely to meet in a church), and acts of kindness. Baptist and Pentecostal congregations are more likely to use traditional evangelistic methods. Urban congregations are more likely to hold BBQs, block parties, carnivals, and Alpha classes, or distribute flyers and make door-to-door calls. They are less likely to run a Daily Vacation Bible School, hold a service at another location, or place an ad in the phonebook or newspaper. Even here, these differences are not large, with notable similarity across denominations. Less common outreach programs are listed in Table 5.4.[6]

When asked about international missions programs, pastors told us that they primarily supported denominational initiatives where the local congregation sends finances directly to the denomination.

Table 5.4 Less common types of outreach or evangelistic activities, by denomination (%)

	Baptist	CMA	CRC	MB	PAOC	Total
Special event celebrations	21.1	18.6	10.2	25.3	29.2	20.5
Food drive, provide meals	21.1	14.5	12.9	18.3	11.4	15.5
Relationship services, counselling, etc.	13.3	12.4	12.0	16.1	14.6	13.6
Youth drop-in/program	7.8	6.2	11.1	8.0	10.4	8.8
Music/concerts/plays	7.8	7.2	3.7	5.7	18.8	8.6
Gardening	8.9	10.3	3.7	5.7	10.4	7.7
Children's program/activities	8.9	6.2	7.4	2.3	5.2	6.1
Sports programs/games	6.7	5.2	4.6	5.7	6.3	5.6
Women's programs/shelter	6.7	5.2	8.3	3.4	2.1	5.2
Miscellaneous (all < 5%)	37.8	21.6	26.9	27.6	24.0	27.4

Source: CECS, 2009.
CMA = Christian and Missionary Alliance; CRC = Christian Reformed Church; MB = Mennonite Brethren; PAOC = Pentecostal Assemblies of Canada.

Funds are then distributed to the missionaries or used to support programs operated by the denominations. In some cases congregations supported denominational missionaries through the sending of funds directly to the missionary. Often missionaries speak in local congregations and share about the work they were involved in and how it can be supported. They also support independent and transdenominational programs like Youth with a Mission (YWAM), World Vision, Wycliffe (Bible translation), and Serving in Mission (SIM, formerly Sudan Interior Mission).

One Mennonite Brethren pastor in Vancouver said, "We have a number of individuals who either currently are involved in missions here locally or elsewhere around the world, that we continue to try to find different ways to be connected to. I think that's the biggest change I've seen overall in church, the Christian community – recognizing where they can get involved and make a difference and realizing that the church really is one of those answers to the world's problems of poverty, hunger, injustice, whatever."

Evangelical congregations also support para-church mission

Table 5.5 Cooperation of evangelical congregations (ECs) with various other congregations and organizations, by denomination (%)

ECs cooperated with	Baptist	CMA	CRC	MB	PAOC	Total
Other evangelical congregations	82.2	77.3	91.7	80.5	80.2	82.6
Other Christian (non-evangelical) congregations	48.9	48.5	50.0	37.9	42.7	45.8
Non-Christian congregations (Hindu, Muslim, etc.)	4.4	3.1	3.7	4.6	2.1	3.6
Other Christian organization (not congregations)	72.2	58.8	74.1	65.5	56.3	65.5
Other non-Christian organizations (not congregations)	53.3	48.5	44.4	57.5	47.9	50.0

Source: CECS, 2009.
CMA = Christian and Missionary Alliance; CRC = Christian Reformed Church;
MB = Mennonite Brethren; PAOC = Pentecostal Assemblies of Canada.

programs. For example, a Christian Reformed congregation in Calgary financially supports a Wycliffe missionary in Thailand. Wycliffe Bible translators and evangelical congregations partner with other organizations like Canada Institute of Linguistics and Tyndale University College where students study linguistics and gain the skills necessary for work as a Wycliffe missionary. Evangelical congregations see Bible translation as a necessary task for the evangelization of the world and so they financially support their missionaries.[7] A Pentecostal congregation and a Mennonite Brethren congregation in Vancouver support members who volunteer with Youth with a Mission. YWAM is an international program of youth focusing on evangelism and discipleship that began in 1960 when Loren Cunningham, an Assemblies of God minister, had a vision of youth volunteering in mission and evangelizing the world.[8]

Cooperation with other evangelical and non-evangelical local organizations is one way evangelical congregations in Canada serve others locally and across the world. Looking at Table 5.5, cooperation is most common between evangelical congregations (82.6%) and with other Christian organizations (65.5%). The highest level of cooperation is among Christian Reformed respondents at 91.7 per cent with other evangelical congregations and 74.1 per cent with other Christian organizations. In addition, nearly half of the evangelical congregations in our sample cooperated in some way with other Christian but non-evangelical congregations (Catholic and mainline Protestants, 45.8%). They also cooperate with non-Christian organizations, likely secular service providers. By contrast, cooperation with non-Christian congregations is rare. This seems to be the boundary of their ecumenism. Yet overall, evangelical congregations are not shaped by the exclusivism that some may assume. Nearly half cooperate with non-evangelical churches and with non-Christian organizations.

IDENTITY: FROM PROGRAM-BASED TO MISSIONAL FOCUS?

While programs are highly valued by some, our face-to-face interviews revealed that certain pastors were ambivalent toward them. For example, a Baptist pastor in Calgary said, "I'm a big believer in just getting together and not always programing it to death." Another Baptist pastor in Calgary said, "You don't want to be program driven and do the marketing thing." A Pentecostal pastor in the Maritimes qualified his understanding of the role of programs in his congregation saying he was not interested in running "programs for the sake of programs ... I've lived long enough to learn this: a crowd is not a congregation. I'm not interested in getting a crowd." He went on to explain that programs have to be based on "disciple making" and being more relational by serving the community. Another Baptist pastor in the Maritimes expressed it this way, "We're moving away from having the outreach events, to trying to train our people to go, bring Christ with them wherever they happen to be going. We've talked a lot about when you go to work, be open to anything that Christ wants you to do – an act of compassion, talking or listening to somebody, if you're involved in a store, when you go to school, when you go to university. We stress that you don't have to necessarily build new relationships, just bring Christ into the relationships that you already have." Evangelical pastors shared similar sentiments across the country regardless of denominational affiliation.

Many pastors spoke about being "missional," and while this was expressed in different ways their comments typically reflected concerns about the role of programs, the importance of relationships, and an emphasis on serving. A Mennonite Brethren pastor in Toronto said, "It's all relationship. We always start with relationship. I've been spending three and a half years building relationships with people and most of them have never walked into a church service." A Christian and Missionary Alliance pastor in Vancouver, trying to figure out how to connect with his community said, "I think it will be relationally through the small groups. That's the way I see it – not necessarily through program and involvement, although that's secondary and that's good too. But the relational part is important." One Mennonite Brethren pastor in Vancouver said, "We talk about ourselves being a neighbourhood church but not 'neighbourhood' geographically. It's far more [important] that we look, in terms of neighbourhood, relationally." A Christian Reformed pastor in Vancouver said, "I avoid the word program, because program has a connotation of if you fit a demographic, you have to go to that thing and you have to participate. But there's no real community or connection and there's no real growth or discipleship." A Baptist pastor in the Maritimes, who is trying to get his congregation to think differently about mission, asked, "Are we a downtown church geographically, or are we a downtown church missionally?" All across the country from all denominations we heard evangelical pastors speak about what it means to be "missional" and how their congregation was going to respond to the changing social and cultural context of Canada.

However, while many evangelical pastors are wondering how they can be "missional," there are some pastors who disagree with these new movements. For example, a CMA pastor in Vancouver was critical of the "emergent" and "missional" emphasis in churches. He thought that pastors who were following these trends were being led away from the centrality of the gospel, the pre-millennial return of Christ, and were being influenced by liberal ideas: "I think in our endeavours at times to become creative in life and ministry in the church, I think we've been letting some other things come in the back door. Some people might look at me and say maybe I'm just too traditional. I guess I'm ready to wear that." His concerns about being emergent, missional, and seeker-sensitive were, in his view, related to other issues like the ordination of women and liberal theology: "They seem like small things, and insignificant, and I think some leaders don't even see the full ramifications of the decisions. I've talked with some pastors who say this is where I've gone. Do you realize that this allows for that and they themselves have not even processed that. My concern is that ultimately scripture will be fulfilled when it says 'at times the very elect will be deceived.'" While this pastor's concern was not universally expressed, there is a growing body of evangelical literature with similar concerns about how congregations and pastors are being deceived by these current theological trends.[9]

In a study of "emerging" congregations in Canada, Steven Studebaker and Lee Beach (2012) of McMaster Divinity College, McMaster University, in Hamilton, Ontario, describe a number of congregations that are embracing the view that Canada is a post-Christian society that requires new methods and strategies of mission. Based on interviews and observations with a small sample of congregations across Canada, these authors argue that there are thriving alternative congregations embracing a community-based ministry, an incarnational or relational approach to ministry, and a holistic view of spirituality. There is no single model of an "alternative" congregation. Rather, there are different approaches, which include the "artisans" who gather with other like-minded creative types and experiment with different forms of worship. There are the urban technology-driven congregations of "hipsters" and "metros" in their twenties and thirties who are attempting to plant congregations in areas many congregations vacated during their move to suburbia. Finally, there are the "misfits" who never fit in traditional evangelical congregations. These pastors and leaders are starting ministries in coffee shops or living in the poorest neighbourhoods in some communal form or with other people on the margins of society. Studebaker and Beach see these congregations as an "emerging" trend among evangelical Protestants in Canada that is "deeply theological" while critiquing programs and a "cookie cutter" view of Christianity. These congregations are also pragmatic, local, contextual, relational, and holistic.

In our research, it is not always clear how evangelicals self-identify beyond the denomination or the congregation and what the implications may mean for the churches. We asked pastors the degree to which their congregation identifies as evangelical, fundamentalist, charismatic, liturgical, or by more recent trends, as missional, emergent, or purpose driven. These labels are common in the evangelical subculture, the topic of books, magazines, blogs, and conferences for evangelical pastors. Lead pastors were asked, "In terms of overall identity or culture, how well do you feel the following terms describe this congregation? Does this term describe this congregation Very, Somewhat, or Not Very Well?" The percentages of pastors who answered "very well" to items in this question are presented in Table 5.6.

We suspect that many of these identifiers are not well understood by the pastors, if indeed they are clearly defined by denominational leaders, authors, or researchers. Older categorizations – evangelical, charismatic, fundamentalist, liturgical – are more clearly defined, and we have defined what we mean by "evangelical," the most common identity, in our research. After evangelical, the next most common identity was "missional," described above. The "emergent" label was not very popular, with only 7.5 per cent of pastors saying the label described their church very well.

Ranked third is "purpose driven," an identity that follows the strategy laid out in *The Purpose Driven Church* (1995), a best-selling book by Rick Warren. The church, argues Warren, needs to align its purpose with the five biblical purposes of the church, the result of which will be a healthy church that is growing in depth and numbers: "Purpose Driven is a church health model that provides your pastoral team with a unique, biblically-based approach to establishing, transforming, and maintaining a balanced, growing congregation that seeks to fulfill the God-given purposes of worship, fellowship, discipleship, ministry, and missions."[10] While the five evangelical denominations ranked the charismatic identity fourth, this is mostly because of the strong identification among the PAOC congregations (47%). The charismatic movement is a transdenominational movement that began in the 1960s among Catholics and mainline Protestant denominations. It emphasizes the work of the Holy Spirit to empower the individual and the church for service and evangelism. Its adherents emphasize the miraculous and surprising movements of the Spirit, and believe that tongues, miracles, prophecy, etc. are still for the church today (see Wilkinson, 2009).

About one in ten pastors identified their congregations as being seeker-sensitive or fundamentalist. The seeker-sensitive movement is probably best typified by Bill Hybel's Willowcreek Church through much of its history. Seeker-sensitive churches provide a welcoming environment for the unchurched. Seeker services generally have contemporary worship, and a polished multimedia presentation in a non-threatening atmosphere.

Table 5.6 Identity descriptors of evangelical churches, as reported by pastors, by denomination (%)

	Baptist	CMA	CRC	MB	PAOC	Average
Evangelical	73.3	85.6	43.5	81.6	83.3	72.6
Missional	36.7	38.1	17.6	46.0	57.3	38.5
Purpose-driven	11.1	22.7	6.5	19.5	26.0	16.9
Charismatic	3.3	5.2	2.8	6.9	46.9	13.0
Seeker-sensitive	12.2	14.4	10.2	14.9	9.4	12.1
Fundamentalist	12.2	12.4	0.9	3.4	25.0	10.7
Emergent	3.3	7.2	6.5	10.3	10.4	7.5
Liturgical	1.1	0	16.7	3.4	1.0	4.8
Cell-church	0	7.2	4.6	2.3	4.2	3.8
Identifies with denomination (extremely and very closely)	42.2	53.6	64.8	39.6	54.2	51.6

Source: CECS, 2009.
CMA = Christian and Missionary Alliance; CRC = Christian Reformed Church;
MB = Mennonite Brethren; PAOC = Pentecostal Assemblies of Canada.

"Fundamentalist" is a derogatory label for most Canadians, referring to those who are dogmatic, intolerant, and argumentative: in short, fundamentalists are un-Canadian. We wonder if some pastors identified their churches as fundamentalist even though they viewed the term negatively. Most rejected it. Two-thirds (67.4%) of the pastors said the label "fundamentalist" does not describe their churches very well. Using a more precise, scholarly definition, fundamentalists are those who espouse a literal view of the Bible; they are morally strict, separating themselves from worldly influences and sometimes even other evangelicals; and they seek to return to a time when religion was undefiled (Marsden, 1984; Ammerman, 1987). This label is rarely applied to CRC and MB congregations, and is applied to a quarter of PAOC churches. Again, we do not know how accurately the pastors used this and other labels.

Only a few pastors identified strongly with the "liturgical" or "cell church" labels. Eighteen CRC pastors identified their congregations as liturgical, and only 5 other congregations did (three of which were MB). Similarly, only 18 pastors identified strongly with the cell-church movement. The cell-church movement may have its strongest proponent in Yoido Full Gospel Church in Seoul, Korea. In the model, the backbone of the church are its evangelistic and discipleship-oriented small groups. While the CMA were mostly likely to identify as cell church (7 pastors), note that the percentages are too small for accurate comparisons.

Nearly three-quarters (72.6%) of congregations in our study said the label "evangelical" describes them very well, and only 13 congregations (2.7%, 8 were CRC) thought that "evangelical" did not describe their congregation very well. The CRC are least likely to say the term describes them very well, as their identity seems stronger with their denomination (see bottom row of Table 5.6) and less strong with the transdenominational evangelical identity. Likely because of their strong identity with the Reformed tradition, the CRC is least likely to identify with any of the more trendy labels. The "missional" identity is strongest among the PAOC, as is, predictably, the charismatic label. In total, over a third of congregations identify themselves as missional. Less than a fifth of the evangelical congregations identify with any other label in the study.

Once we hold congregational size/attendance constant, those congregations that are growing (higher attendance in 2008 than in 2007) and have more programs are more likely to be considered "missional" and "purpose driven" (see Table 5.6). It is surprising that "missional" congregations would have more internal programs, since the missional movement is more external-focused. However, the term "missional" seems to be used by pastors who are positive about the overall vitality of the congregation. Most of the internal programs are positively correlated with a "missional" description. Congregations with a lot of internal programs (controlling for average attendance) are rated more positively by the pastor ($r = .267^{***}$), as are congregations that are regarded as "missional" ($r = .393^{***}$). Educated and younger congregations also have more programs, and the pastor tends to be older in these congregations. Denomination, race of congregation, gender of pastor, region, and income/expenditures (and many other possible predictors) were not significant predictors of missional identity.

What can we conclude from these findings? First, evangelical congregations show uniformity in internal programs. Evangelical congregations offer Bible studies, religious education, prayer meetings, rites including marriage and baptism, youth and children's programs, classes on Christian spirituality, spiritual gifts, and other similar programs. This shows a level of commonality across these particular denominations or what may be referred to as a generic evangelicalism. Evangelicals share a subculture that supports their many activities lending to many similarities (Reimer, 2003).

Second, some evangelical congregations in Canada have shifted away from traditional approaches to evangelism and toward more holistic ministry, which includes a greater emphasis on social action. While there is some variation between the groups on what activities are emphasized, nearly all congregations provide services to their communities. This may reflect some of the recent discussions about the importance of a holistic approach that emphasizes both "good news and good works" (Sider, 1999). Donald Miller and Tetsunao Yamamori (2007) have also put forward the idea of "progressive Pentecostalism" to describe a more holistic approach among Pentecostals from Africa, Asia, and Latin America. A holistic Pentecostalism is also explored in North America with some evidence to support these changes (Wilkinson and Studebaker, 2010).

Third, these findings may also be related to external or cultural and societal changes where evangelical pastors believe that Canada is a post-Christian society. As a result, they have moved toward a "missional" focus, with a focus on relational, "incarnational" ministry in their neighbourhoods, with a corresponding move away from prioritizing internal programs. Since most Canadians rarely enter congregations, evangelical churches are shifting their rhetoric (and in some cases their activities) to impacting people outside the walls of the church. Will such a missional, external focus add vitality and growth to the churches? We wonder. On the one hand, a more holistic ministry among unchurched neighbours may increase the authenticity and attractiveness of church participation. On the other hand, increased cooperation and engagement may soften subcultural boundaries, causing evangelical churches to lose distinctiveness. There is a balance between relevance and distinctiveness that can enhance vitality, but it is a difficult balance to maintain.

6

Leadership and Pastoral Well-Being

Institutional religion in Canada is not just finding fewer people in the pew; there are also fewer clergy to fill the pulpit. Shortages of Catholic priests have been well documented since at least the 1960s for North America (Carroll, 2006; Fichter, 1968; Greeley, 1972; Hoge et al., 1988, 1995). Some have claimed that mainline Protestant denominations face a similar shortage (Berton, 1965; Carroll, 2006; Jud et al., 1970; Towler and Coxon, 1979; Randall, 2004) although most evidence is from the United States. It is hard to recruit qualified young seminarians, and many leave the ministry disenchanted or stressed out. As a result, denominations are trying to figure out how to recruit and retain qualified clergy. One creative effort to recruit comes from Halifax: "The shortage of Catholic priests in the West has been well documented. The archdiocese of Halifax decided to put up billboards to try and attract men into the priesthood. Billboard messages include 'Yes, You Will Combat Evil. No, You Don't Get To Wear a Cape' and 'White Collar Workers Wanted'" (Pauls, 2001).[1]

By 2001 a few media sources were saying that all Canadian denominations were facing clergy shortages, yet their examples related to Catholics and mainline Protestants (Todd, 2001; Hiebert, 2001). In 2010, the *Globe and Mail* wrote, "Clergy shortage affecting all denominations in Canada," stating,

> As Canada becomes increasingly secular, many faith groups are searching high and low for young people willing to do God's work. In some cases that has meant recruiting from abroad, where instead of preaching for converts congregations are returning to former missionary lands to harvest

clergy. In other cases, they're bypassing the young entirely, welcoming older people in their second or third careers. A vocation used to begin straight out of school, but faith groups are now marketing themselves to the teacher, the biochemist, even the spy. Other groups, particularly the rapidly growing minority faiths, are struggling to find Canadian clergy who understand the cultural context in which their congregations live.[2]

Again, examples in the article were from mainline Protestant denominations. So, are evangelical Protestants facing a shortage as well? The evangelical denominational leaders we talked to certainly think so. All five denominational leaders were concerned about clergy shortages in the future and were looking for innovative ways to keep pastors, particularly young pastors, and to attract new gifted leaders. Some told us that it was difficult to recruit young people. The number of graduates, they claimed, is inadequate to replace the pastors who are retiring. A Pentecostal (PAOC) leader, for example, explained that while clergy are aging there are fewer young people stepping up to take their place. Some young people do not understand what "calling" means, he said, and are questioning what ministry entails.[3] A French Baptist leader told us he would not be able to retire at retirement age because there were too few young pastors to replace him. Another Baptist leader (CBOQ) said that 100 of their pastors (roughly 365 total congregations) would reach retirement age in the next five years, and a Mennonite Brethren (MB) leader said they would need to replace 40 per cent of their pastors in the next five years due to retirement and burnout.

Denominational leaders also discussed issues about congregational leadership and clergy needs. There is agreement that "good" leaders do well and "successful" congregations, they argue, are successful because of the leadership. Yet, there are also a number of challenges evangelical churches are facing. For example, the denominational leaders all talked about young leaders who did not seem to fit into traditional models of congregational life. One denominational leader commented on how the church "was packaged for a generation passing away" and pondered about "how are we going to be faithful in the future?" Another leader also wondered how "age-related tensions" would be resolved when young theological graduates do not feel they fit and older congregants seem to be less amenable to change. Some leaders questioned whether or not new young graduates "were selfish" and "immature." Other leaders wondered about the role of theological education and whether or not the seminary or Bible college was doing a good enough job in training leaders to face the challenges. Some denominations were rethinking the role of pastoral training and moving away from colleges and seminaries to a lay leadership program that was church based. Others criticized their seminary for being too "research based" and moving away from training pastors.

Some researchers say the cost of being a pastor is increasing, while the benefits are decreasing (e.g., Finke and Stark, 1992). Since the move away from institutional religion, clergy work has become more demanding. Canadians are more likely to leave a congregation if they do not get what they want, and "shop" for religion elsewhere. They are demanding consumers of religion, evaluating the religious "products" presented by clergy to see if they suit their needs. Clergy calls for institutional commitment often fall on deaf ears. Individualism results in less deference to clergy. While the position has lost prestige, the costs are at least as high as ever. Catholic priests are required to be celibate, pastors are expected to be on call day and night, and the pay in other helping professions is perceived to be better. There are some benefits. The hours may be long, and the pay poor, but the retirement plan is "out of this world," quipped one preacher.

Clergy shortages have much to do with demographics. A high percentage of pastors are baby boomers who are taking early retirement or will be reaching retirement age shortly. With a moderately small cohort of young people who are comparatively less interested in ministry, there are not enough new clergy to replace them. Demographic reasons point to clergy shortages among evangelicals as well, because, like most Canadians, they are having fewer children over time and there are many aging evangelical boomers.

Some say that the problem is distribution. In fact, in the United States, researchers claim there is no shortage of clergy (except for the Catholics). For instance, Stanford sociologist Patty Chang (2003) explains that there is actually a glut of pastors – nearly two pastors for every empty pulpit – available at the same time as there are many congregations without pastors. On the one hand, denominational leaders, who tend to count empty pulpits, are decrying shortages, while graduating seminarians are finding considerable competition for empty pulpits. Who is right? They both are. New seminary graduates often have limitations on where they can pastor. Higher percentages of seminarians are older, pursuing a second career, have families, and sometimes they carry a significant amount of debt (Carroll, 2006). There may be plenty of part-time positions available, and possibly even full-time positions in small, rural congregations. However, limitations due to children, spouse's work, student debt, and other factors make taking such positions impossible or unattractive. Many seminarians also want to stay near or in the city, where their spouses work and/or their children go to school. As we shall see below, part-time positions are becoming more common, and full-time positions less common. Note also that roughly half of all evangelical congregations are small, with average attendance under 100 people.

Yet, evangelicals are least likely to have vacancies, and they also have the highest ratio of pastors to parishioners (Chang, 2003; Davidson, 2003). Data from the United States show that most evangelical denominations actually saw an increase in the number of clergy between 1981 and 2001, and the ratio of clergy to lay adherents also increased. In 2001 the overall ratio was 189:1 with Catholics at 1,429:1 and Assemblies of God 103:1. In Canada, Bibby (2004) estimates that there are more evangelical ministers and ministerial staff in Canada than Catholic and mainline Protestant ministerial personnel combined.

Even if evangelical clergy are more plentiful, the flow of new clergy candidates coming through the seminaries may not be adequate to fill the need. There are thirty-nine seminaries in Canada affiliated with the largest accrediting body, the Association of Theological Schools (ATS), and over half of them (56%) have a student body (full-time equivalent, or FTE) of less than 75. Figure 6.1 presents head-count data (which is the number of students enrolled, including both full-time and part-time students) based on whether the seminary is evangelical (EV), mainline Protestant (ML), or Catholic (RC).[4] ATS has sixteen evangelical, sixteen mainline Protestant, and seven Catholic affiliate seminaries in Canada.

The number of seminary students in Canada is down substantially over the past decade, with overall enrolment declining from 6,254 students in 2001 to 5,234 in 2011 (a 16% drop). This represents a decline of roughly 23 per cent for mainline Protestant, 20 per cent

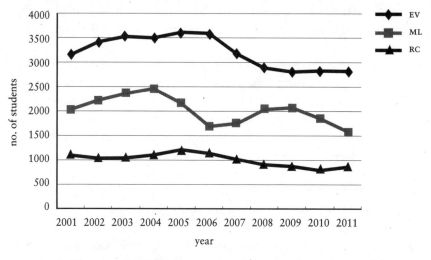

Figure 6.1 Number of seminary students in Association of Theological Schools schools in Canada.

EV = evangelical Protestants; ML = mainline Protestants; RC = Roman Catholics.
Source: Association of Theological Schools data, 2011.

for Catholic, and 11 per cent for evangelical seminaries over the eleven-year period. We think this actually underestimates the evangelical decline. Data from seven leading evangelical seminaries (ACTS, Regent, Tyndale, Briercrest, Ambrose, Providence, and Taylor) show a 20 per cent decline in head count (2,419 to 1,907) in the past decade (2002–11), and a 30 per cent decline in full-time equivalent counts, indicating an increase in the proportion of part-time students.[5] Add to this the fact that many students who attend seminary are not training specifically for work as pastors, and even some who are training for professional Christian service will end up pursuing other occupations. In other words, the number of seminary graduates is greater than the number seeking positions as pastors. For argument's sake, let's assume that the number of seminarians is fairly reflective of the number of pastors/priests available. Based on Outreach Canada's (2010) estimates of 11,000 evangelical congregations, 6,000 Catholic and 7,500 mainline Protestant congregations, the ratio of seminarians to congregations is about 1 to 4 for evangelicals, 1 to 5 for mainline Protestants, and 1 to 7 for Catholics. Overall, evangelicals seem to be slightly better off in terms of available leadership, but their pool of seminarians is declining rapidly (particularly if the number of congregations holds steady, as it seems to be doing).

While we lack definitive evidence, it seems reasonable to suggest that there is, or will soon be, a shortage of evangelical clergy in Canada. Yet seminary enrolment numbers do not tell the whole story, and there are other reasons for concern. Research in the United States shows that those entering seminaries are not as talented as previous cohorts (Chaves, 2003). While academic prowess is probably not the most important predictor of future clergy success, it does suggest that ministry may not be as attractive as it once was to the brightest young people. We also heard from the denominational leaders that the talented, theologically trained youth are less interested in congregational ministry than before, and more interested in working with other non-profit or for-profit organizations. A shortage of talent does not bode well for the future of the congregations. Yet, a balanced perspective is required. Bruce Guenther, president of Mennonite Brethren Biblical Seminary Canada, agreed that there are more available positions for pastors than there are seminary graduates to fill them, but he doubts there will be a "crisis" in the near future because congregations tend to find leaders, even if they are not graduates of their seminary. Congregations are resourceful, and many have intentionally developed leaders from within. Canadian evangelicals continue to recruit clergy from a network of Bible colleges across the country.[6]

CLERGY DEMOGRAPHICS

Clergy shortages and historical changes in gender equality and immigration have created a more diverse clergy in Canadian evangelical pulpits. Traditionally, seminarians used to be young white men. In the past thirty years, there has been growing diversity in terms of age, gender, and race/ethnicity. Now, there is a majority of women in some programs, and the percentages of older, second-career, and ethnic students are increasing. In addition, seminaries are becoming more interdenominational (Coggins, 2011).[7]

Regarding women clergy, many denominations have officially changed their policies over time, offering full ordination to women.

In 1936 the United Church of Canada ordained its first woman minister, with the Presbyterian Church in Canada following in 1967, the Anglican Church of Canada in 1975, and the Evangelical Lutheran Church in Canada in 1976. Of course, Catholic priesthood is still limited to men. Some evangelical denominations have ordained women since they started, others very recently, and still others not at all. Three denominations in our sample ordained women recently, the Mennonite Brethren in 2006, the Christian Reformed Church in 2007, and the Christian and Missionary Alliance in 2012.[8] Two others have been ordaining women for a long time, and we look more closely at these.

In the early 1900s Pentecostal women enjoyed access to a variety of ministerial roles, including that of pastor. However, as the movement institutionalized, "the early freedom of gifted women [was] quickly eclipsed by the coexisting patriarchal assumptions and practices" (Holmes, 2009, 175). It was not until 1984 that the Pentecostal Assemblies of Canada officially began ordaining women, and it was 1998 before women were allowed to hold leadership positions at the national and district levels (Holmes, 2009; 2010). The Convention Baptists also ordained women early on, with the first ordained woman (Muriel Spurgeon Carder) in 1947 by the CBOQ and in 1956 by the CABC (Josephine Moore) (McNally, 1987). Data from these denominations, however, show that female clergy still make up but a small percentage of lead pastors and pastors overall, as can be seen in Table 6.1.

Table 6.1 shows that 901 of the 3,555 (25%) credential holders in the PAOC are women, but only 43 of the 964 lead pastors are women (4.5%). Out of 646 CABC ordained pastors, 79 are women (12.2%), and 26 of 366 senior/lead pastors are women (7.1%). In our interviews, we spoke to only 18 female pastors in all five denominations (4%). The numbers are low partly because we asked to speak to the "senior or lead pastor." Indeed, 182 of the 478 lead pastors told us that there was at least one female on their staff of pastors. There were 810 other pastors (not counting the lead pastor) working in the congregations we interviewed, and 313 (38.6%) were women. Of the 100 youth/children's pastors we interviewed, 34 were women. Thus, women fill about one-third of pastors' positions, although few are lead pastors. Women lead pastors tend to have small congregations, with a median congregational size of 60, compared with the male median of 140.

With an increasing proportion of ethnic congregations, the number

Table 6.1 Women pastors in the Pentecostal Assemblies of
Canada and in the Convention of Atlantic Baptist Churches

	Ratio (n/n)	Women (%)
Pentecostal Assemblies of Canada		
All pastors (men/women)	2,654/901	25.3
Lead pastors (men/women)	921/43	4.5
Convention of Atlantic Baptist Churches		
All pastors (men/women)	567/79	12.2
Lead pastors (men/women)	340/26	7.1

Source: Pentecostal Assemblies of Canada website and in the Convention of
Atlantic Baptist Churches denominational staff.

of non-white clergy is growing as well. Minority pastors are probably
underrepresented in our data, as roughly fifteen pastors we contacted
were unable to participate in the survey because they did not speak
English or French well enough to complete the interview. However,
evangelical denominations also face specific challenges with recruiting
and training new immigrant pastors. For example, a PAOC leader
spoke to us about the challenges of finding culturally appropriate
courses and faculty for ethnic pastors, since they are generally not
attending Bible college or seminary. The BC and Yukon District of
the PAOC operates a "college" for ethnic pastors that focuses specifically on issues related to them. A leader for the CMA spoke about
the challenges of finding and training ethnic pastors for new immigrant congregations, specifically pastors who can speak Mandarin
and understand Chinese culture. A CRC leader also expressed the
need for ethnic pastors to assist with new congregational initiatives.
As seen in Table 6.2 roughly 90 per cent of pastors in our sample are
white (non-minority) (430) and about 10 per cent (48) are members
of visible minorities, the largest group being from Asia. Of the 48
minority pastors, 27 ministered in congregations where the majority
of attendees matched their ethnic category (e.g., 22 of the 28 Asian
pastors ministered in congregations where over half of the attendees
were Asian), and 14 ministered in majority white congregations (the
remaining 7 were in multi-ethnic or in non-matching ethnicity congregations). In our data, 49 congregations had a majority of non-
white attendees.

142   A CULTURE OF FAITH

Table 6.2 Ancestry of pastors of
evangelical congregations in Canada

Ancestry	Pastors (n)
European or North American	430
African	7
Asian	28
Aboriginal	4
Latin American	2
Caribbean	1
Pacific Islands	2
Other	4
Total	478

Source: CECS, 2009.

Regarding education, many evangelical denominations have a history of prioritizing calling and gifting above educational achievement. Yet, our sample does not show a poorly educated clergy. Table 6.3 divides educational achievement between theological (seminary) and non-theological (university) education, and by denomination. Each cell gives the proportion of pastors in that educational category. Regarding pastoral training, nearly two-thirds (62.7%) of pastors achieved a Master's degree or higher (53.8% Master's, 8.9% doctorates), with only 14.2 per cent having less than a Bachelor's degree. In addition, nearly half (46.7%) have a non-theological Bachelor's degree or more. The least educated denomination is clearly the PAOC, with the most educated being the CRC. Roughly 95 per cent of CRC lead pastors in our sample had a Master's degree or more, compared with only 10 per cent of PAOC lead pastors. This may be because PAOC pastors receive theological education at the undergraduate level in contrast with CRC pastors who obtain their first theological degree at the graduate level.

While attention has focused on shortages of pastors and growing demographic diversity, one other important trend has been unnoticed, that is, the move toward part-time and lay leadership in congregations. This trend is growing internationally across organizational types (Bardoel, Morgan, and Santos, 2007) and is increasingly typical

Table 6.3 Theological and non-theological educational achievement of evangelical lead pastors, by denomination (%)

	Baptist	CMA	CRC	MB	PAOC	Total
Theological training						
None	5.6	1.0	0	4.6	4.2	2.9
< BA	4.4	4.2	0.9	6.9	41.1	11.3
Bachelor's	17.8	34.4	3.7	14.9	45.3	22.8
Master's	64.4	44.8	86.1	66.7	5.3	53.8
Doctorate	7.8	15.6	9.3	6.9	4.2	8.9
Non-theological training						
None	32.2	41.1	18.5	37.9	62.5	37.9
< BA	15.6	18.9	7.4	11.5	22.9	15.1
Bachelor's	44.4	35.8	61.1	43.7	10.4	39.3
Master's	5.6	2.1	13.0	4.6	3.1	5.9
Doctorate	2.2	2.1	0	2.3	1.0	1.5

Source: CECS, 2009.
CMA = Christian and Missionary Alliance; CRC = Christian Reformed Church;
MB = Mennonite Brethren; PAOC = Pentecostal Assemblies of Canada.

in Canadian organizations (Pupo and Duffy, 2000). Several factors contribute to this trend. Service jobs require more flexibility and are more likely to be part-time. Financially tight businesses find the cost-saving benefits of part-time work attractive, since part-time work often comes without benefits and other perks. The increasing number of women in the paid workforce means a higher percentage of two-earner families. The result is more people looking for part-time work.

On the one hand, congregations face similar pressures. They are often financially strapped because of decreased participation among laity, including voluntarism, giving, and attendance. And they are often trying to hire clergy with a working spouse. On the other hand, evangelical and Catholic clergy are still dominated by white, educated males, who are less likely to work part-time. Thus, one would expect there to be fewer part-time workers in these traditions.

Today, many congregations cannot afford a full-time pastor, or some choose to hire multiple part-time pastors even if finances allow for a full-time position. Besides the cost benefits, multiple part-time pastors may have an advantage over a full-time person in that part-timers can work in areas of strength. Full-time pastors and staff, often responsible for tasks as diverse as bookkeeping, working with children, and marriage counselling, struggle to perform tasks that they dislike or lack the skills to do well, as we see later in this chapter. In *God's Potters*, Jackson Carroll (2006) notes that 29 per cent of conservative Protestant clergy in the United States are bivocational, largely because small, rural congregations cannot find or afford full-time ordained clergy.

Using Canada Revenue Agency data, Hiemstra (2011) found that there is a trend over the past decade toward part-time positions in congregations in Canada, including Catholic, mainline Protestant, and evangelical denominations. By 2010 almost a quarter (24.1%) of Christian congregations in Canada had no paid full-time staff. Roughly 20 per cent of Catholic and evangelical congregations have no full-time staff, compared with over 30 per cent of mainline Protestant congregations. In rural areas, which tend to have smaller and older congregations, the proportions are even higher (roughly 28% evangelical, 37% Catholic, and 50% mainline). Our sample also has evidence of part-time and lay leadership. Among lead pastors, 47 of the respondents (10%) work a secular job as well. Fourteen have no theological training, and 54 more have some theology courses, but less than a Bachelor's degree. Nine lead pastors are unpaid and another 22 are part-time. If trends continue as they are now, we expect an increasing percentage of part-time and lay pastors in evangelical congregations, even though they lag slightly behind other denominations in this regard.

CLERGY WELL-BEING

With all the concern about pastor shortages and dropout, it is not surprising that there are a myriad of studies on clergy well-being. Fewer studies have focused on evangelical denominations, and one is hard-pressed to find published Canadian data for any of these groups.[9] Nonetheless, it is reasonable to assume that pastors from different traditions face similar threats to their well-being and job satisfaction.

One of the most commonly cited threats to the well-being of pastors is too many time demands. Studies show that the vast majority of pastors spend more than 40 hours a week at work. The full-time paid pastors in our sample averaged 51.7 hours a week. Furthermore, since they are always on call, they find it difficult to balance work and family time (Lehr, 2006). "Being a pastor is like being a dog at a whistlers' convention," quipped Michael Jinkins (2012) of the Alban Institute, who found 74 per cent of its sample of Austin Seminary graduates raised the concern of time pressures (12). Several studies indicate that criticism and conflict are another major threat. This conflict is rarely over theological issues, even if there are a lot of disagreements in congregations. Instead, it is generally over interpersonal tensions, gossip, backstabbing, snide comments – all of which have a corrosive effect on a pastor's enthusiasm for ministry. A third common issue is loneliness. Past studies reveal that many pastors long for a safe confidant who can relate to their personal struggles. As a result of the need to maintain professional boundaries (which limits how emotionally vulnerable a pastor can be with those under his or her pastoral care), and the concern that sharing problems with superiors or congregants will be perceived as "unspiritual" or incompetence, pastors tend to avoid conversations about their own personal well-being. A 2007 study by Duke University found that clergy were significantly more likely to "report excessive job demands, criticism, feelings of loneliness and isolation" than their congregants (Zylstra, 2009, 17). A fourth threat is the headlong collision between an idealistic view of what ministry should be and the cold realism of human frailty and fickleness experienced by many young pastors. Pastors invest in congregants, only to find that congregants may not, in turn, invest back in the congregation.

Closely related to applied studies on the well-being of pastors are the social scientific studies of clergy job satisfaction, stress, and burnout. Some studies have found that clergy evince high job satisfaction in comparison with other occupations (Goetz, 1997; Dart, 2008), and relatively low stress (Barna, 1993). Nonetheless, clergy seem to be susceptible to burnout (Francis et al., 2008), just like social workers, teachers, nurses, and others in helping professions. Research indicates that factors influencing burnout can be divided into four main areas: personality factors, demographic factors, work environment, and period effects. Personality factors focus on personality traits and personal coping mechanisms. Some studies show that personality factors are the strongest predictors of burnout

(Rutledge and Francis, 2004; Hills et al., 2004; Francis et al., 2009). Demographic factors suggest that stress and burnout are more common among younger, less educated, and unmarried pastors (Francis et al., 2009). Work environment factors address both the unique nature of clergy tasks (common to all clergy) and those special factors attributed to the particular congregation they serve. Work environment factors common to most pastors include regularly dealing with major life transitions (such as funerals, conversions, family crises, and personal traumas), repetitive tasks, coping with the daily operations of organizations (meetings, budgets, and financial pressures), and theological disagreements. Pastors tend to be highly dedicated and invested in their work, which can increase stress and burnout. Pastors perform "people work," which is emotionally demanding. A pastor's job performance is difficult to measure concretely, and thus good performance often goes unrecognized and uncelebrated. Congregations are voluntary organizations; thus pastors must work with the lay volunteers in the congregation regardless of ability or performance (they cannot be fired, only the pastor can). Lay volunteers may show lack of commitment by dropping tasks, "church hopping," participating intermittently, causing dissension, and so on. Congregations often lack clear channels of communication, functional structures, and committees, and these dysfunctions inhibit positive change that the pastor is trying to implement.

Finally, period effects are related to evidence showing that clergy burnout and turnover is increasing over time (Jenkins and Maslach, 1994). This issue could be related to changes in the pastors themselves or in the people in the congregations, or both. If pastors have changed over time, it may be because they grew up in a time of relative plenty – unlike those pastors who experienced the Great Depression, for instance – and thus lack perseverance or a willingness to make do with very little. The growing tendency toward greater individualism, immediate gratification, and increased educational credentials (which tend to correlate with higher job expectations among pastors) may also have an effect (Jenkins and Maslach, 1994). Incoming pastors may have lower levels of psychological health or resilience than previous generations of pastors, possibly because the healthiest youth are seeking more prestigious occupations. On the other hand, it might not be the pastors who have changed but the people or the society around them. For example, Milner et al. (2006) argue that in a secularized society, clergy have less control and therefore less ability to do their jobs well because their position is no longer highly esteemed. Secularization also means that people privatize their religious views (they are "spiritual, not religious") and are less committed to organizational forms of religion (they participate selectively and "shop around"). As a result, clergy work with uncommitted laity and have less influence in their lives. They have more tasks to cover, less pay, and less job security. Hence, Milner et al. speculate that clergy who have an "external orientation" (i.e., finding legitimacy and motivation through growing congregations numerically, or through positive support from their congregants) experience lower job satisfaction than those clergy who have an "internal orientation" to ministry (i.e., based on a sense of professional competence, personal integrity, and spiritual connectedness to God).

While evangelical pastors we interviewed expressed a fairly high level of job satisfaction, certain aspects of their work were draining. One Christian Reformed pastor from Calgary spoke about the stress on his children and family when other people's issues spill over into his family life. A Pentecostal pastor in Calgary shared how the "pettiness of people" can sometimes be very negative. He also spoke about congregational financial pressures that are stressful. A Baptist pastor in the Maritimes shared how he finds managing staff, especially with different personalities, particularly stressful. He also talked about trying to find balance in his life: "The other thing that causes the most tension is that I am a workaholic – and to keep balance between here and home – the ministry is draining." A Mennonite Brethren pastor in Toronto expressed some dissatisfaction over paperwork and administration wishing he could pass it on to someone else so he could focus on what he really enjoys, being with people. A Baptist pastor in Vancouver struggles with trying to help his congregation catch a new vision to reach out to the community. Overall, many pastors express some stress and tension over issues about finances, staff, leading people, resolving conflict in the congregation, and desiring more time with family.

To broaden our interview data, our survey looked at stress as experienced by pastors, their job satisfaction, and their pastoral tasks (whether the pastor works in areas of strength or weakness). Stress refers to environmental factors that are perceived as straining or exceeding the adaptive capacities of the individual and threatening

148   A CULTURE OF FAITH

his or her well-being. It should be distinguished from burnout, which is marked by emotional exhaustion (fatigue caused by extensive interaction with others), depersonalization (uncaring and cynical attitudes toward others), and lack of personal accomplishment (deterioration in perceived competence and personal satisfaction with achievements) (Maslach and Jackson, 1981).

STRESS AND JOB SATISFACTION

We asked pastors, "On a scale of 1 to 10, where 1 is no stress and 10 is extremely stressful, how stressful is your pastoral work right now?" The average score was 5.86, although nearly a quarter of the pastors (23.8%) rated their stress at 8 or more, and another 20 per cent rated it at 7.

In spite of the moderate to high levels of stress, pastors rated their job satisfaction fairly highly. Job satisfaction is normally understood as the fit between personal needs/desires and the work performed (Jenkins and Maslach, 1994). Using the same scale (1–10), we asked pastors to give their level of satisfaction in a variety of work-related areas. In keeping with the pastoral concerns raised in previous research, the list emphasizes time constraints and relationships. Table 6.4 gives the averages for each question and for overall job satisfaction. It also gives the percentage of respondents who gave a high job satisfaction rating for each item (8 out of 10 or higher). Besides study leaves and sabbaticals (which we suspect many pastors rarely have), "workload and work expectations" has the lowest rating while "relationships with church staff" is rated the highest.[10] However, there is little variation between the averages, and most items are rated fairly high. The overall job satisfaction is 7.9 for the evangelical pastors in this study.

Next, we asked pastors about the duties they performed at least monthly, followed by "I will now read through those duties you said you were involved in at least monthly. Please identify those areas that you consider strengths, areas of satisfaction and enjoyment, and those areas you consider weaknesses, areas that you find draining. If the area is neither a strength nor weakness, just say 'neither.'" All the tasks in the survey are listed in Table 6.5. In the second column, the percentage of pastors who said they were involved in that activity is

Table 6.4 Job satisfaction scores for evangelical pastors in Canada

Satisfaction with ...	Average score	Respondents scoring 8 or above (%)
Study leaves/sabbaticals	6.26	41.5
Workload/expectations	7.45	57.3
Support from denomination	7.46	59.2
Time off each week	7.56	58.5
Support from congregation	7.96	67.2
Salary and benefits	7.98	69.2
Relationship with lay leaders	8.22	77.0
Vacation time	8.39	79.3
Relationships with church staff	8.48	82.4
Overall job satisfaction	7.9	67.8

Source: CECS, 2009.

given. The subsequent columns give the percentage of those pastors who considered that activity an area of strength and those that considered it an area of weakness (the remainder considered it neither a strength nor weakness).

Not surprisingly, the vast majority of lead pastors are involved in visitation, preaching, administration, greeting/meeting newcomers, vision casting, and counselling. Less common tasks may be covered by another pastor or volunteer, or may not be offered in the congregation. Administration is the most common area of weakness for just over a third (34.8%) of the pastors, and nearly all are involved in it. Visitation, counselling, working with children, and connecting with newcomers are considered areas of weakness by between 15 per cent and 20 per cent of the pastors. On the other hand, nearly all pastors consider preaching and teaching adults to be areas of strength.

We then asked, "Roughly what percentage of your work time do you spend on areas of weakness?" and "Has your church hired staff or positioned volunteers to help with these areas of weakness?" Answers to the first question ranged from no time spent in areas of weakness (the default for all those who did not consider any of the tasks they did to be areas of weakness, 36.8% of the sample) to 70 per cent of their time, with 10.5 per cent as the average. Of those who said they did some task that was a weakness, 57 per cent said

Table 6.5 Canadian evangelical pastors' self-perceived areas of strength and weakness

Tasks	Respondents who perform this task monthly or more frequently (%)	Respondents who consider this task an area of strength (%)	Respondents who consider this task an area of weakness (%)
Visitation	97.5	58.3	19.4
Sermon preparation and preaching	93.7	94.5	0.8
Administration	93.5	39.2	34.8
Greeting/meeting newcomers	87.0	61.7	15.4
Developing vision/goals	86.4	61.2	12.1
Counselling	86.0	52.2	17.8
Leading small groups	60.0	73.8	4.9
Teaching adult Sunday school	49.1	81.2	3.0
Working with youth	42.1	51.7	12.4
Leading worship	41.5	66.2	8.1
Working with children	24.9	57.1	16.8

Source: CECS, 2009.

that staff or volunteers helped in these areas of weakness. Those who did not have help in their areas of weakness (43%) had slightly lower job satisfaction.[11] They also viewed their congregation more negatively, which we analyze further below.

Finally, in light of the fact that pastors often voice concerns about loneliness, we asked pastors, "Do you have close friends in your area with whom you share your personal or spiritual struggles?" and 77.4 per cent of the pastors said they did. Still, nearly a fifth said they did not, and those who did not had lower job satisfaction.[12] There was no clear demographic difference between those who had a confidant and those who did not.

We have described the data, but more informative are the correlates of job satisfaction, because they hint at the causes. To examine causes, nine of the satisfaction items from Table 6.4 were combined to create a scale of job satisfaction.[13] Satisfaction is not significantly correlated with gender, congregation size, recent increases in attendance, whether the pastoral position is paid or not, length of time at the congregation, denomination, province, or educational level of pastor. Table 6.6 shows the most important correlates of job satisfaction, including some questions that tapped the pastor's subjective evaluation of his or her congregation. Pastors were asked to respond to twenty "opinion of the congregation" statements that were combined into one scale. The twenty statements, to which all of the responses were "strongly agree" (1) to "strongly disagree" (5), are the following:

1   "In general, this congregation is wary of change and innovation."
2   "The vast majority of laypeople are *not* aware of the goals and direction of this church."
3   "Everyone enthusiastically participates in congregational singing."
4   "The pastors and staff of this church often scramble to complete tasks that are dropped by the layperson responsible for them."
5   "Newcomers find it hard to form friendships with people in this church."
6   "The lay leaders are committed to this church and fully endorse its mission."
7   "The participants in this church are pessimistic about its future."
8   "I think we have problems with communication between the clergy, lay leaders, and the congregation."
9   "Attendees frequently invite unconverted friends and family to this church."
10 "The contributions of our youth and children are appreciated in this church."
11 "I don't think we are doing enough for our children and youth in this church."
12 "In general, the congregation is satisfied with the quality of the programs provided for the adults in this church."
13 "The congregation is committed to praying for this church's ministry and programs."
14 "People in our church are encouraged to ask questions and challenge ideas."
15 "The laity expect the pastors and other church staff to do most of the work in this church."

16 "This church is very committed to leadership development and formation."

17 "It is often difficult to fill voluntary positions in this church."

18 "Overall, I would consider this to be a very healthy church."

19 "I am worried about the long-term future of this church."

20 "This church tends to burn out its leaders."

A question on congregational finances was also included, which asked, "How would you describe your congregation's financial health currently? Would you say it is excellent, good, tight but manageable, in some difficulty, or in serious difficulty?" This subjective financial item was also strongly correlated with the job satisfaction scale. In order to interpret the numbers in Table 6.6, note that correlations range from 1 to −1, with stronger correlations being further from zero. (The asterisks [*] beside each correlation indicate roughly the degree to which the correlation is statistically significant, which means that we can be sure that the correlation is not simply the result of sampling error. Regarding the pastor's characteristics, the positive and significant correlation with age indicates that those who are older are more satisfied. Pastors of European/North American descent (white) tend to be slightly more satisfied than members of ethnic minorities. Ethnic (non-white) minority pastors are significantly less satisfied with their vacation time, the only single-item difference that reaches statistical significance. We had only ten French-language interviews, but these pastors ranked their satisfaction lower overall, and they were particularly less satisfied with their salary/benefits, time off, and vacation time.[14] Carroll's (2006) study of US pastors gives similar results. He found that white, male, older clergy who have been in ministry for many years are more satisfied.

Not surprising is the negative relationship with pastoral stress, hours worked, and hours spent in areas of weakness. The "hours worked" correlation is almost identical ($r = .115$) if we include only those pastors who work full-time ($N = 446$). Equally unsurprising are the positive correlations between job satisfaction and relational support, such as having help in areas of weakness and having a confidant. The last three items are the strongest correlates of job satisfaction in the survey. It appears that the pastor's view of his or her congregation's health has the greatest effect on the pastor's satisfaction. The financial well-being of the congregation and particularly the tendency of the

Table 6.6 Evangelical pastors' self-perceived areas of strength and weakness correlated with job satisfaction scale

	Correlation with satisfaction scale
Age	0.163***
White	0.091*
French	-0.087
Pastor's stress level	-0.287***
Hours spent in pastoral work per week	-0.118*
Percentage of time spent in areas of weakness	-0.133**
Staff/volunteer help in areas of weakness (N = 305)	0.139*
Has close friends to share personal struggles with	0.151***
Congregations current financial health	0.268***
I consider this a very healthy church	0.336***
I am worried about future of church	-0.319***
Church tends to burn out its leaders	-0.364***
Opinion of the congregation scale	0.510***

Source: CECS, 2009.
*$p < .05$; **$p < .01$; ***$p < .001$.

congregation to stress pastors suggest that the congregation's vitality is key to the pastor's health. The strongest correlation with job satisfaction is clearly the 20-question "opinion of the congregation" scale. On the positive side, this probably indicates that pastors care about their congregations. On the less positive side, unhealthy congregations are hard on pastoral well-being.

These measures, however, are not free of bias. Although we would expect the vitality of the congregation and the health of the pastor to be related, the pastor's subjective valuation of the congregation, like his or her job satisfaction, is in the eye of the beholder. Negative valuations of congregations (òr of job satisfaction and stress levels) could indicate a less vital congregation, or pastor, or both. The lower job satisfaction (and lower opinion of their congregation) of younger pastors is disconcerting for denominations that face a shortage of young leaders. Surely this would indicate that young pastors are more susceptible to burnout and leaving the ministry. The key question is why do these correlations with age exist? Is this because of "pastor" factors such as idealistic expectations, or poorer emotional health, or newer visions of ministry that do not mesh well with current congregational realities? Or is it related to "congregational" factors? Younger pastors may be more likely to find work in less healthy congregations (because the older pastors do not want those jobs) or less established congregations (such as a recent church-plant) that negatively affects their job satisfaction.[15]

In Table 6.7 the effect of age is illustrated, both with the twenty-item "opinion of the congregation" (ranges from 20 to 100) scale and the job satisfaction scale (ranges from 9 to 90). For pastors aged 30 or younger, their opinion of the congregation is a full 14 points lower than for the ≥ 51 age category. The really big jump is between the youngest category of pastors (only 8 respondents in this category) and everyone else. However, each age category shows increasingly positive views of the congregation. The same pattern exists for job satisfaction, but the age differences are less extreme. The Canadian Evangelical Churches Study (CECS) data provide a unique opportunity to parse out the "pastor" from the "congregation" effects because we interviewed pastors and youth pastors in the same congregation. The average age for youth pastors is 34.4 years,[16] 14.8 years younger than their lead pastors on average (49.2). There are 13 identically worded "opinion of the congregation" items in the two surveys, which were added together to form a scale ("Opinion2").[17] The average Opinion2 score for youth pastors is 47.25 and for their lead pastors it is 50.01. The difference is statistically significant, which means that we can be sure that youth pastors are more negative about their congregations than are the lead pastors. Furthermore, the younger the youth pastor, the more negative he or she is about the congregation (age and Opinion2 correlation is −0.196*).[18] Obviously, the difference in job satisfaction and opinion of the congregation are at least partly due to "pastor" effects, particularly the age of the pastor.[19] However, the difference does not mean that "pastor" effects explain all the differences and "congregational" effects explain none. Rather, it is likely that both factors are important predictors. What we can say is that the correlation between lower opinions of the congregation and younger pastors is at least partly related to age. One positive here for evangelical churches is that they may have a better fit between clergy and congregation, likely because the congregational polity of evangelical congregations allows them to

Table 6.7 Congregation satisfied with its pastor and pastor's job satisfaction, by pastor age groups

	Age group of pastors (years)			
	30 or less	31–40	41–50	51+
Congregation satisfied with pastor	62.8	72.6	74.1	76.9
Pastor satisfied with job	63.1	67.8	67.7	71.0

Source: CECS, 2009.

select their own pastors, while the Roman Catholic Church and some mainline Protestant denominations assign clergy to churches (Carroll, 2006). There is also less theological variation in evangelical churches, which often means the pastor matches the theological conservativeness-liberalness of the church more closely (Reimer, 2011). Carroll (2006) found that 57 per cent of conservative Protestant lay members strongly agreed that there is a good match between clergy and congregation, compared with 37 per cent of Catholics, with mainline Protestants in between.

In conclusion, organizations like congregations rise and fall on the quality of their leaders. If there are too few qualified clergy, the congregations will suffer. Sociologists are not good at predicting the future, but Canada's aging clergy and small cohorts of young pastors do point to growing shortages. Following the growing diversity of evangelical congregations, pastors are becoming demographically more diverse as well. Racial/ethnic and gender diversity gets all the attention, but another important change is the move to part-time staffing of congregations.

The Canadian evangelical pastors who participated in this study claim to have a high level of job satisfaction. Typical of those in helping professions, however, these pastors also find their jobs moderately stressful. This combination of moderate stress with high job satisfaction probably indicates that they are deeply committed to their work. Pastors who are older (and to some extent white and English-speaking), who spend less time in areas of weakness, who work fewer hours, who have a close confidant, and who perceive their congregation to be healthy also have less stress and higher job satisfaction. In addition, younger pastors have both lower job satisfaction and lower opinions of their congregations. Why is this?

One possibility is that the congregation is the problem. The pastor's opinion of his or her congregation is the most powerful predictor of job satisfaction in this research. The congregation can be the problem if younger pastors get more dysfunctional congregations than older pastors, whether because they are more idealistic ("I can fix this congregation") or because they are less discerning ("I didn't realize this congregation was so messed up when I came"), or because the healthiest congregations already have pastors in place and the younger ones get whatever is available.

This research indicates that it is not just the congregation, however, since young pastors have lower job satisfaction and are more critical of their congregation than the older lead pastor in the same congregation. Of course, this does not mean young pastors are the problem. They are more critical of their congregations and maybe they are right to be so. Yet, how do we explain it? This may be an "aging" issue, such that younger pastors become less idealistic or more competent as they age. Or this could be a "period" issue, where young pastors today have less job satisfaction than pastors of previous generations, and they are not going to grow out of it. Another possible explanation is related to "dropout" effects. Job satisfaction may be inflated because those with low job satisfaction are more likely to quit the pastorate, or not respond to the survey. There may be less job satisfaction on average among young pastors simply because those who would have become dissatisfied older pastors have already left the ministry, and thus they are no longer in the sample (Francis et al., 2008).

Finally, it is possible that neither the congregation nor the pastor is the problem. A vital congregation and healthy pastor may not work out simply because of a poor fit between them (disagreement over vision, theology, etc.). One study found that pastoral job satisfaction suffers when the pastor is more theologically liberal than the congregation, but not when the pastor is more conservative (Mueller and McDuff, 2004). Furthermore, young pastor dissatisfaction can be caused by a lack of fit between pastor and the denominational leadership, because they disagree theologically or in purpose, or because the pastor senses a lack of support from the congregation (Rugenstein, 2005). Possibly there exists a gap between young pastors and typically older congregational lay leadership or denominational leadership.

Whatever the cause of the dissatisfaction of younger pastors, their attitude toward the congregation is highly correlated with their job satisfaction. Healthy leaders seem to make for vital congregations and vice versa. The relative institutional commitment and higher private religiosity of evangelicals spawns congregational leaders because the churches provide the institutional base from which potential leaders can be developed. Likewise, strong pastoral leadership energizes congregations to further vitality. Certainly, part of the reason for the relative strength of evangelical congregations is their leadership.

7

Youth and Children

with James Penner

Unless evangelicals can keep their children and youth in the pews, their future is precarious; and they know it. As we showed earlier, evangelical congregations are likely to prioritize ministry to youth and children over anything else. And this is not just talk. Evangelical congregations of sufficient size have active youth and children's programs. Virtually all congregations (98%) in our sample with 100 regular attendees or more hold Sunday School for children and at least three-fourths have youth activities for teens.[1] Among evangelicals, having children (fertility rates) and keeping them in the congregation (retention rates) has a greater effect on congregational growth than does evangelism: "The surest source of new adult members for a denomination is in the pews already – among the children of the present members of that denomination" (Greeley and Hout, 2006, 105). Since children's and youth programs are so important to congregations, we wanted to know what they were doing for the young and how well they were doing it. What programs do congregations run for their youth and children? Who are these pastors that lead them? What is their opinion of their congregation's youth/children's work? Do these programs attract children and youth from outside the congregation?

In addition to phone interviews with nearly 500 lead pastors, we completed another 100 phone interviews with youth/children's pastors. We asked the lead pastors if their congregation had a youth/children's pastor (we asked for a youth pastor first) and for contact information for this pastor. In this way, we interviewed both youth/children's pastors and lead pastors in 100 congregations. Eighty-nine youth and 11 children's pastors were interviewed, and we reached our quota of 100 interviews long before lead pastor interviews were completed. The youth/children's pastors interviewed are spread across the country, with each denomination well represented (16 Baptist, 24 CMA, 14 CRC, 25 MB, and 21 PAOC). There are 25 part-time pastors, and 5 more that are unpaid volunteers, with the remaining 70 being full-time paid clergy (see Appendix). We asked these pastors questions about the programs they lead.

We also wanted to know if the youth that are raised in a congregation attend as adults. While evangelicals prioritize their youth and most churches have programs for them, it does not mean that these efforts result in higher retention rates. As noted in chapter 2, the lifestyles of "emerging adults" – a term used to designate that lengthening period of time between high school and settling down to a family and a regular job – is not conducive to religious participation. In order to answer this question, we make use of the "Church and Faith Study of Young Adults" (CFYA) conducted by James Penner and Associates (2012) for the Evangelical Fellowship of Canada. In 2010 and 2011 this project interviewed seventy-two young adults from across Canada who were raised in Christian churches. Then utilizing an online Angus Reid panel, it surveyed 2,049 18- to 34-year-olds who had attended a mainline Protestant, evangelical Protestant, or Catholic church in childhood. The research produced findings on the religious trajectories of these emerging Canadian adults including their present levels of religious commitment and the characteristics of the congregations they tend to abandon – or continue to attend.

RESEARCH ON YOUTH AND EVANGELICAL FAITH

When we look at all the Christian traditions as a whole, youth religiosity and participation in organized religion has decreased across Canada and elsewhere.[2] In Canada from 1984 to 2008 there was a precipitous decline in the proportion of Canadian teens who identify themselves as either Protestant or Catholic – from 85 per cent to 45 per cent (Bibby, 2009). Regarding church participation, Bibby reports that while weekly attendees stayed at about 21 per cent for three decades, there was a marked increase between 1984 and 2008 in those who never attend (from 28% to 47%). Even in the United

States, where religiosity among youth is more robust, there is evidence of faith deterioration during and immediately after high school. The National Study of Youth and Religion (NSYR) found that 75 per cent of America's 13- to 17-year-olds self-identified as Christian, yet only one in two practised Christianity or deemed it important (Smith with Denton, 2005).

How can we make sense of this decline in institutional religiosity among the young? Pluralism, individualism, and consumerism are frequently linked to diminished institutional religiosity among the younger generation (Bellah et al., 1985; Hoge et al., 1994; Bibby, 2006; Wuthnow, 2007; Smith with Snell, 2009). Others point to emerging adulthood, a distinct stage in life for 18- to 25-year-olds (Arnett, 2004). Life stage markers traditionally associated with increasing religiosity (e.g., getting married and having children) are now postponed as other activities associated with young adulthood, like greater mobility, shift work, late night parties, drug and sexual experimentation, are not conducive to piety (Uecker, Regnerus, and Vaaler, 2007; Mason, Singleton, and Webber, 2007): "Because these ideals are out of sync with religious mores, it is easier to put off faith participation" (Smith with Snell, 2009).

Other research points to weaknesses in the churches themselves in keeping the youth that do attend, including weakness in the following areas: (a) the religious vibrancy of congregations; (b) the competence of leaders; and (c) age-specific programming (Bowen, 2010; Dean, 2010; Ji and Tameifuna, 2011; Smith, 2003; Penner et al., 2012; Webber et al., 2010). Churches seem to be particularly weak on servicing young adults after high school (Wuthnow, 2007).

In short, the future of institutional religiosity of Canadian youth looks grim, and the broader culture is not helping, according to the research cited above. Yet, there is fairly consistent evidence that evangelical congregations and denominations are doing better than others. Bibby (2009) found that about two-thirds (68%) of evangelical teens attend at least monthly, far above the one-third (33%) Canadian average. Nonetheless, it would be unrealistic to think that the larger cultural influences are not making any inroads into the evangelical youth subculture. What is at the root of this change? Evidence from the United States shows that evangelical youth are replacing an external locus of authority for a personal one, which in chapter 2 we argued undermines institutional religiosity: "Older evangelicals tend to believe that God is the source of moral authority, and young evangelicals believe that their own personal conscience is the arbiter of right and wrong" (Farrell, 2011, 528). Still, the institutional participation of evangelical youth is higher relative to their mainline Protestant and Catholic counterparts.

Does keeping youth connected to a congregation matter? Research suggests that religious participation among youth has diverse pro-social effects. Smith (2003) argues that these effects are far reaching from intergenerational satisfaction to psychological well-being to educational success and civic involvement. Religious youth also develop *learned* competencies uniquely available in religious settings. These include organizational and leadership skills, coping abilities and cultural capital that bring motivations, competencies, and performance-enhancing attitudes that young people carry into diverse settings (22–5). Last, religious youth benefit from social and organizational ties normally inaccessible to non-religious youth. In an increasingly age-stratified society where there is a prolongation of adolescence, faith communities remain largely intergenerational sites that provide youth with social capital for pro-social outcomes, a closed network that discourages anti-social behaviour, and a vast array of life-enhancing national and international networks (25–7). Smith acknowledges that not all religious influences are positive and that there are non-religious functional alternatives for many of these outcomes. Yet, the vast majority of the social evidence is pointing in the direction of pro-social religious effects on young people, and these effects have been documented in religious settings in Canada (Bibby, 2009).

YOUTH AND CHILDREN'S MINISTRY IN CANADA

Evangelical Protestants are very concerned about their children and youth. They take seriously the biblical mandate to "Train a child in the way he should go, and when he is old he will not turn from it" (Prov. 22:6, NIV). Evangelicals desire to provide "good ministry" throughout the life cycle, in both the home and the church. What we wanted to know is what do evangelical congregations do with their young people? We asked all 100 youth and children's pastors to answer general questions about programing in their congregation.

Table 7.1 Events for youth and children offered weekly by evangelical congregations

Events for youth	Congregations (n)	Events for children	Congregations (n)
Youth group	91	Sunday school or children's church	91
Bible study	56	Midweek events	49
Musical/artistic	51	Musical/artistic	21
Other	10	Other	9

Source: CECS, youth pastor subsample, 2009.

Table 7.1 gives the actual counts, or number of congregations that held specific events. Since we interviewed 100 pastors, the counts are conveniently the same as the percentages.

Considering we were interviewing youth and children's pastors, it is not surprising that nearly all the congregations had youth and children's programs. Of the 100 churches, the most common activity for youth was a youth group. In evangelical congregations, youth groups often happen on a weekday evening (typically Friday), and involve games and activities, snacks, and a teaching time from the youth pastor or volunteer. Often these groups are directed toward having fun while providing an alternative to less wholesome entertainment options available to youth. Fifty-six congregations had separate Bible studies. Over half (51) of the congregations also had youth choirs, bands, or other musical and artistic groups. Other events include Sunday School for youth (4) and sports-related groups (6). Although we did not specifically ask pastors about Sunday School, it seems the traditional program has given way to evening youth group events in evangelical youth ministry. Youth leaders may be finding it difficult to get youth to come to any event on a weekend morning.

Children's ministry, in comparison, focuses on Sunday morning, either as Sunday School (often before the main worship service) or children's church (children meet separately during the main church service). Mid-week events, like Teamkid, Awana, or Pioneer programs were also held in about half of the churches (49) in our sample.

Musical or artistic groups were less common (21). A few other events were also mentioned.

We asked youth pastors specific questions about their youth ministries, and children's pastors specific questions about their children's ministry. These leaders also plan special or less regular events for youth and children, which are listed in Table 7.2. We asked them if their congregation had sponsored a variety of such events in the past twelve months. Recall that 89 youth pastors were asked about the issues summarized on the left of the table, and while we had only 11 children's pastors, there were a number of pastors (designated as youth pastors) who oversaw a wider set of ministries, including children's ministry. There were 35 pastors in our sample who answered questions regarding children's ministry, and the results are shown on the right side of the table. Because of the small sample size, these results should be viewed with caution.

Congregations offer a surprisingly wide range of events. We suspect that many of these were not separate events, but occurred as part of the regular youth group. Nearly all respondents said their congregations (91%) held classes or meetings where they discussed youth issues such as dating, consumerism, sex, peer pressure, and the like. Congregations also commonly offered teaching on spiritual disciplines like Bible reading or prayer (84.3%), baptism or confirmation (71.9%), ministry training (68.5%), and classes where young people are encouraged to discover their spiritual gifts (50.6%).[3] However, youth work focuses not only on religious teaching. Most youth ministries sponsored community service events (88.8%), which often included working in a soup kitchen or cleaning up an area in the neighbourhood. Outreach events (78.6%), where youth were encouraged to bring their friends to hear a special speaker or to a youth rally, were common as well. Events related to social justice (69.7%) focused youth on the plight of the less fortunate, either in Canada or overseas. A popular evangelical youth event was the 30-Hour Famine, sponsored by World Vision[4] where youth were to eat nothing for 30 hours and raise money and awareness for the world's hungry.

Youth Sundays (69.7%) feature youth as the focus of the main Sunday worship service. Often the youth are involved in leading the worship music, speaking, and other roles. Such Sundays raise awareness and appreciation for youth ministry among the adults, as well as give youth an opportunity to develop their leadership skills. Short-term

164   A CULTURE OF FAITH

Table 7.2 Events for youth and children offered by evangelical congregations in the previous twelve months (%)

Youth Events	%	Children's Events	%
Youth issues classes	91.0	Christmas programs	88.6[a]
Community service	88.8	Outreach (invite a friend)	74.2
Spiritual disciplines classes	84.3	Vacation Bible school	65.7
Outreach (invite a friend, etc.)	78.6	Children's Sundays	62.9
Baptism or confirmation classes	71.9	Service projects	57.1
Social justice (30-hour Famine, AIDS awareness, etc.)	69.7	Training for parents with children	31.4
Youth Sundays	69.7		
Nature/wilderness events (camping trips, hikes, etc.)	69.7		
Ministry training classes	68.5		
Mission trips	64.0		
Spiritual gifts classes	50.6		
Intergenerational connections	44.9		
Future planning classes	23.6		

Source: CECS, youth pastor subsample, 2009.
[a] Some pastors answered this question even though they did not answer other children's ministry questions, so we adjusted the number based on the 35 pastors who answered the majority of questions about their congregation's children's ministry.

mission trips are also common (64%). Groups of youth and leaders travel to countries in the developing world or elsewhere, often to participate in service projects, like building a school or facility for worship, or in other ministries run by local congregations, like evangelism or feeding programs. Less than half of these congregations sponsor intergenerational connections, where youth are paired with adults who are not their parents, for mentoring or for prayer support (44.9%). Only a minority of congregations help youth process future decisions, like choosing a college or selecting an occupation (23.6%). Other events (not shown) mentioned by youth pastors include camps (8%), social events (12%), sports activities (6%), other youth group events (20%), retreats/conferences (15%), concerts/movies (11%), special speakers (8%), fundraisers (5%), and partnering with other congregations (9%).

Common children's events, listed on the right side of Table 7.2, included Christmas programs (88.6%) and outreach events, where kids are encouraged to invite a friend (74.2%). Vacation Bible schools have a long tradition in evangelical congregations, and were offered by 65.7 per cent of the congregations for which we have data. Held during summer vacation, churches put on a program for neighbourhood children that includes games, crafts, snacks, speakers, Bible stories, and lessons. Often these are half-day (morning or afternoon) events that last for a week, led by pastors and volunteers. Congregations have in mind discipleship and evangelism, possibly even reaching out to parents through their children. Parents may have in mind free child care and getting their rambunctious children out of the house.

Many evangelical churches also provide children's Sundays, service projects, and parenting skills for adults. Christmas pageants and children's Sundays are other ways to recognize children and the ministries of the congregation. Nearly two-thirds of congregations (62.9%) had such Sundays, which is similar to the 69.7 per cent of congregations that held youth Sundays. Pre-teen children are not thought to be too young to engage in service projects, and over half (57.1%) of the congregations sponsored such events. Less common is parental skills training for families with children, offered by about one-third of the congregations (31.4%), sometimes as a way of serving the broader neighbourhood.

The range of activities suggests that evangelical congregations are committed to investing in their children and youth. As we note below, non-parental adult investment in children and youth, by youth pastors or adult lay members, for example, is one factor that promotes institutional involvement into adulthood. The data also show that engaging the youth in congregational activities and participating in camps and mission trips correlate with institutional retention. These are precisely the kinds of activities sponsored by evangelical churches.

In Table 7.3 we look at the size and composition of the youth groups. The table shows that evangelical youth groups in our sample have a median number of 30 youth (different youth, those who participate in multiple events are counted once) attending youth events each week. A median number of 8 volunteers regularly support youth programs. The variation was great, however, from a small church with 2 youth and no volunteers to a large church with 500 youth and 65 volunteers. About two-thirds of the youth participants had

Table 7.3 Description of those attending youth events offered by evangelical congregations

Who attends?	Median n (%)
Youth participants/week	30.0
Youth volunteers/week	8.0
Youth with at least one regularly attending parent	20.0 (68.2)
Youth with parent(s) who also attend main worship services regularly	20.0 (66.7)
Youth from un-churched families	9.0
Un-churched youth attending regularly	2.0 (6.2)
Percentage of churches where youth participants increased (% decreased)	52.2 (12.0)

Source: CECS, youth pastor subsample, 2009.

at least one parent participating in the congregation (median of 20 or 68.2%). Two-thirds of the youth also attend the congregation's main worship services (20.0 or 66.7%). The remaining third of the youth attending youth events were from unchurched families (median of 9). If these numbers are generalizable, then clearly these youth groups have a significant outreach to unchurched youth, and do not only service their own. However, these youth are usually "youth group only" participants. Only 1 in 15 youth (6.2% median) with non-attending parents regularly go to religious services. For those youth who have a parent or parents who regularly attend Sunday services, two-thirds attend regularly themselves. This means that one-third of the youth are not attending Sunday services. Research shows that youth who do not attend Sunday services when they are young are less likely to attend later. Parents' regular attendance is a necessary, but not a sufficient cause of their youth attending regularly, supporting the finding of others (Myers, 1996; Bader and Desmond, 2006; Penner et al., 2012).

About half (52.2%) of the youth pastors claimed that the number of youth participants in the last two years had increased (since 2007, interviews completed in 2009). Only 12 per cent said participation was decreasing (the remaining 36% said it had remained the same). This growth variable is not correlated with whether the pastor works full-time or part-time or is unpaid, the size of the youth group,

Table 7.4 Description of those attending children's events offered
by evangelical congregations

Who attends?	Median n (%)
Child participants/week	50.0
Volunteers/week	15.0
Children with at least one regularly attending parent	25.0 (84.4)
Children from un-churched families	5.5 (14.6)
Percentage of churches where child participants increased (% decreased)	48.6 (3.0)

Source: CECS, youth pastor subsample, 2009.

the number of volunteers, or the percentage of youth who attend
Sunday services. While we do not expect youth leaders to undersell
their own youth programs, it seems that the youth programs are
vital for those who participate.

In Table 7.4 we look at similar data for children's ministries.
Results are based on only 35 respondents, so we need to caution
readers that such small samples have large margins of error. Note
that children's ministries are larger than youth ministries, involving a
median of 50 (different) children in an average week and 15 volunteers. Again, the range is great, varying from 5 to 700 children and
from 2 to 150 volunteers. Not surprisingly, children are more likely
to have parents who attend than youth. The median proportion of
children with at least one parent regularly attending the church is
84.4 per cent, with few (only 14.6%) being unchurched. Half (48.6%)
of the pastors told us their children's ministry was growing, while
only one church (3%) told us the number of children participating in
the events offered for children was decreasing (the rest said no change).

YOUTH AND CHILDREN'S PASTORS

Of the 100 pastors we interviewed, 34 were female, a much higher
proportion than lead pastors (4%). However, half of these women
were either part-time or unpaid (4 of the 5 unpaid positions were
women), and 10 of the 11 children's pastors were women. The average

age for all youth/children's pastors is 34 years but the range is significant, from 19 to 64 years. Like the lead pastors, these pastors are also well educated. Of full-time youth/children's pastors, 87 per cent had some education or training as pastors (79% of all youth/children's pastors), and 73 per cent have Bachelor's or Master's degrees. In addition, 41 per cent of full-time and 68 per cent of the part-time pastors have some non-pastoral post-secondary education, and over half (55%) of these have Bachelor's or Master's degrees.

The tenure of youth pastors is notoriously short. One study in the United States found that the average tenure of youth workers is about two and one half years (Rouhlkepartain and Scales, 1995). Many do not stay in youth work very long, because the position is viewed as a stepping stone to a lead pastor position, or because of stress, other job offers, or spousal or family needs. In our study the median youth worker had been in his or her position for 3 years (4 years on average), and the previous pastor had held his or her position for a median of 2 years (3.1 years on average). Not all youth pastors have a quick turnover, however. One youth pastor we interviewed had held his position since 1952 (57 years). Nonetheless, there seems to be fairly quick turnover for youth pastors, even if it is likely longer than the two years commonly cited.[5]

Why is this? Youth pastors are commonly given a wide range of tasks, some of which they consider areas of weakness. Many oversee a broad range of ministries, including both high school and junior high ministries (87%), and/or young adult ministries (43%), outreach/evangelism (58%), small groups (50%), administration (60%), and leading music in the main worship service (22%). Since youth/children's pastors are often the second pastoral hire after the lead pastor, their workload is diverse, as often two pastors carry the full load of responsibilities (depending on volunteer support). Clearly, these youth/children's pastors cannot be equally adept at all these tasks. Overall, youth/children's pastors spend about 15 per cent of their time in tasks they consider weaknesses, particularly administration (Posterski et al., 2011), and only about one-third (35.5%) received support from other staff/volunteers in such tasks. In fact, not having help in areas of weakness is correlated with both lower job satisfaction ($r = -.235^*$) and lower opinion of the congregation ($r = -.267^*$).[6] We noted in chapter 6 that younger pastors had a more negative attitudes toward their congregation than the lead pastors of that same congregation, and lack of support for areas of weakness is part of the reason for this. Other factors obviously contribute as well, but we wonder if this may also be part of the reason for their high turnover rates.

RETENTION AND YOUTH

How well do evangelical congregations retain their youth? What are the factors linked to whether evangelical children stay or leave their churches in youth or young adulthood? To answer these questions we turn to the data from the Church and Faith Study of Young Adults (CFYA; Penner et al., 2012).[7] Table 7.5 presents pre-screened data on the present religious identification of 2,722 18- to 34-year-olds who were raised Christian. Those with missing data and those not raised Christian were removed. Of note, out of 697 respondents raised in evangelical congregations,[8] 63.1 per cent still identify as evangelical in young adulthood. This is significantly higher than the retention rate of Catholics (46.9%) or mainline Protestants (34.4%). The data show that evangelical Protestants hold on to more of their children and youth than other Christian groups, even though the attrition is significant for all groups.

When we look at switching patterns between Christian traditions, we find that more survey participants moved to evangelicalism than switched into other faith communities. Further, more childhood Catholics (3.8%) and mainline Protestants (8.8%) became evangelicals in young adulthood than evangelicals turned Catholic (1.7%) or mainline Protestant (2.3%). As a result, two out of every three children who were raised evangelical (67.1%) maintained a Christian affiliation in young adulthood. This is higher than for Catholics (51.2%) or mainline Protestants (44.7%).

Those who do leave are not going to other faiths, but to the unaffiliated. Evangelicals in Canada lose very few of their childhood members (0.6%) to other world religions. Only 4 out of 697 evangelicals joined other world religions. This is similar to the rate of loss among mainline Protestants (4 of 674 or 0.6%) and Catholics (5 of 1,351 or 0.4%) to other world faiths. Evangelicals lose 32.3 per cent to the non-institutionally unaffiliated, which is a lower percentage than mainline Protestants (58.4%) and Catholics (48.4%). Childhood

Table 7.5 Religious affiliation of young Canadian adults "raised Christian," by childhood family religious affiliation

Childhood Family Religious Affiliation	Religious affiliation as young adult (%)								
	Christian affiliations				Other world faiths	Non-institutional affiliations			
	EP	MP	RC	Total cbr		Atheist	Agnostic	No religion	Spiritual, etc.
EP (N = 697)	63.1	2.3	1.7	67.1	0.6	6.9	5.7	12.8	6.9
MP (N = 674)	8.8	34.4	1.5	44.7	0.6	14.7	12.6	18.4	9.1
RC (N = 1,351)	3.8	0.6	46.9	51.2	0.4	15.8	9.4	15.2	8.0
Total (N = 2,722)				53.7	0.5	13.2	9.3	15.4	8.0

Source: CFVA, pre-screen dataset (Penner et al., 2012).
EP = Evangelical Protestant; MP = Mainline Protestant; RC = Roman Catholic

evangelical defectors self-identify in young adulthood as no religion (12.8%), atheist (6.9%), agnostic (5.7%), or spiritual (6.9%).

Although not captured in Table 7.5, the pre-screening also identified any childhood non-attendees who began attending congregations (at least sporadically) in their teen/young adult years, and who ultimately identified with a Christian tradition as young adults. This minority of youth go against the trends of decreased attendance and disaffiliation. There are 49 young adult evangelical reaffiliates/re-attenders, which is considerably higher than the 9 young adult mainline Protestant additions or the 18 Catholics.

How do defection rates compare between Canada and United States? Mark Chaves (2010) compared the growth trajectories of mainline and evangelical Protestants in the United States and found that evangelicals lose fewer of their youth to the unaffiliated. In their National Study of Youth and Religion, Smith and Snell (2009) found higher retention rates for evangelicals than for mainline Protestants, but even higher retention for Catholics and Mormons. Table 7.6 compares their 18- to 23-year-old respondents with the 18- to 24-year-old age group from the CFYA data. The table shows that retention is higher in the United States than in Canada for most Christian groups, and that Canadian Christian youth are much more likely to move to the "no religion" category than found in the American sample. Note that these data stem from different research methodologies – the NSYR relied on phone interviews instead of an Internet panel – so they are not perfectly comparable. Also note that the CFYA analyzes Canadian retention between "childhood" and young adulthood, while the NSYR examines retention between affiliation at age 13–17 and age 18–23. The higher retention rate in the United States may be partly because of the shorter time span. Still, we think that the Canadian defection rates are higher than in the United States as there are fewer cultural supports for church attendance in Canada. However, more research is needed.

ATTENDANCE RATES

In Table 7.7 we describe attendance rates. These data are for 1,977 young adults who were childhood evangelicals, mainline Protestants, or Catholics who completed the survey. Note that this sample is

Table 7.6 Retention and switching rates of younger/emerging adults by Christian tradition, Canada–USA comparison

Age 18–24[a]	% Canadian-Raised Christian Affiliation			% Christian Affiliation at age 13–17, USA		
	Evangelical Protestant (N = 125)[c]	Mainline Protestant (N = 81)	Roman Catholic (N = 196)	Evangelical Protestant (N = 750)	Mainline Protestant (N = 277)	Roman Catholic (N = 652)
Evangelical Protestant	**72.0**	3.7	5.1	**64.0**	20.0	6.0
Mainline Protestant	0.8	**32.0**	0	10.0	**50.0**	3.0
Catholic	1.6	8.6	**45.9**	2.0	2.0	**66.0**
No religion[b]	25.6	54.0	48.9	20.0	26.0	23.0
Other world religions	0	1.2	0	1.0	1.0	2.0

Source: For Canada, the CFYA dataset (Penner et al., 2012), and for the United States, the National Survey of Youth and Religion 2007–08 dataset (Smith and Snell, 2009, 109).
Note: Interesting denominational differences are highlighted in bold face.
[a] Canadian data includes 18- to 24-year-olds; USA data includes 18- to 23-year-olds.
[b] Canadian No religion data includes: Atheist, Agnostic, Spiritual, None, and Other.
[c] Canadian unweighted; USA weighted.

YOUTH AND CHILDREN   173

Table 7.7 Attendance at religious services of young Canadian adults "raised Christian," by childhood family religious affiliation

Childhood Family Religious Affiliation	Attendance at Religious Services in Young Adulthood n (%)		
	Weekly or more	Less than weekly	Never
Evangelical Protestant (N = 497)	193 (38.8)	159 (32.0)	145 (29.2)
Mainline Protestant (N = 507)	60 (11.8)	247 (48.7)	200 (39.4)
Catholic (N = 973)	90 (9.2)	490 (50.4)	393 (40.4)
Total (N = 1,977)	343 (17.3)	896 (45.3)	738 (37.3)

Source: CFYA survey dataset (Penner et al., 2012).

limited to those who were raised Christian, meaning they identify as Christian and attended a congregation at least occasionally while growing up (weekly or more often, weekly, monthly, or seldom). Evangelical youth were much more likely to have been weekly attendees as children. 56.3 per cent (193 of 343) of the survey's childhood weekly attendees were raised evangelicals, even though they account for only 25.1 per cent of the sample. Mainline Protestants added 17.5 per cent and Catholics added 26.2 per cent. Of those raised as evangelicals, 70.4 per cent attended weekly or more as children (n = 350) compared with 12.5 per cent of Catholics and mainline Protestants. In addition to their higher levels of institutional participation as children, evangelicals enjoy considerably higher attendance retention rates. Over one in three (38.8%) evangelicals attended weekly as young adults, compared with about one in ten mainline Protestants and Catholics. If we limit our sample to only those who attended weekly or more often as children, 55.1 per cent of raised evangelicals are weekly attendees as young adults, compared with 27.2 per cent of mainline Protestants and Catholics.

Again, the institutional retention rates of evangelicals are higher relative to Catholics and mainline Protestants, but many evangelically raised young adults attend less or have dropped out altogether, and many others do not even identify with an evangelical denomination. While 29.2 per cent of children who were raised as evangelicals never attend as young adults, 46.2 per cent (67 of 145) of these never-attendees used to attend weekly or more often as children. Another 70 former weekly attendees now say they seldom attend. In other words, 39.1 per cent of those who regularly attended evangelical congregations as children attend seldom or never as young adults. This is sobering news for the future of evangelical congregations.

However, we want to know more than these raw numbers show. What contributes to retention and non-retention? Previous research shows the importance of parents, peer networks, congregational characteristics, and personal religious experiences to religious retention. Table 7.8 highlights how those raised as evangelicals experienced God, congregational life, and religious instruction. These are just some of the items used in the survey, but enough to demonstrate how these experiential themes relate to the attendance levels of these young adults. We are not arguing that these experiences cause church attendance. We suspect these associations are mutually reinforcing.

It appears that attendance at worship services by evangelical young adults hinges on the way that God is experienced by them. If God is perceived to be present in tangible ways, young adults are much more likely to be found inside congregations. Sometimes this experience is a memory of an earlier time that keeps being inspirational. An evangelical young adult, raised as a Catholic, who now attends an evangelical congregation, speaks of a "joy ... inexplicable" from a conversion experience in university that still motivates him:

And I started to become really, really depressed in university and addicted to sex and suicidal ... I had some good friends ... And they invited me out to hear someone share about [the possibility of a] relationship with God ... And I was so intrigued and it sounded exactly what I wanted ... So the next day I went back to my dorm room and read something that she gave me which had Scripture on it and basically the gospel message. And for the first time ever I really felt like God was speaking to me and this was truth, that I really felt his presence and his peace in a very dramatic way ... So ... I received his forgiveness ... That day was the beginning of my new life, and it was dramatic – like black and white, night and day, for me ... I was a new person; anyone who knew me would've just been weirded out almost because I just had a joy that was inexplicable, and purpose in life that could not be thwarted. [9]

Table 7.8 Religious experiences of young Canadian adults "raised evangelical," by attendance at religious services

Religious Experiences	Attendance at religious services in young adulthood		
	Weekly or more N = 193	Less than weekly N = 159	Never N = 145
Percent "strongly" or "moderately" agreeing:			
Experience of God			
I have experienced God's love personally.	99.0	70.4	24.1
I believe God answers my prayers.	99.0	73.0	28.3
Experience of Church			
In my experience, the opinions of youth matter to church leaders.	82.9	57.2	35.9
In my experience, church is a place where my talents go unappreciated.	10.9	25.2	41.4
I have experienced emotional healing through help received from a church.	77.7	38.4	7.6
Experience of Teaching and Beliefs			
In my experience, the church addresses tough topics in their sermons.	89.6	53.5	36.6
Those in church leadership are able to help me explore my toughest questions.	90.2	47.8	24.8
I feel free to ask questions of church leaders.	93.7	56.6	40.0

Source: CFYA survey dataset (Penner et al., 2012).

Raised evangelical weekly attendees are much more likely than non-attendees to report experiencing God as loving (99.0% vs. 24.1%) or someone who answers their personal prayers (99.0% vs. 28.3%). Virtually no young adults who were raised as evangelical attendees (1.0%) continue to attend without this relational view of God.

Young adults who were raised as evangelicals also seem to be more likely to attend when certain things are experienced in the faith community. They desire, for example, that their voice be heard. One evangelical young adult who stayed with the church said, "It's hard to trust leadership that doesn't even really know that you exist. It's hard to be a part of a congregation whose members can't hold a five-minute conversation about my day or even show interest in it ... Somehow an environment has to be created where people know that their voice matters." Regular attendees are more likely than those who never attend to report that their opinions matter to church leaders (82.9% vs. 35.9%). They are also less likely to report that their talents go unappreciated (10.9% vs. 41.4%). Another young adult laments her inability to contribute in her congregation after returning from a season of overseas mission work. She no longer attends: "Even though I said, look, this is what I am good at, this is my experience, this is what I can help you with. And I became familiar with their ministries, and, and put myself out there, and I had new ideas, and shared them. But nothing was being received or accepted. It wasn't that they said, 'No, you can't do that,' it was just that nothing ever really happened with my ideas. Nobody gave me a job." Her experience of not being valued by the leadership coincided with "a crisis of faith" surrounding her mother's sudden death. Her inability to make sense of this tragedy raises another key issue. Young adults want congregations to be places where their emotional needs are met. Regular attendees are much more likely than non-attendees to report experiencing personal emotional healing at church (77.7% vs. 7.6%) and for the church to have a positive impact on others inside (and outside) the church walls.

Another young adult spoke enthusiastically about her congregation: "When I get back in my car after [church] I'm on fire, not necessarily because of the messages, even though they are great, but because of seeing other people who love others, love sinners as though they were their own family members and what I retain from this, is this massive fire that reaffirms my faith. I exit the church utterly encouraged in my faith." She is a young adult evangelical who has been a regular attendee since childhood. Leadership plays a key role in how evangelical young adults perceive church. As one young adult said, "My youth pastor was just always speaking to our lives ... I always felt valued by him. You know, I always felt like he saw our potential and invested in us as leaders and treated us with respect. Like, he never talked down to us or anything. I always appreciated that and, just the idea of how mentoring is important."

The way in which church teaching is delivered appears to be important to young adults raised in an evangelical congregation. They desire space to ask questions and leaders who address their toughest topics. One young adult said, "I feel like I [want] time to pick through the bones I have before I have a solid grasp of what I actually do believe." Meanwhile, another evangelical childhood attendee stopped attending in part due to claims of hypocrisy and judgment as well as an inability for people in her congregation to handle her questions and doubts. She saved her harshest criticism for her catechism class, where the focus was memorization of church doctrine: "Don't get me started ... it felt like school of the worst kind ... I'm sorry. It felt like we should have been wearing uniforms. I found it very boring, dry and not very open for discussion. Memorize for the next class." Another evangelical young adult attendee described the poor teaching practices of a congregation he at one time attended and said, "It feels as if they were brainwashing me with incorrect things that religion should be about. So I feel that maybe that's why youth today are turned off of religion in general, or certain religion, because it is too aggressive, it's like a sales approach." Regular attendees were much more likely than non-attendees to agree that churches addressed tough topics in their sermons (89.6% vs. 36.6%), that leaders were able to explore tough question (90.2% vs. 24.8%), or that church was a place they felt free to ask their hard questions (93.7% vs. 40.0%).

EXPERIENCE OF PARENTS

In Table 7.9 we look at the relationship between parents' church attendance and young adults' attendance. Of respondents who reported that both their parents attended "regularly" while they

Table 7.9 Young Canadian adults "raised Christian" who attend weekly or more, by parents' attendance (non-divorced parents only)

Childhod family religious affiliation	Parents' attendance at religious services			
	HIGH – Both parents attend regularly (%)	MODERATE – One parent attends regularly (%)	LOW – Neither parent attends (%)	Weekly+ attendees (n)
Evangelical Protestant (N = 354)	64.6	34.0	7.7	48.0
Mainline Protestant (N = 394)	21.8	11.2	2.7	11.4
Roman Catholic (N = 697)	22.0	7.2	3.5	11.2

Source: CFYA survey dataset (Penner et al., 2012).

were growing up, 64.6 per cent of those young adults who were raised evangelical currently attend weekly or more, compared with roughly 22 per cent of mainline Protestant and Catholic young adults who had parents who attended worship services regularly. If only one parent regularly attended (more often the mother), the percentage of young adult weekly attendees drops roughly in half. Very few young adults still attend if neither parent attended regularly when they were young.

Present-day religious attendance is powerfully correlated with parental attendance. Note how one young adult describes the personal piety of her mother: "And my Mom who lived it, like, I would see her reading her Bible every night and praying. And I knew that her relationship with Jesus was something that was real ... I think seeing how real my Mom's relationship with the Lord was, did, and continues to really challenge me and inspire me to consider the way that I live." Spiritual role modelling by parents, of course, is no guarantee of young adult religiosity, but its importance was clear in the CFYA interviews. Young adults pick up on the subtleties of their parents' faith. Note, for example, how one evangelical young adult who left the church, mentions her ongoing intrigue about her own father's personal Bible reading: "And my Dad, I only ever really saw him reading his Bible in church. And I mean, I'm sure he did it. My Dad's

Table 7.10 Religious practices of young Canadian adults "raised evangelical," by parental religious practices

Religious behaviours in young adulthood	Parental religiosity		
	HIGH – Both parents pray, read Bible, attend services regularly (N = 192)	MODERATE – Religious inconsistency in one or both parents (N = 202)	LOW – Neither parent prays, reads Bible, or attends religious services (N = 102)
% of young adults who:			
Pray privately weekly or more often	82.8	39.6	19.6
Read Bible weekly or more often	60.9	17.8	3.9
Attend religious services weekly or more often	72.4	23.8	5.9

Source: CFYA survey dataset (Penner et al., 2012).

just much more of an inward person than my Mom is. So, I'm sure he did it on his own time. But I never really saw it when I was younger and I always kinda wondered because he wasn't as open about it as my Mom was."

In Table 7.10 we see how current levels of personal prayer, Bible reading, and attendance at religious services among young adults who were raised as evangelicals correspond with the same religious practices of their parents while they were growing up. If evangelical children witness high levels of consistent religious practices in the home, they are much more likely to practise their faith as well when they grow up. Four in five still pray weekly (82.8%), two in three still read their Bible weekly (60.9%), and seven in ten still attend church weekly (72.4%). Where parents exhibited inconsistent levels of spirituality (either because only one parent practises these disciplines regularly or both did not practise certain disciplines regularly), the long-term transmission of spiritual disciplines to their children dropped off considerably. As expected, when parents are irreligious in behaviour despite identifying with an evangelical religious tradition, the religious practices of their children are minimal. Various researchers point to the lifelong effect of early religious socialization (Vaidyanathan, 2011). Cornwall (1988), for example, found that parents played a significant role in the religiosity of their children by intentionally channelling their youth into settings where they could form close ties with co-religionists. Bader and Desmond (2006) found that consistency in the home, like regular religious attendance by both parents, was needed for effective faith transmission. Furthermore, homes with two religious parents who exhibit "belief hegemony" have a greater impact on the religion of their children than households where children receive mixed messages (Myers, 1996). Our findings here mirror what these researchers have reported.

In conclusion, evangelical congregations prioritize youth and children's ministry. The data in this chapter clearly show that the evangelical congregations put significant resources – youth pastors, volunteers, programs – into developing faith in their children and youth. Evangelical pastors told us that their congregations prioritized highly youth and children's ministry more consistently than any other priority. Research shows that the efforts of the congregation matter considerably for youth retention.

Evangelical congregations provide the space for the development of faith and institutional commitment. The data show that those youth who experience God in a meaningful way are much more likely to attend through young adulthood. Evangelical congregations encourage such experiences. They organize mission trips and send children to camps, which provide particularly important religious experiences (Penner et al., 2012). Relationships are also important. Youth need relationships with non-familial youth and adult mentors to show them an authentic faith. Congregations provide opportunities in their weekly meetings and activities for such bonds to form.

Of course, not all congregations foster faith commitment or future institutional commitment equally well. Those congregations that allow youth to ask questions and explore their faith, to have input into congregational life, and provide leadership and service opportunities do better than those that do not. Youth are watching the adults around them. They are looking for examples of faith that is genuine. Not all congregations provide examples that are compelling. The presence of adults like youth pastors and volunteers who invest in the youth are those with greatest opportunity to provide such examples. Programs structure time for faith emulation.

Yet, in spite of all these efforts, what happens at home may be more important than what happens within the congregation. In a regression analysis, we compared the relative strength of various influences on young adult attendance. What we found was the parental religiosity – whether or not both parents attended, prayed, and read the Bible regularly – was the most powerful single predictor of the young adult's attendance pattern. If an evangelical child saw all three of these from both parents, retention is just over 80 per cent. The next most important factor was whether or not their youth leaders "did a great job modelling Christianity" for them, followed by whether or not their faith was experienced at camp or on a mission trip. Taken together, these three institutional-experiential factors – youth leader modelling, revitalizing camp experience, and mission trips – are even stronger than the parental effect.[10] The point is clear: congregations and parents are both important to the institutional commitment of the next generation. Obviously, the two spheres are linked. The congregation shapes parental faith and commitment, just as parental commitment to the faith enhances the congregation. Positive religious experiences in youth group, camp, or a mission trip can only further enhance retention.

8

Financing Evangelical Congregations

with Rick Hiemstra

Church congregations, like all organizations, need a continuous stream of money to operate. Most congregations are largely dependent on the giving of the individuals who attend them. Without their generosity in both volunteer time and money, the ministries of most congregations would cease. Yet, even with generous parishioners, many congregations struggle. Financial pressures are a perennial problem (Chaves, 2004), and congregations often find creative ways to add to what is put in the offering plate. Congregations have used, or now use pew rents, yearly dues, rummage or yard sales, renting their building, car washes, interest from investment income or endowments, and many other ways to increase revenue. Yet, one wonders if societal pressures and cultural changes make it harder on churches financially. In this chapter we investigate the finances of evangelical congregations. We begin by looking at giving in Canada, and draw from research on generosity in the United States. We then examine the revenue, expenditures, and assets of evangelical Protestant congregations in Canada, comparing them with mainline Protestant and Roman Catholic churches. We see evidence for present and future institutional vitality by following the money.

Historically, some evangelical organizations followed George Muller (1805–1898), who "prayed in" millions of dollars to set up orphanages in Bristol without telling anyone of his ministry's financial needs, except God. He even went without a regular salary, claiming to trust God for his "daily bread." Such "faith missions" are rare now. Since 1945 most evangelical organizations have followed the entrepreneurial practices of D.L. Moody (1837–1899), founder of the Moody Bible Institute in Chicago, who actively asked for money and sent out fundraising letters (Hamilton, 2000). Over time, the methods of corporations – advertising, direct solicitation, professional managers, hierarchical structure – were adopted by evangelical organizations. Values of efficiency, rationality, and consumption from the secular world were sometimes contested since they did not match well with the self-denial and frugality of the Protestant ethic. In many cases, however, they were adopted without much critique (G.S. Smith, 2000). Such methods were justified because more money made for more ministry (Hamilton, 2000). Parishioners or supporters give more when solicited.

Today, however, many clergy do not like asking for money. Pastors do not want to turn people off, or they do not know how to ask for money, so they tend not to. As noted in chapter 3, evangelical pastors talked about financial giving and tithing, with a median of twice (3.46 times on average) in the past six months. To avoid offence, talk of money is often couched in broader themes of generosity and stewardship, rather than direct appeals to meet the congregation's budget needs. Even if pastors tiptoe around the topic of money, many Canadians still give generously to their congregations.

GIVING IN CANADA

Canada has excellent data on charitable giving and volunteering, available from the Canada Survey of Giving, Volunteering and Participating (CSGVP) conducted by Statistics Canada, which polled over 15,000 Canadians in 2010 (Statistics Canada, 2012). We can also look at trends over time in these data, since the first poll on charitable giving and volunteering was completed in 1997, and it has been repeated roughly every three years since then (2000, 2004, 2007). In 2010 about 24 million (84%) Canadians aged 15 years or more made a financial donation to a charity or non-profit organization, for a total of $10.6 billion. While income tax data from Statistics Canada show a much lower number of givers (5.6 million or 23% of tax filers in 2009), the amount of giving claimed on income tax returns is still substantial, at $7.75 billion.[1] Besides financial donations, Canadians gave donations of food (62%) or items like clothing (79%), so that nearly all Canadians (94%) gave goods, food, or money to charity (Turcotte, 2012). Fewer Canadians, 13.3 million

(47%) volunteered. Nonetheless, the amount of time volunteered was substantial, totalling 2.1 billion hours, which is roughly equivalent to 1.1 million full-time jobs (Statistics Canada, 2012). In addition, the numbers of volunteers are growing faster than the population (Vézina and Crompton, 2012). These high levels of giving time and money are important for charitable organizations.

Even youth are active in voluntarism. In fact, young people, aged 15–24, have higher rates of volunteering (58%) than older Canadians, although older Canadians volunteer more hours (Vézina and Crompton, 2012). Giving money is widespread as well. Among young Canadians, 73 per cent made at least one charitable donation in 2010, with an average amount of $143. Again, this is below the Canadian average of $446 in charitable donations. Whether amounts of giving will increase as they age (and earn more) is still to be determined, but giving and volunteering is widespread among Canada's youth.[2]

While the rate of giving money and volunteering is high in Canada, the amount of giving and volunteering is highly skewed. The majority of Canadians give, but most do not give very much. The median is $123, meaning half of Canadians give more and half gave less than that per year. The average is much higher at $446, partly because there is a small percentage that give (and volunteer) a lot. The top 25 per cent of donors account for 83 per cent of the total value of donations, and the top 10 per cent contributed 63 per cent of the dollars given; the top 10 per cent gave $995 or more in 2010 (Turcotte, 2012). For volunteering, the top 10 per cent account for 53 per cent of all the volunteer hours; these top volunteers contributed 391 hours or more per year, equivalent to nearly 10 weeks of full-time work (Vézina and Crompton, 2012). Those who tend to give financially are also generous with their time, indicating that volunteer work is not a substitute for, but a correlate of financial giving. In 2010 those who volunteered for 60 hours or more had a higher rate of making donations (91%) and gave substantially above the average ($784). By comparison, non-volunteers averaged $288 (Turcotte, 2012). These data show that there is a relatively small percentage of Canadians who are very generous with their time and money, and they account for the majority of both hours and money given to charity.

Who are these generous Canadians? They tend to be older, university graduates who have high incomes, and most importantly for our purposes, are frequent attendees of religious groups (Turcotte, 2012). The strong correlation between religious participation and generosity is long established in Canada. To quote Carleton University researcher Nick Scott (2007):

> A "civic core" of uniquely engaged Canadians, in fact, accounting for disproportionately high amounts of volunteering, giving, and associating – 29% of the adult population in 2000, responsible for 85% of volunteer hours, 78% of total charitable dollars, and 71% of associational activity – are defined in part by their atypical religiousness (Reed and Selbee, 2001). Religion seems to help infuse their participatory worldviews with a commitment to contributing to the common good while providing access to social networks through which to do so. (5)

Why are religious participation and generosity linked? Some say it is the pro-social values taught by religions. Religion inculcates the faithful with love for each other and compassion for the less fortunate. No doubt this is part of it, but we think habits and practices developed through regular civic participation are much more important. After all, most Canadians agree that generosity and "concern for others" are very important virtues (Bibby, 2006). What supports generosity is the institutional and community setting that provides opportunities (or pressure) to give, the relational networks that promote pro-social behaviour, and the socialization processes that make helping normal. Of course, the congregation is not the only place these habits are developed, but it is obviously an important one when we look at the data (Bibby, 2011). That is why research finds that religious participation is more important than religious beliefs when it comes to giving (Bowen, 1999; Scott, 2007; Berger, 2006). Selbee and Reed (2000) state,

> We repeatedly find that groups with higher rates of volunteering also show higher levels of participation in other spheres of community life such as membership in civic organizations, interaction with family and friends, church attendance, length of residence in the community, number of organizations volunteered for, and informal helping.

Beliefs matter, but levels of association and participation matter more. (1–2)

In the United States, Vaidyanathan, Hill, and Smith (2011) found that giving to congregations, non-congregational religious organizations, and secular organizations were all higher for those involved in religious organizations. They argue that what makes people generous is not specific ideology, but regular involvement in religious, political, and civic practices. Qualitative research shows that people learn giving behaviours in church (and through other associations) in childhood socialization, and sometimes they transfer these habits into other charitable settings (see Vaidyanathan and Snell, 2011). Giving to congregations, then, should be strongly correlated with attendance. In Table 8.1, we summarize findings from Statistics Canada's 2010 Survey of Giving, Volunteering and Participating, comparing those who attend a congregation weekly or more often with those who attend less often. Weekly attendees gave, on average, $688 to religious organizations, compared with $61 for those who attend less than weekly. Note that this average of $61 includes those who attend monthly or less often. While the difference is stark, there is even a greater difference between weekly attendees and those who never attend, as giving decreases with attendance (McKeown et al., 2004).

Even though they account for only 16 per cent of the population, regular attendees provide 71 per cent of the giving to religious organizations. That weekly attendees give more to religious organizations is not surprising. More surprising is that they also give more to non-religious organizations ($306 vs. $247). All told, a higher proportion of weekly attendees donate (93% vs. 83%), and they give over three times as much as those who attend less often (average $1,004 vs. $313; median, $350 vs. $100). They also volunteer more time (Vézina and Crompton, 2012).

There are important implications of generosity, particularly for evangelical congregations. As previously noted, evangelical Protestants attend, volunteer, and give at much higher rates than other Canadians, even other weekly attendees (Bowen, 2004). Berger (2006) found:

On virtually all measures, with or without "economic" corrections, conservative Protestants give more dollars, give a larger proportion of total income, volunteer more hours,

Table 8.1 Generosity in relation to evangelical church attendance

	Attend weekly+ (16%)	Attend < weekly (84%)
Average annual donation to religious organizations	$688	$61
% of total donated to religious organizations	71	29
Average annual donation to non-religious organizations	$306	$247
Average total average donation	$1,004	$313
Median total median donation	$350	$100
Donor rate (% who made a donation)	93	83
Average total hours volunteered annually	202	141

Source: Turcotte (2012).

and volunteer for a larger proportion of their available hours. Moreover, conservative Protestants are more likely to give through all giving methods, and are more likely to volunteer for all kinds of activities. Particularly interesting is the fact that almost 60% of conservative Protestants give through their church collections, with fully 75% of their giving going to religious causes, while those measures are only 40% and 46%, respectively, on average for other religions. (122)

The proportion of donations going to religious organizations, however, is declining over time. Of all giving, 40 per cent or $4.26 billion went to religious organizations in 2010, compared with 46 per cent and $4.8 billion in 2007 (Turcotte, 2012).[3] In 2000, 49 per cent of all giving went to religious organizations (McKeown et al., 2004). In addition, religious motivations for giving seem to be on the decline. In 2007, 32 per cent of donors said they were motivated to give to fulfil religious obligations, compared with 27 per cent in 2010. Among the many motivations for giving (feeling compassion toward people in need and believing in the cause were the top motivations), declining religious motivation was the only significant change (Turcotte, 2012). Of course, these changes are not surprising considering that the percentage of weekly attendees is shrinking over time. Yet, even among weekly attendees, the average annual donation was higher in 2007 ($1,085) than in 2010 ($1,004), if only slightly (Turcotte, 2012).

If many Canadians give time and money but the majority of giving is done by a relative few, one may conclude that these few are generous by any standard. This small percentage of generous Canadians, many of them regular participants in congregations, however, is not that generous by religious standards. Most Christian groups teach "tithing," or donating 10 per cent of your income as the norm (Smith and Emerson, 2008). If we take the median total family income in Canada in 2010 ($69,860)[4] compared with the median yearly giving ($123), we find that the typical Canadian gives less than two-tenths of one per cent (0.18%). Even among the weekly attendees – the majority of whom are Christians, and who have incomes roughly the same as the national average (Bowen, 2004; McKeown et al., 2004) – the median ($350) is 0.5 per cent and the average of $1,004 is just over 1.4 per cent. Evangelical Protestants give at a similar level of 1.4 per cent (Berger, 2006), far below the 10 per cent "tithe."

In their study of (the lack of) Christian generosity in the United States, Smith and Emerson (2008) conclude that the greatest impediment to generosity is consumerism, which focuses attention on what one does not have, not on what one has. Second, as noted above, clergy do not talk about money since it is often not appreciated, and when they do, they communicate low expectations (not a 10% tithe). Third, some laypeople lack confidence that non-profits will use their money wisely and efficiently. Fourth, there is a tension between individualism ("my money") and divine ownership ("God's money") among Christians. Interview respondents said contradictory things because they had trouble harmonizing American autonomous individualism and private property with God's ownership and stewardship of all things. Fifth, there are few consequences for not giving because giving is a private matter. Corporate "shirking," where a minority do the majority of the work or giving yet all enjoy the same benefits, likely comes into play. Finally, they noted that Christians perceive that they cannot give more (which the authors felt was more perception than reality), and that giving was not routine. Instead, attendees decide what they can afford or want to give each week. In Canada, the CSGVP asked about "barriers to giving" and found that the most common reasons for not making more financial donations were that the person felt she or he could not afford it (71%) or she or he was happy with what had already been given (64%) (Turcotte, 2012, 33).

Is there evidence of a crisis of religious giving in the future? There is good reason for concern. We know that religions have less authority than they used to, so they have less sway over the pocketbooks of Canadians. We also know that religious participation is declining, so Canadians are less likely to hear of congregational financial needs. In addition, Bibby (2006, 57) shows that only about one-third of Canadians have "a great deal" or "quite a bit" of confidence in the leaders of religious organizations in 2005, compared with one-half in 1985. With little confidence in religious institutions, they may not trust them with their money. The CSGVP found that 37 per cent of Canadians did not give more because they "did not think the money would be used efficiently" by the organization, up from 33 per cent in 2007 (Turcotte, 2012, 32).

The problem is not just related to decreasing institutional religion. Consumerism, individualism, and other factors seem to make people less generous in North America. The richest countries and their citizens are not very generous when we look at proportion of income. The median donation of $150 for Canadian wealthy donors (with annual incomes of $100,000–119,999) is a smaller proportion of their household income (0.14%) than that of low-income donors (with annual incomes of $20,000–39,999) whose median donation is $80 (0.27% of their household income).[5] As a proportion of its Gross Domestic Product, in 2010 Canada gave about one-third of one per cent (0.33%) in foreign aid, and the United States even less (0.21%).[6] Increased competition for donation dollars is another factor that may reroute money that traditionally went to congregations. The proliferation of religious organizations (other than congregations) and non-governmental organizations (Wuthnow, 1987) means that there are more religious groups vying for donation dollars. Evangelical Protestants receive pleas for money from private Christian schools, missions or philanthropic organizations, and many other non-profit groups besides their congregations.

One way congregations can weather the change in Canada is for the shrinking number of faithful attendees to give more. That is what is happening in the United States, says Chaves (2004), as the typical attendee digs deeper to keep the congregation afloat. This is evident in Canada as well. In 1969, 58.7 per cent of Canadian households made contributions to religious organizations that averaged $470 (in constant 1996 dollars). In 1996, only 37.9 per cent made religious donations, but the average amount was $683. According to Statistics Canada, "Fortunately for religious charities, the average value of these contributions has been increasing at almost the same rate as the percentage of households making them has decreased" (Reed, 2001, 4).

Even though the faithful are giving more to keep their churches operational, they seem to be fighting a losing battle. Faith Communities Today (FACT), a study of some 11,000 congregations from over 120 denominations in the United States in 2010, released a report called *Decade of Change in American Congregations 2000–2010*.[7] The FACT survey found that 31 per cent of congregations reported excellent financial health in 2000, compared with 14 per cent in 2010. The rate of decline has actually increased in the latter part of that decade, partly because of the 2008 recession, which we look at below.

FINANCES OF EVANGELICAL CONGREGATIONS

In our Canadian Evangelical Churches Study, we asked several questions about finances. These included questions on total income and expenditures, percentage of expenditures that went toward certain areas, and the pastor's subjective evaluation of the financial situation. Much more detailed financial information, however, is available through the Canada Revenue Agency (CRA). Every one of the roughly 85,917 Canadian registered charities is required to complete an annual Charitable Information Return (T3010 or CIR) for the federal government's Charities Directorate within six months of their fiscal year end. Of these charities, two-fifths (33,412) are classified by the Charities Directorate as religious, and we estimate that 24,000 of them are Christian congregations. Further, about 94 per cent of religious organizations in Canada are registered charities.[8] The CIRs collect over 200 pieces of information covering fundraising, program descriptions, directors, and political activity; however, most of the information collected is financial.[9] Most of the CIR data are posted publicly on the Charities Directorate website beginning with the

2000 fiscal year. The data are both available through access to information requests and directly from the Charities Directorate website.[10]
Using denominational directories and the assistance of denominational officials, Rick Hiemstra matched 6,199 evangelical congregations, 2,973 mainline Protestant congregations, and 1,078 Roman
Catholic parishes to their registered charity numbers (see Appendix).
We also matched the CECS congregations to their registered charity
numbers to compare the dataset's financial information. Using these
registered charity numbers we compiled the congregational CIR information from 2000 to 2010 for analysis.[11] We use these data to show
details of how congregational income, expenditures, and assets have
changed over time.

Before we look at the CIR data on income, expenditures, and
assets, we start with a measure of overall financial vitality from the
CECS data. The nearly 500 CECS pastors were asked to give their
opinion on the overall financial situation of their congregation.
They were asked to rate it as "excellent," "good," "tight but manageable," "in some difficulty," or "in serious difficulty." Two-thirds
of the pastors rated their congregational financial vitality as "good"
(34.1%) or "tight but manageable" (34.9%). Another 17.6 per cent
said it is "excellent" and 13.4 per cent that their congregation was
in "some difficulty" or "serious difficulty" financially. Table 8.2
shows the correlations between perceived financial vitality with several other variables.

It is important to note that perceived financial vitality is not
significantly correlated with income or expenditures separately (not
shown), or whether income is higher than expenditures ($r = .079$). It
is strongly and negatively related to the percentage of the income
spent on salaries ($r = -.242^{***}$). It is also negatively correlated with
the percentage spent on the maintenance of buildings and grounds.
Clearly, evangelical pastors do not consider it financially healthy for
their congregations to spend a high percentage of their incomes on
salaries and maintenance, even if they are receiving the salaries themselves (and enjoying the building improvements). They consider it
better for money to be spent externally, like for missions ($r = .179^{***}$).
The percentage spent on local outreach is positively correlated with
financial health as well, and almost reaches significance ($r = .089$).
Even if a higher percentage of money is going toward the internal
costs of operating a congregation that is not because the pastors

192   A CULTURE OF FAITH

Table 8.2 Correlations with perceived financial vitality, evangelical congregations

	Correlation
Income – expenditures	.079
% spent on salaries	-.242***
% spent on maintenance	-.095*
% spent on mission	.179***
Size (no. of regular attendees)	.110*
Attendance increase	.170***
Giving increased at beginning of 2009	.306***
Positive opinion of the church	.359***

Source: CECS, 2009.
*$p < .05$; ***$p < .001$.

want it that way. Perceived financial health is weakly correlated with congregational size ($r = .110^*$), and more strongly correlated with growth, both in attendance and financially. It is most strongly correlated with the pastors' overall positive attitude toward their congregations. Not surprisingly, pastors are positive about their congregations' finances if they are growing in attendance and offerings. Pastors may be reflecting their focus on people and the overall vitality of the ministry, not on budgets.

Even if pastors are more focused on people and ministry, and less focused on budgetary numbers, their general perceptions of the congregation's finances are fairly accurate. Because we were able to match congregations in the CECS sample with their CRA numbers and combine the datasets, we looked at the trajectory of tax-receipted gifts (roughly equal to individual giving or offerings) for the CECS congregations based on their CRA reports. The average yearly change in dollars (or the "slope" for the statistically inclined) shows that congregations rated as having an "excellent" financial situation by their pastors saw median giving gains of 7.0 per cent per year between 2003 and 2008 (based on 2003 total receipted gifts), a median gain of $13,078 per year. In comparison, those rated as having "good" (3.9%) or "tight but manageable" (4.8%) financial health showed small yearly gains, while those reporting "some difficulty" only gained 1.7 per cent a year (below cost of living increases). Those

Table 8.3 Annual change in giving in relation to perceived financial health, evangelical congregations

	Total receipted gifts slope – median ($)	Total receipted gifts slope – as % of 2003 total giving median
Excellent (*n* = 80)	13,078	7.0
Good (*n* = 157)	7,140	3.9
Tight but manageable (*n* = 155)	6,607	4.8
Some difficulty (*n* = 50)	2,707	1.7
Serious difficulty (*n* = 10)	-956	–0.7
Total (*n* = 452)	6,971	4.5

Source: CECS/CRA combined dataset, 2009.

reporting "serious difficulty" saw decreased giving over the time period, at an annual –0.7 per cent. The actual numbers are given in the Table 8.3.

INCOME

In his study of the income of evangelical congregations between 2003 and 2008, Hiemstra (2010) found that the period leading up to the 2008 recession was not particularly good for evangelical congregations. Their income was rather flat, increasing only 1.5 per cent per year after adjusting for inflation. Two-fifths of congregations faced income declines during that time. Income growth was greatest in the province of Alberta (26% growth, adjusted by median income), with very modest growth in Ontario (3%) and Nova Scotia (4%).

In Figure 8.1 we look at the giving trajectory for the five denominations in our CECS sample, using the CRA data, as it gives a larger sample and a view of change over time. The figure gives the median total for tax-receipted gifts for the denominations from 2000 to 2009 in constant dollars. It is clear that giving is fairly flat over this period. The slight gains shown by some denominations do not necessarily mean growing congregations, since we know that faithful attendees are giving more to maintain budgets even while attendance is declining (this is true of Canadian congregations overall; we are

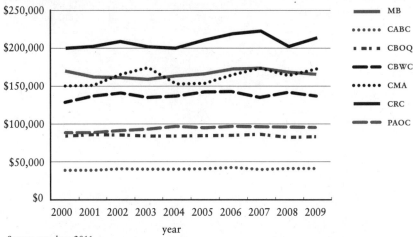

Figure 8.1 Median tax receipted gifts (line 4500) 2000–09 by denomination in 2000 dollars

Source: CRA data, 2011.

MB= Mennonite Brethren
CABC= Convention of Atlantic Baptist Churches
CBOQ= Canadian Baptists of Ontario and Quebec
CBWC= Canadian Baptists of Western Canada
CMA= Christian and Missionary Alliance
CRC= Christian Reformed Church
PAOC= Pentecostal Assemblies of Canada

not sure if it accurately reflects these evangelical denominations or all evangelical congregations). The differences in giving are largely related to church size, with western and urban congregations tending to be larger. The eastern Baptist conventions (CABC and CBOQ) have smaller congregational incomes and are showing negative income trajectories, whereas the PAOC has smaller incomes but a slight positive trajectory. In comparison, the larger congregations of the CRC, MB, and CMA denominations are fairly flat, with slight gains shown by the CMA.

THE RECESSION

We were particularly interested in the effect of the 2008 recession on giving. In the United States, where the recession was worse, the negative effects of the recession on religious giving was documented in "Holy Toll: The Impact of the 2008 Recession on American Congregations," based on the FACT survey. The authors found that 57 per cent of congregations reported their income had declined due to the recession, and that the number of congregations that reported being in serious financial difficulty doubled to almost 20 per cent. It surprised the researchers that the recession affected both mainline and evangelical Protestants in similar ways. For evangelical congregations, the congregations dealt with lower income by delaying capital campaigns or projects (29%), reducing monies for mission and benevolence (27%), reduced savings and investments (25%), salary freezes or reductions (25%), delaying the filling of staff positions (17%), and laying off staff or giving staff furloughs (9%). Obviously, staffing took a hit.

In Canada, Hiemstra's examination of CRA data (2010) showed that evangelical congregational incomes, once adjusted for inflation, grew slowly from 2003 to 2006, hit their ceiling somewhere around 2007, and showed slight decline into 2008. So, overall, evangelical congregations were already facing declining incomes coming into 2008. Over the first four months of 2009 as compared with the same period in 2008, more CECS pastors told us that their congregational giving had remained the same (43%) or increased (34%) than those who said their giving had decreased (20%). Thus, the effect on overall giving seems to be minor. The best conclusion seems to be that the recession may not have made for a sudden change in giving, yet it added to a longer trend of declining income. Like the United States, however, the recession seemed to have a significant effect on staffing. As we note under "Expenditures" later, there seems to be an increase in staff layoffs in 2009, possibly due to tighter budgets in 2008 and earlier.

Figure 8.1 shows that not all denominations were negatively affected by the recession, at least not in their receipted gift income. The CRA data show that rural (and smaller) congregations actually weathered the recession better than urban congregations (Hiemstra, 2010), possibly because rural economies and their congregants (who tend to be older) were less affected by the recession. While rural congregations may have more stable incomes, they have about one-half the median income of urban congregations, just as eastern congregations have about half the income of larger congregations in western Canada (Hiemstra, 2010).

A more detailed picture of income is given in Table 8.4, which looks at median dollar amounts of gifts and total revenue between the years 2000 and 2010, in constant 2000 dollars. In 2010 the

Table 8.4 Median tax-receipted gifts (line 4500) and total revenue (line 4700) by Christian tradition in 2000 dollars, 2000 and 2010

	Tax-receipted gifts			Total revenue		
Tradition	2000 ($)	2010 ($)	% change	2000 ($)	2010 ($)	% change
Evangelical Protestants	93,394	97,910	4.8	111,664	119,193	6.7
Mainline Protestants	83,024	80,169	-3.4	106,065	110,876	4.5
Roman Catholic	119,613	124,409	4.0	171,682	177,658	3.4

Source: CRA data, 2012.

median evangelical congregation received $97,910 in offerings and $119,193 in total revenue. The median evangelical congregation brings in more money than the median mainline Protestant congregation, but less than the median Catholic church. In constant 2000 dollars, evangelical congregations have increased their giving slightly, by 4.8 per cent, which is similar to the Catholic increase of 4.0 per cent. While these figures do account for inflation, we doubt that such a tiny increase does much to improve the financial vitality of churches. In fact, this small change may actually signal tighter budgets. For instance, occupancy costs (see Table 8.5) for evangelical congregations have increased at a much greater rate, which likely puts a squeeze on other line items in many churches. Giving in mainline Protestant congregations is down slightly, by 3.4 per cent. These minor changes in revenue further support the previous statement that faithful attendees are digging deeper to increase their giving, since the decline in attendance is greater than changes in offerings and revenues.

Congregations, as noted above, are largely dependent on the financial gifts of regularly attending individuals. For evangelicals, offerings account for at least 82.1 per cent of total revenue in 2010. Comparatively, mainline Protestant offerings accounted for 72.3 per cent, and Catholic offerings 70.0 per cent of total revenue. Table 8.4 shows that revenue is increasing more quickly than offerings for the evangelical and mainline Protestants. The difference is very slight for evangelicals and more noticeable for mainline Protestants.

FINANCING EVANGELICAL CONGREGATIONS 197

Mainline congregations are obviously finding other ways to bring in money to make up for lower offerings.

Part of the gap between receipted gifts and revenue is related to rental and fundraising income. Mainline congregations, in particular, have greatly increased the amount of money from rentals and to a lesser degree, fundraising, and are much more likely than evangelical congregations to claim income from these sources. These sources account for less than half of the non-giving revenue for mainline Protestants and much less than that for evangelicals and Catholics (even less when we consider that many churches did not claim rental or fundraising income). Other sources could include money from investments, endowments, the denomination, and even the government. For example, the Salvation Army is unique among evangelical denominations in the amount it receives from government sources.

EXPENDITURES

How do evangelical congregations spend their money? In Table 8.5 we break down expenditures based on the itemized lines in the 2010 CRA data. Those expenses that account for 10 per cent or more of total median expenditures are included in the table. The table also includes the percentage change in the item between 2000 and 2010 based on constant dollars, and the percentage of the total expenditures accounted for by the item. The final column gives the percentage of congregations that filled out that line of the CRA form in 2010. Not surprisingly, the largest expense is related to staff compensation. The total compensation amount would include all staff, whether pastoral, administrative, custodial, part-time or full-time. In many congregations compensation costs are largely the salary and benefit packages paid to one pastor, but in others compensation may cover multiple staff or more than one congregation can share the compensation cost of one clergy person who oversees more than one congregation. Table 8.5 shows that the median spending on all compensation is $57,453 for evangelical congregations, which is 45 per cent of total expenditures (identical to the 45% found in CECS data).[12] Mainline congregations spend a bit more, and Catholics a bit less. The percentage change column shows that evangelical staff compensation has increased by 19.4 per cent above inflation between 2003 and 2010, with lower increases

Table 8.5 Median expenditures 2000–10 by Christian tradition in constant 2000 dollars,[a] select charitable information return expenditure lines

Expenditure	Tradition	2010 median ($)	% change 2003–2010 (constant $)[a]	% of total expenditures 2010 (median)	% churches reporting this line in 2010
Total compensation (Line 4880/0390)[b]	Evangelical Protestant	57,453	19.4	45.0	81
	Mainline Protestant	61,572	9.2	49.3	81
	Roman Catholic	54,985	10.3	30.9	85
Occupancy costs (Line 4850)	Evangelical Protestant	23,531	32.0	14.9	69
	Mainline Protestant	22,878	12.3	17.5	71
	Catholic	42,106	13.2	22.9	79
Gifts to qualified donees (Line 5050)	Evangelical Protestant	14,380	14.1	11.7	71
	Mainline Protestant	11,127	-3.5	9.8	64
	Catholic	23,351	11.1	12.0	71
Total expenditures (Line 5100)	Evangelical Protestant	115,158	6.7	100.0	92
	Mainline Protestant	109,136	3.5	100.0	92
	Catholic	171,023	5.3	100.0	94

[a] Calculations based on Consumer Price Index: CANSIM Table 176-0003 (accessed 16 July 2012) http://www5.statcan.gc.ca/cansim/pick-choisir?lang=eng&p2=33&id=1760003)
[b] Line 4880 was cross-listed as line 0390 starting in 2009.

for mainline Protestants and Catholics. The reader should not conclude that pastors are paid a considerably higher income or that evangelical congregations are adding positions. Part of the apparent increase is due to the negative effects on staffing during the recession, as noted above. A minority of small congregations no longer reported compensation in 2009 (missing data), and so median compensation went up for the remaining congregations because they tended to be larger.[13] Other evidence of the recession is the proportion of congregations that claim compensation expenditures. In the final column, note that 81 per cent of evangelical and mainline congregations and 85 per cent of Catholic churches claimed compensation expenses. This suggests that almost 20 per cent of evangelical and mainline congregations have no paid staff.[14] In addition, the proportion of congregations claiming compensation is decreasing with time, indicating that staff have been laid off. This is particularly true of mainline Protestants. In 2003, 90 per cent claimed compensation expenses, a decline of 9 per cent by 2010. In comparison, evangelical Protestants declined 4 per cent and Catholics 7 per cent.

Occupancy costs include costs associated with the buildings owned or rented by the congregation. As a proportion of total expenditures, occupancy costs are lowest for evangelicals, at 14.9 per cent. This is partly because they tend to have smaller and newer buildings, and we suspect they are also more likely to rent. In the CECS sample, about 14 per cent of the evangelical congregations did not meet in the building, but in a school (22 congregations), or community centre (18 congregations) or other places like a home, mall, or store. As noted before, less money going into occupancy costs is likely good for congregational vitality, as more money can go into staff and various ministries.

The "gifts to qualified donees" mainly includes gifts to other charitable organizations, which could include donations to the denomination, local charities, and other mission or philanthropic organizations. These account for roughly 10 per cent of total expenditures. We know some evangelical congregations tithe 10 per cent of their income to other charitable organizations or the denomination's head office. More evangelical and Catholic churches claim this line than mainline Protestants (71% vs. 64%), and these donations are growing for Catholics and evangelical Protestants, but shrinking for mainline Protestants.

Most important is the last line, the total expenditures, where evangelicals are spending slightly more than mainline Protestants but much less than Catholics, in keeping with their income. However, the difference between median total revenue (based on Table 8.4) and spending is considerably less for mainline congregations ($1,740, or 1.6%) compared with evangelical Protestants ($4,035, or 3.4%) and Catholics ($6,635, or 3.7%). Overall, expenditures are indicative of the tighter finances of mainline congregations. In comparison, evangelical congregations are more likely to see more money spent on discretionary costs like compensation increases, gifts to other charities, and increased spending on "other expenditures" like advertising and education. Yet, the evidence is mixed, because increased compensation is partly due to a declining number of churches claiming the expense, evangelical and otherwise.

Finally, there are some revealing CRA data related to total assets. First, there is a significant increase in cash in the bank, especially for evangelical congregations. It appears that congregations prefer to put away some cash for a "rainy day." No doubt, many congregations realize that next year's forecast does not include growing congregational budgets. Second, regarding the reported market value of land and buildings, evangelicals report a median value of $526,724, which is roughly three times (311%) their total median income. Both mainline Protestant and Catholic congregations claim their property assets are about five times their income. This suggests that Catholics and mainline Protestants have more elaborate buildings. On the down side, it also suggests that if they were in the market for a new building of equal value, it would be more difficult for them to pay for it. The lower than expected proportion of congregations reporting this asset (52% evangelical, 48% mainline Protestant, and 28% Catholic) likely means that denominations or dioceses hold the deeds to many church buildings.

In conclusion, the picture emerging from all this financial detail is that evangelical congregations are in better financial health than mainline congregations particularly. Evangelical median congregational incomes are higher and growing slightly while mainline congregational incomes are declining slightly. As a result, evangelical congregations have more money to spend on discretionary costs like donations to other non-profits, education, and promotion. They spend a lower percentage of their total expenditures on occupancy costs, freeing up more money for other ministry options.

Yet, in many ways they are the same. There is plenty of evidence that the recession negatively affected congregations in all three traditions. Staffing compensation, the largest single expenditure area, seemed to be particularly hard hit. There was a significant decline in the proportion of congregations claiming compensation costs between 2003 and 2010. Some of these churches let go of staff. Similarly, giving to evangelical churches is fairly flat. The total revenue growth is similar for all three traditions, and evangelicals are doing only marginally better than the others.

What of the future? Generous Canadians are disproportionately members of congregations and are giving more to help meet congregational budgets. The problem is that there are fewer people giving. There are many signs that congregations are tightening their budgets, with less discretionary spending. Evangelical Protestants are doing comparatively well, but are showing minimal financial growth. Many factors affect their financial future, but probably none as much as whether the spiritual journeys of the younger generation will take them back to institutional religion.

Conclusion

The roughly 11,000 evangelical congregations in Canada are diverse. From the white, clapboard-sided Baptist churches of rural New Brunswick to the Chinese Alliance churches in downtown Toronto, the Aboriginal Pentecostal churches in northern Manitoba, the Christian Reformed churches on the Alberta prairie, and the large Mennonite Brethren congregations in the Vancouver area, evangelical congregations seek to build God's dominion from coast to coast to coast. Some have modern worship styles with electric guitars and drums while others have traditional organ-led hymns. Some are charismatic and some are liturgical. Some are growing quickly and planting satellite congregations; others are greying and some are closing their doors. They represent over one hundred different denominations; many others belong to no denomination at all. They are cooperative, but they also are internally divided. Heated disagreements exist within and between denominations and congregations. Many evangelical congregations have split from nearby congregations (James, 2011). They are not a unified or monolithic group.

In spite of all this diversity, however, evangelical congregations show some surprising similarities. Roughly 80 per cent of evangelical churches list ministry to youth and children as a top priority, and they have extensive youth and children's programs. The vast majority have Bible studies, prayer meetings, and other small group meetings during the week. They emphasize the authority of Scripture, that the only way to heaven is through faith in Jesus Christ's salvific work on the Cross, that a conversion experience is central, and that Christians need to actively live out their faith. They live out their faith through evangelism, acts of compassion and care toward those around them, and through regular church attendance, Bible reading, and prayer. These similarities, and many others, point to the presence of a pervasive evangelical subculture that spawns such interdenominational similarities and cooperation. We argue that the congregations are the hub of this subculture, and that to understand evangelicals, we need to understand their congregations. In this book, we described these congregations, drawing from over 500 interviews with evangelical pastors from across Canada.

The evangelical subculture, of course, is not impervious to the social currents around it. Rather, the walls of the subculture are permeable, so congregations take on local colour even while resisting (selectively) some of the influences of the "world." These evangelical congregations, then, are also Canadian. Yet, they remain distinctive in important ways, like in their exclusive beliefs about salvation, their sexual ethics, and their ability to reinforce an institutional form of religious devotion.

While roughly half of evangelicals claim to be in church on a given Sunday, many are not institutionally committed. They form a continuum: at one extreme are those who are evangelical only in claiming affiliation, resembling non-evangelical Canadians and fully embracing the broader culture; at the other extreme are those who aggressively resist the broader culture and commit themselves to distinctive evangelical beliefs, practices, and attitudes. Where evangelical persons find themselves along this continuum has a lot to do with their level of participation in an evangelical congregation.

We note that the Canadian culture is not supportive of its churches, as weekly attendance continues to decline. We also cannot ignore the fact that younger generations are less likely to go to church than older generations, and that young adults show high levels of dropout, as we showed in chapter 7. We see few reasons to think that any native-born Christian population will grow, including evangelicals. These numbers may stabilize depending on future immigration patterns and retention. Of course, whether evangelicals experience slow growth in numbers, slow increase in number of congregations, or stability also depends on the vitality of the churches.

Related to their resistance of some cultural influences, evangelical congregations are doing *comparatively* well. Canadian evangelical congregations are maintaining a strong institutional religiosity at a time when most other Christian traditions are facing declining church participation, and have been for roughly half a century. In this book, we have suggested that the relative vitality of the evangelical subculture has a lot to do with evangelical congregations themselves. The congregations are central to evangelical life. Obviously, the congregations are not the only reason for evangelical resilience. Other organizations – Christian day schools, denominations, para-church organizations – matter as well. So do evangelical individuals – clergy, other leaders, artists, authors, media producers – who also energize the subculture and the congregations. However, our argument is that the congregations are centrally important to both the micro (individual) and macro (subcultural) strength.

We have given many reasons for their relative institutional strength. They are part of a distinct subculture that is salient enough to hold the primary identity for many evangelicals. Their subculture emphasizes an external locus of authority, leading them to defer to biblical authority and the injunction to continue to meet corporately. And, because the Bible requires interpretation and application, individual evangelicals often defer to pastors and church leaders because of the authority of the Bible (and ultimately, God) in their lives. Their diversity allows evangelicals to choose from an array of churches, increasing the likelihood of finding one that they like. Internally, these churches benefit from congregants who give and volunteer at high rates, adding to their vitality. Churchgoers are among the most generous Canadians giving time and money; and evangelicals lead other Christian groups in terms of generosity. They not only give money and volunteer more time to their churches, but also they give to and volunteer more for non-religious causes. The people in the pews tend to be younger, and have incomes and education levels similar to adherents of mainline Protestant and Catholic traditions. Their congregations are only forty-five years old on average, and newer churches tend to be less costly to maintain and tend to be located in growing areas. Financially, evangelical congregations are in a better position than mainline Protestant congregations.

Evangelical pastors we talked to indicated that many of their congregations have a clear vision and most attenders are committed to it. Congregational mission statements centre around the Great Commandment – to love God, and to love others – and the Great Commission – to evangelize, or more accurately, to make disciples of Jesus. At least four in five evangelical pastors said that their

CONCLUSION 205

congregation has a mission statement that shapes their current priorities, and the lay leaders are invested in it. Research suggests that a compelling vision or mission is important to organizational vitality. These congregations prioritize the young and offer extensive programs for children and youth – Sunday schools, youth groups, mission trips, camps, youth choirs, and many more activities. Most evangelical congregations have youth and children's events. The children are top priority in both word and action. All these factors benefit evangelical institutions.

Yet, there is evidence that evangelical congregations are no longer growing, but that many (we think most) evangelical denominations have plateaued in both numbers and in finances. While evangelical denominations are in a better place in terms of qualified pastoral leadership than mainline Protestant and Catholic groups, the denominational leaders we talked to are concerned about future leadership shortages. Many congregations struggle to retain their youth, others are closing, and many face aging memberships, aging clergy, and financial pressures. In addition, there are few demographic reasons to predict continued growth. A quick look at Statistics Canada projections clarify what the religious demographics will look like based on current growth/decline trajectories.

In 1981, 90 per cent of Canadians were Christian, of some stripe. In 2006, this proportion was 75 per cent. By 2031, Statistics Canada (Malenfant, Lebel, and Martel 2010) projects that roughly two-thirds (64%–66%) of Canadians will be Christian. Between 2006 and 2031, the number of Muslims in Canada will triple, accounting for nearly half (48%) of all non-Christian religious affiliates. Over the same time, most other non-Christian religious groups will double, and those with no religion would increase from 17 to 21 per cent of the population. If these projections are correct, the proportion of Christians would decline, even though they will remain the dominant religion for the foreseeable future. The Statistics Canada report does not distinguish between mainline and evangelical Protestants, so the evangelical future is unclear. While the proportion of Protestants overall will decline over time, the proportion of those in Statistics Canada's "other Christian" category (which includes those who identify simply as "Christian," "Apostolic," "Born-again Christian," or "Evangelical"), will increase from 3 per cent of the population in 2006 to 4.6 per cent in 2031. It is difficult to know what percentage of this "Other Christian" category is evangelical, or if their increase might correspond to an increase in evangelical affiliates (Malenfant, Lebel, and Martel, 2010; see also Mata, 2010).

Because the Canadian natural birth rates are below replacement levels, most population growth for Canada is now due to immigration (Trovato, 2009). Statistics Canada data show that about 10 per cent of immigrants arrive as Protestants, and roughly another 6 per cent identify within the "other Christian" category (see Beyer, 2008). While not all of these immigrants will find their way into evangelical churches, many will. Evangelical leaders tell us that the majority of their new churches are ethnic churches. Yet, even if most evangelical immigrants join evangelical churches, their proportion of the immigrant population (less than 16%, but we're not sure how much less) is not much higher than the current evangelical population of 10 per cent. Of course, some evangelicals may be converts to Christianity, but evidence shows that the growth of immigrant conversion is slight (Beyer, 2005). Add to this that evangelicals are having difficulty attracting the Canadian-born while evangelical families also have fewer children. The demographic future does not look bright.

South of the border, there are rumblings that evangelical congregations are no longer growing. Is there reason to think that North American institutional evangelicalism has reached its peak and is headed for slow decline? Yes. Many of the same cultural forces that make church participation less conventional are happening in both countries, even if church attendance has fewer cultural props in Canada than in the United States. Furthermore, evangelicals in the United States and Canada show many similarities as they share a similar evangelical subculture (Reimer, 2003).[1]

In his overview of American religious trends, Duke University sociologist Mark Chaves (2011) compares the long trend of liberal (mainline) Protestant decline and the comparative growth of conservative (evangelical) Protestant denominations in the United States. He thinks the trend will change. Since evangelical birth rates are declining, fewer of their youth are participating, and the society is becoming less supportive of their conservative politics and sexual mores, so evangelical growth may slow or stop. "It seems likely that the trajectories of conservative and liberal Protestant denominations will not be as different over the next several decades as they have been over the last several decades. Conservative denominations are losing their competitive edge" (91). In fact, the 2012 *Yearbook of American and Canadian Churches* (Lindner, 2012) is already showing that some large evangelical denominations in the United States, notably the Southern Baptist Convention and the Lutheran Church-Missouri Synod, are declining. Since birth and immigration rates no longer benefit evangelical congregational growth to the degree they did, we do not see that changing. For these reasons, the evangelical congregations are susceptible to the same demographic patterns that led to mainline Protestant decline in the 1960s. This raises questions not only about the future of evangelical churches but also about the future of institutional Protestantism in North America.

In his book, *The Great Evangelical Recession* (2013), journalist and pastor John Dickerson predicts the worst. Due to inflated statistics on the number of evangelicals in the United States, along with growing antipathy, internal divisions, and other factors, he sees a "megatrend" toward "massive regression" (22). He states, "The decline in evangelical Christianity is not *just* that we are failing at evangelism or *just* that we're failing to keep our own kids or *just* that we'll lose 70 percent of our funding in the next thirty years. Its all those factors (and more) combined" (22, original emphasis). Although alarmist,[2] Dickerson's book correctly identifies demographic signs of decline. While there are too many factors involved to perfectly predict future growth trajectories, we doubt that evangelical congregations will experience the same rate of decline as the mainline Protestant traditions did over the past half-century. There are several reasons for this. Many maintain a strong evangelistic impulse, which will lead to some converts. Although few joiners are converts, even a few can energize the church. They are attracting and integrating a sizeable minority of Canadian immigrants. And the shift in global Christianity is such that immigration is contributing to a wider transformation of Christianity. Whether or not these new immigrant Christians will be able to hold off the tide of Canadian cultural and social trends that they see as eroding faith, we can only speculate. There are Christians arriving from Africa, Asia, and Latin America who are shaped by the notion of reverse mission whereby they claim to be called by God to push back secularizing trends (see Aechtner, 2012). We are not convinced they can do so, and the second generation will likely lose some of this fervour as it conforms to Canada's tepid religiosity. While the majority of immigrants are non-Christian, the strength of evangelicalism worldwide – especially its Pentecostal/ charismatic manifestations – implies that evangelical immigrants will continue to come to Canada and that many will join evangelical congregations. And, although they are having fewer children, evangelicals work hard to help their children keep the faith. For these reasons and others, we think any prediction of inevitable decline is premature. In the end, the future fate of evangelicalism in Canada, and the United States, will likely follow the fate of the evangelical congregations. We think that all religious traditions require a strong organizational base for long-term viability and to maintain religious commitment among the individuals in that tradition. In spite of a Canadian milieu of weakening institutional religiosity, the current resilience of evangelical congregations indicates that their future is not a fait accompli.

PRACTITIONER POSTSCRIPT

While this book is primarily written for those interested in the academic study of religion in Canada, we expect that some practitioners – pastors, denominational leaders, etc. – will read these pages. We are glad for that. However, a word of caution is in order. Sociologists are tasked with telling "what is" in the social world, not what "should be." Yet, more often than not, it seems that social science books like this one are understood as prescriptive instead of descriptive. From at least the start of the church growth movement fifty years ago, evangelical leaders have used social scientific methods to measure success quantitatively – for example, the number of people in the pews, the number of sinners saved, and/or the size of the church budget. Furthermore, they use social science to prescribe technique. For example, churches should target those groups of people most likely to give time and money, and they should offer a worship service that attracts the unchurched. What "should be" becomes conflated with "what works" to grow quantitatively.

The tendency of evangelical practitioners to borrow (selectively) from the broader culture is nothing new. Bebbington (1989), Smith (1998), and others have argued that evangelicalism is in dynamic tension with the broader society, adjusting their technique in light of modern practice. The evangelical subculture has somewhat uncritically embraced the fundraising techniques (Noll and Eskridge, 2000), technological advances like radio, television, and the Internet, business structures and marketing techniques, and even corporate language. In short, evangelical churches are thoroughly modern. They seem to believe that with the right research, and the correct techniques, and the correct business model, good leadership, and attractive buildings and programs, they will grow and succeed. Thus, practitioners will often read books like this, hoping to find some knowledge from science that will help them "succeed" using the same definition a secular business might use.

Unfortunately, we wonder if we are unintentionally feeding a tendency within evangelicalism that encourages practitioners to prioritize questions like "What can I do to grow my church?" This is not necessarily a bad question; it just may not be the most important one for practitioners to ask. By its own logic, evangelicalism prioritizes the Bible as the final authority, and Jesus as the primary example – not numerical growth. Their ecclesiology suggests they first ask different questions, like "What does it mean to be a faithful witness of the reality of Jesus?" Sometimes the answer to that question may require the church to do things that will not add to its numerical or budgetary success. Meeting the physical and emotional needs of those in the congregation or community may not promote numerical growth. Supporting congregations that serve older or poorer congregants in small towns will not help denominations grow, but it may be an example of faithfulness. Spending time in prayer may not show the same strong correlations to measureable outcomes as cutting-edge technology or the latest worship songs in the worship service. Our point is that we are not trying to prescribe how churches should define success or what churches should do.

At the start of this project, we asked two respected evangelical theologians how to measure church health. This was their joint reply:

Because the Church is the presence of the divine-human Christ on earth and His infinitely beautiful bride, it is impossible to measure her health. We are particularly concerned that theological categories not be taken over by (neutral) empirical measurements. These measurements lead us away from theological concerns and assume that we can find some other, neutral ground on the basis of which to measure the "health" of the Church. For example, we might be tempted to measure the health of the church by the presence or absence of a nursery, youth group, or hospitality committee. Each of these categories may be seen as transcending any theological viewpoints that exist (infant baptism or the meaning of the Eucharist).

It is for this reason that we have not talked about church "health" in this book. Nor have we prescribed techniques for health, however defined. Instead, we have looked at vitality, defined quantitatively. We do not assume that evangelicals will, or should, agree that these are correct measures of church health or vitality.

Yet churches are also institutions, like factories or banks. They depend on human actors to maintain their buildings, pay their budgets, run their programs, and define their goals. They need people (attendees and volunteers) and money to be viable, regardless of how spiritual their purposes. It is within the limited scope of these mundane, earthly factors that this book may be helpful to evangelical practitioners.

Appendix

The appendix contains the telephone questionnaire, which was administrated by Advitek in English and French. It also has the questions we asked of the denominational leaders. Attention is given to the response rates and representativeness of the data. Further attention is given to questions about the Church and Faith Study of Young Adults (CFYA) data and the Canada Revenue Agency (CRA) data.

CANADIAN EVANGELICAL CHURCHES STUDY

The "Canadian Evangelical Churches Study" (CECS) included interviews with the lead pastors (the senior pastor or only pastor) of 478 evangelical congregations by phone in 2009. These phone interviews were completed by Advitek, a data collection firm in Toronto, in both English and French (the English version of the survey is given below). The response rate for these interviews was roughly 40 per cent. Advitek also performed 100 youth and children's pastor phone interviews in these same congregations. The congregations contacted were randomly selected from lists of congregations provided by denominational leaders. The denominations were the Pentecostal Assemblies of Canada (PAOC), the Christian Reformed Church (CRC), the Mennonite Brethren (MB), the Christian and Missionary Alliance (CMA), and the four Baptist Conventions – the Convention of Atlantic Baptist Churches (CABC), the Canadian Baptists of Ontario and Quebec (CBOQ), the Canadian Baptists of Western Canada (CBWC), and the French Baptist Union/Union D'églises Baptistes Françaises au Canada (FBU).

212   APPENDIX

Prior to the phone interviews, we conducted face-to-face interviews with 50 other lead pastors in major regions across Canada (Maritimes, Toronto area, Calgary area, and Vancouver area). Finally, we interviewed the national leaders from the denominations in our study.

RESPONSE RATES AND REPRESENTATIVENESS

Our 40 per cent response rate on the CECS main pastor survey raises questions about representativeness. While it is not what we hoped, people inside the phone polling industry tell us that a 40 per cent response rate is a very good response rate for phone polls. Figure A1 gives the response rate breakdown.

The 73 "wrong numbers" (fax numbers, disconnected, etc.) and the 130 "inaccessible pastors" can be subtracted from the total response rate because these had no possibility of a successful completion. We attempted to resolve wrong numbers by searching the Internet for an alternate number, and this effort resulted in some correct numbers. Regarding the "inaccessible pastor" category, our requirement was that we interview a lead pastor who had been at the church for 6 months or more; 104 congregations did not meet this criterion. The remainder of this category (26 out of 130) were unable to complete the interview either due to language limitations (15 interviews could not be completed in English or French) or long-term illness of the pastor (11). Of the numbers called that were possible to complete, there were many where the pastor was never available. We suspect that some of these numbers were bad numbers (because there was never an answer), but this was not tracked. So, we can conservatively say that the response rate is somewhere around 40 per cent for the pastor interview. A minority of the eligible phone numbers had a minimum of 8 callbacks, with the majority of the sample receiving up to 23 callbacks. When we discovered that we would not reach our quota with the present sample, we added more churches and that group only received up to 8 calls. Only 4 pastors terminated the interview partway through.

In light of the large number of unavailable respondents, our main concern for the representativeness of our data was that we would miss some smaller churches (and to a lesser extent, ethnic

Figure A1. Response rates flowchart.

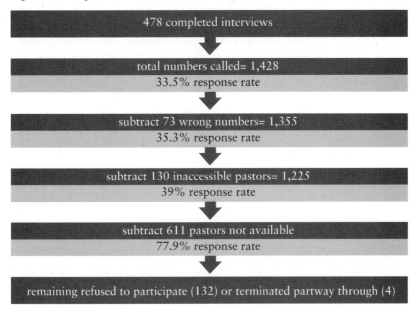

churches), since churches without administrative help or part-time/volunteer pastors would be less likely to be available. The two sources of data that give some indication of the quality of the data – denominational data and CRA data – are mentioned above. Hiemstra's Canada Revenue Agency data involved matching each church from the CRA data with denominational lists, resulting in 5,822 congregations (see Hiemstra, 2009).

We should be clear that both sets of data have their problems. First, denominational data vary in quality. Many churches do not send annual reports to their denomination, a few churches will close or move before data are updated, and so forth. We note that the denominational data suggest that our data underrepresent small congregations. While this may be true, it is not true to the extent indicated, because of problems with the denominational data. In fact, we were able to fully reconcile the data.

First, since we sampled roughly 100 congregations from each denomination, we have roughly equal numbers of congregations from denominations with larger congregations, such as the CRC, as

Table A1. Congregational incomes, CRA and CECS data

	2008 CRA data			CECS data		
Denomination	Churches (n)	Average Income ($)	Median Income ($)	Churches (n)	Average Income ($)	Median Income ($)
PAOC	966	301,170	126,253	94	247,602	125,563
CRC	241	357,800	285,617	103	292,274	240,000
MB	209	444,758	224,802	85	440,268	240,000
CMA	390	461,752	219,423	93	399,815	254,000
CABC	473	105,010	57,314	32	215,560	122,500
BCOQ	329	201,799	113,109	24	191,100	120,549
CWBC	145	322,359	200,079	24	381,231	188,000
French[b]	N/A	N/A	N/A	5	–[a]	–[a]
Total	5,822[c]	291,038	143,205	460	323,749	204,245

Source: CRA data (2012) and CECS (2009).
N/A = not available.
[a] Sample too small for accurate estimates.
[b] French Baptist.
[c] The total includes all evangelical churches (from all evangelical denominations) in the dataset who reported total income.

we have from small-congregation denominations such as the Baptists. In reality, there are many more Baptist congregations in Canada (about 1,070) than CRC congregations (about 250). If each of the five denominations had an equal number of churches, we would expect an average attendance of 181.9 and median of 115.4 based on denominational counts, which is closer to, but still a bit smaller than, the CECS congregational sizes.

Second, we think the denominational counts are probably too low. We think this because we are able to match the average attendance of most churches in the CECS sample with those in the denominational data (we were not able to match all because sometimes denominational attendance data were missing). Note that the CABC and CBOQ estimates in the CECS seem much too high compared with denominational data, so we matched churches for these conventions. For the 45 CABC and CBOQ congregations that we were able to match, the denomination reported an average attendance of 100.5 and a median of 75.0. The pastors of these same congregations told us that their average attendance was 120.6 with a median of 90.0. Similarly, for the 71 MB churches we were able to match, the denomination reported an average of 206.8 with a median of 140. The MB pastors told us their average attendance was 235 with a median of 170. This means that the pastor estimates were about 20 per cent higher than the denominational figures. This makes our data look fairly good, but which is correct? Well, we suspect in most congregations, it's the pastor who reports the statistics to the conference, and if he or she does not, then a staff member would be drawing from the same data the pastor would use. We think our data are closer to accurate, since we know they're based on up-to-date information, recognizing that pastors may give slightly optimistic attendance counts (note that we asked pastors to consult their official documents when reporting the attendance of the previous year, although only 15 per cent did so). If the denominational data are 20 per cent too low, the denominational median would be 107 and the average 180. Applied to our sample of 100 from each denomination, we would get 138.5 as a median and 218.3 as an average, which is nearly identical to what we found. Still, we think we were somewhat more likely to miss small congregations, and that is why our estimate for the median size of congregations in these five denominations is about 100 instead of 107.

One reason we still think the CECS sample underrepresents small churches is based on how they compare with the CRA data. Of course, the CRA data are not perfect either, even if we have more confidence in them. The CRA will miss churches that do not claim separate charitable status, and there will likely be some churches that were not included in the evangelical fold because of the obscurity of the information available, and because Hiemstra could not match them with current denominational lists. Nonetheless, they provide a foil to at least check the issue of size. In Table A1, we compare the average and median income of congregations based on the CRA data and our data, both reported for the year 2008.

Table A1 shows that the CRA and CECS data match very well across denominations, giving us much more confidence in the representativeness of our data. The CABC data again suggest that the CECS data missed some of the smaller congregations, but the other Baptist regions are very close. Finally, the CRA data suggest that congregations in the denominations we chose are somewhat larger than the median for all denominations.

216   APPENDIX

CANADA REVENUE AGENCY DATA

This sample represents approximately two-fifths of the Christian churches in Canada or about one-third of all congregations in Canada. The largest portion of the sample congregations is evangelical because the dataset was built on a pre-existing dataset of evangelical congregations maintained by the Evangelical Fellowship of Canada (EFC). While the mainline Protestant and Catholic subsamples represent a smaller proportion of their respective set of congregations than the evangelical Protestant subsample, we nevertheless believe that these subsamples represent at least one-third of mainline congregations and about one-sixth of Catholic congregations.

Congregations were included in the sample if they met the following criteria:

- At least one charitable information return was posted on the Charities Directorate website for the fiscal years ending in 2003–10.[1]
- The congregation could be positively matched with its Registered Charity Number (RCN).
- The congregation could be positively identified with one of the religious code values included in Table A2.

Congregations were matched to their denominations by comparison with denominational directories, both printed and online. Where possible electronic versions of directories were obtained and electronic scripts were used to make preliminary matches of the Charities Directorate's contact information with the denominational contact information.[2] After preliminary electronic matches were made the matches were reviewed and validated by Hiemstra.

Given that the authors relied heavily on electronic means for preliminary matching the data is biased toward congregations where the contact information registered with the Charities Directorate was similar to that published in their directories. There are a variety of reasons why this contact information may vary. These include:

- A congregation may have changed its name without updating the name it registered with the Charities Directorate.
- The contact address provided to the Charities Directorate may

Table A2 Congregational frequency counts by denomination and tradition

Denomination	Tradition		
	Evangelical	Mainline	Catholic
Pentecostal Assemblies of Canada	987		
Convention of Atlantic Baptist Churches	488		
Christian and Missionary Alliance in Canada	404		
Fellowship of Evangelical Baptist Churches	372		
Canadian Baptists of Ontario and Quebec	340		
Christian Reformed Church in North America	247		
Salvation Army Canada/Burmuda Territory	246		
Canadian Conference of Mennonite Brethren Churches	221		
Mennonite Church Canada	199		
Church of the Nazarene in Canada	184		
Canadian Fellowship of Churches and Ministers	179		
Canadian Baptists of Western Canada	151		
Baptist n.o.s.a	151		
Canadian National Baptist Convention	149		
Associated Gospel Churches of Canada	129		
Evangelical Free Church of Canada	127		
Evangelical Missionary Church of Canada	122		
Free Methodist Church in Canada	119		
North American Baptist Conference	105		
Vision Ministries	95		
Wesleyan Church of Canada	92		
Baptist General Conference of Canada	85		
Pentecostal Assemblies of Newfoundland and Labrador	84		
Fellowship of Christian Assemblies of Canada	83		
Seventh Day Adventist Church in Canada	59		
Apostolic Church of Pentecost	58		
Evangelical Mennonite Conference	57		
Foursquare Gospel Church – Canada	49		
Churches of Christ in Canada	44		
Reformed Church in America – Canada	42		
Vineyard Resource – Canada	41		
Canadian Conference of the Brethren in Christ Church	38		
Plymouth or Christian Brethren	37		
Church of God – Cleveland	32		
Church of God – Anderson	29		
Reformed n.o.s.a	25		
Fellowship of Evangelical Bible Churches	24		
Evangelical Covenant Church of Canada	21		
Evangelical Mennonite Mission Conference	20		

218   APPENDIX

Table A2 (cont'd)

Denomination	Evangelical	Mainline	Catholic
		Tradition	
Pentecostal n.o.s.	19		
Canadian Reformed Church	17		
Anglican Network in Canada	14		
United Brethren Church	11		
Grace Communion International	5		
Moravian Church in America – Canadian District	5		
Pentecostal Holiness Church of Canada	4		
Holiness n.o.s.a	3		
Netherlands Reformed Church	3		
Evangelical Christian Church in Canada (Christian Disciples)	3		
Apostolic Church in Canada	2		
Partners in Harvest	1		
Association of Chinese Evangelical Ministries	1		
United Church of Canada		1,073	
Anglican Church of Canada		647	
Presbyterian Church in Canada		366	
Evangelical Lutheran Church		346	
Presbyterian n.o.s.[a]		205	
Lutheran Church in Canada		151	
Missouri Synod Lutheran Church		13	
Presbyterian Church in America – Canada		1	
Roman Catholic			1,016
Ukrainian Catholic			59
Total	6,023	2,802	1,075

Source: CRA data (2012).
n.o.s. = not otherwise specified.

be that of the congregational treasurer rather than that of the church building.

- A congregation may have merged with one or more other congregations forming a circuit or parish that subsequently takes on a new address.
- A congregation may provide the Charities Directorate with a mailing address while publishing a street address in its denominational directory.
- A congregation may be known by a fuller name with the

Charities Directorate and an abbreviated name within its denominational directorate, e.g., Newington Presbyterian Church vs. Newington.

The absence of published, accessible directories caused some denominational traditions to be underrepresented. Within the broader evangelical traditions these include Restorationist traditions such as the Plymouth Brethren, and smaller Anabaptist, Pentecostal, and Reformed denominations. Within the broader mainline tradition these include smaller Presbyterian and Anglican denominations.[3] Within the broader Catholic tradition Ukrainian Catholic Churches are underrepresented because of the difficulty the authors had matching these congregations to Registered Charity numbers. Congregations were also coded as urban or rural. A congregation was identified as rural if the second character of its postal code registered with the Charities Directorate was a zero (per Canada Post procedures) and as urban otherwise.[4]

CHURCH AND FAITH STUDY OF YOUNG ADULTS

The Church and Faith Study of Young Adults (CFYA) study, also called the "Hemorrhaging Faith" study, was conducted by James Penner and Associates along with the Evangelical Fellowship of Canada. This project interviewed 72 young adults who were raised in Christian churches from across Canada in 2010 and 2011. Then utilizing an online panel, it surveyed 2,049 18- to 34-year-olds who attended a mainline Protestant, evangelical Protestant, or Catholic church in childhood. The Angus Reid online panel, which has close to 100,000 panelists, includes both anglophone and francophone participants. The panelists sign up for the panel, and they complete a profile that focuses on common demographic data. The data from each subsequent survey are used to augment these profiles. Surveys can subsequently be targeted to groups with particular characteristics. Our research team was interested in two kinds of young adult respondents (currently aged 18–34):

1 Those who were raised Christian.
2 Those who were not raised Christian, but came to identify themselves as Christian by the time they were young adults.

First, a pre-screen survey asked several questions to identify who was raised Christian; 2,886 respondents who matched the above criteria were sent a questionnaire, with 2,049 responses.

There are good reasons to be confident in these data. Angus Reid closely matches the panel to Canadian census demographics. It has had an excellent record of outperforming or matching the results of phone polls 16 out of 17 times. In 10 of 17 elections since 2007, the predictions from this online panel have been the most accurate out of all pollsters who published a prediction (Angus Reid Global, 2014). The data have an exceptional 71 per cent response rate. While we have confidence in the general findings of this report, the panel data may somewhat underestimate retention rates. First, we know that young adults are in a period of life when they are less likely to participate in religious institutions, and that some (but probably a clear minority) will increase their religious participation once they have settled into family life. Second, the panel somewhat underrepresents immigrant young adults (who tend to be more religious); see Bibby (2012) or Penner et al. (2012). They were slightly more likely to be urban, highly educated, female, and fully employed. There was also a small non-response bias, with fewer religious service attendees than non-attendees filling out the survey. The Appendix in Penner et al. (2012) gives more detail on the panel characteristics and the project's methodology.

SURVEY

A: *Telephone Survey Questionnaire* – CECS

1. I just want to confirm that you are the senior or lead pastor of this church, and that you have been pastor at this church for 6 months or more. Is that correct?
2. In what year did you become the lead or senior pastor at this congregation?
3: Have you always been the lead pastor at this church, or did you hold another pastoral position at this church prior to becoming lead pastor?
4. In that case, what year did you first join the pastoral staff in this congregation?
5. What year was this congregation officially founded? I am looking

APPENDIX   221

for the year this congregation officially started, even if it began at
another location.

6. How long did the previous lead pastor serve this congregation?

7. How about the lead pastor before that?

8. Has this congregation ever started another church in your local
area, either as a new church plant or as another site of this church?

9. How many plants/sites?

10. What year was the most recent plant/site started?

11. Does your congregation meet in a church building, or in
another type of facility like a community centre or gymnasium?

12. What type of building does your congregation meet in for
its primary worship services? School, Community centre, Hotel,
Mall/shopping centre, Private home, Storefront,
Other (Specify) _____

13. Does this building belong to your congregation, or does it
belong to another group that loans or rents space to you?

14. Now I would like to ask some questions about average
attendance and changes in average attendance over the last year.
Will you be referring to your official records or just giving your
best estimate for these questions on attendance?

15. About how many different people, including both children and
adults, attend church worship services at this congregation during
an average week?

16. Compared with two years ago, that is, this time in 2007, has
the total average attendance Increased, Decreased, or Remained
about the same?

17. What would you say is the main cause of this?

18. NOT INCLUDING INFANTS, how many people, if any, officially
joined this congregation as members in 2008?

19. How many people, if any, started regularly attending this congregation in 2008, but did not officially become members?

20. Of those who joined in 2008 as members or regular attendees,
how many were converted to Christ by someone in this congregation, if any? Please do not count children of church families in this
number, but only new converts in the last year who came from outside the congregation.

21. In total, how many people left this church in 2008, if any?
Please include people who passed away or moved.

22. Now I would like to ask some questions about this church's

purpose, priorities, and programs. Does this church have a mission or purpose statement?

23. In your view, does this mission or purpose statement shape the priorities and goals of this church at the present time, or not?

24. Has the leadership set specific goals for the next 6 months, year or 2 years for this congregation?

25. Has the leadership designed ways to measure these goals, so that one can determine whether or not the goals have been reached?

26. Are there set times or dates when the leadership will evaluate the extent to which these goals have been reached?

27. Are those responsible for implementing these goals held accountable by someone or some group within the church?

28. Does this congregation have any organized effort, committee, or designated individual whose purpose is to follow up on new-comers and visitors?

29. Does this congregation have any organized effort, committee, or designated individual whose purpose is to reconnect with those who used to attend this church but have not done so for a while?

30. Does this congregation have any organized effort, committee, or designated individual whose purpose is to provide help to members or regular participants, e.g., by cooking meals for a new mother or someone who just got home from the hospital, or providing financial assistance to someone who needs it?

31. During the last year, has this congregation held Sunday school or other RELIGIOUS EDUCATION classes for children age 12 and under that meet at least weekly?

32. In an average week this year, how many children under the age of 12 attend these religious education classes?

33. Other than regular youth group meetings, does this church have RELIGIOUS EDUCATION classes for teenagers age 13 to 18 that meet at least weekly during the last year?

34. In an average week this year, how many teens attend these religious education classes?

35. WITHIN THE PAST 12 MONTHS, have there been any groups or meetings or classes or events at this church that specifically focused on the following purposes or activities ...

New member classes

Marriage enrichment classes or premarital counselling

Training for religious education teachers

Classes in preparation for baptism

Training for worship leaders or music ministers

Classes on parenting skills or parenting issues

Classes to train people in evangelism or community outreach

Classes focused on discovering and using spiritual gifts

Still thinking of the past 12 months only, has your church held Bible studies for people in the church?

Prayer meetings?

Groups on spirituality and the spiritual disciplines?

Discussions on the purpose and direction of the church?

Groups that prepare missionaries or mission teams?

NONE OF THE ABOVE?

36. Now, I would like to find out what COMMUNITY SERVICE activities are sponsored by this church. By this I mean those activities run by your church where most of the people who benefit are in your local community but are not part of your church. At any time IN THE LAST YEAR, has this church provided...

A food pantry or soup kitchen?

Visiting the elderly or those in hospitals that are not part of this congregation?

Day care, pre-school, or before/after school programs?

Giving cash or vouchers for individuals or families that do not attend this church?

Counselling for people in the community?

Programs to help people find jobs or cope with unemployment?

Substance abuse programs or Community workshops on a topic of interest, like financial planning, parenting, or youth issues?

Language training, tutoring, or other educational services for adults?

Still thinking of the past 12 months only, has your church been involved in prison ministry?

NONE OF THE ABOVE?

37. You said this church was involved in COMMUNITY SERVICE ACTIVITIES. About how many laypeople in this church are involved in these activities (this activity) in the past year ...

38. Does this congregation receive government funding for any of its programs or activities?

39. Does this church officially support, with either volunteers or finances, community service activities that are run by other

churches or community service organizations?

40. How many laypeople in this congregation, if any, would you say are involved in volunteering for activities run by other churches or community service organizations?

41. IN THE PAST 12 MONTHS, has this congregation done any of the following outreach activities in the community ...

Community BBQs, block parties or children's carnivals in the last year only?

Distributing flyers or door hangers to promote the church or a church event?

Daily Vacation Bible School?

Placed a church advertisement in the newspaper or phone book?

The Alpha program?

Gone door to door to promote this church or evangelize?

Neighbourhood Bible studies or small groups, which are focused on reaching people outside this church?

Street drama or singing?

Held a church worship service in an alternate location in the community, like a park or a building that is not a church?

Acts of kindness, like free car washes, raking leaves, or handing out free drinks?

NONE OF THE ABOVE?

42. Has this church run any other outreach or service activities in the community?

43. What other outreach or service activities? (PROBE FOR UP TO THREE)

44. Does this congregation have any organized effort, committee, or individual focused on foreign missions?

45. Does this church have a website?

46. Thinking now of the top lay leadership team in this church, do the members of this leadership team receive training, possibly from the denomination or from the church?

47. As you know, congregations operate according to certain values or priorities, even if they are not explicitly stated. In your view, what are the actual priorities of this church, based on how they function, even if they are different from your priorities? As I read out some possible priorities, please tell me whether you feel it is a Very High priority, Somewhat High priority, or Not a Priority for this church. The first item is ...

47a. Maintaining an active evangelism and outreach program, encouraging members to share their faith?

47b. Protecting people in the church from the negative influences in the world?

47c. Promoting deeper spirituality through the spiritual disciplines like prayer, fasting, meditating on scripture, etc.?

47d. Promoting the faith development of our children and youth?

47e. Working to preserve traditional morals and family values?

47f. Encouraging people to serve according to their gifts?

47g. Providing care, counselling, and other services for our members?

47h. Serving the poor and needy in the community?

47i. Promoting cooperation between the churches in the community?

47j. Providing a worship service that is welcoming and comfortable to non-churched visitors?

47k. Enhancing the beauty of the church building and grounds?

47l. Building volunteer leadership within the church?

47m. Helping members get ahead financially or promoting success in business?

47n. Strengthening marriages and family relationships?

47o. Preserving our ethnic culture or language?

47p. Teaching the theological distinctives of our religious tradition?

48. Now for some questions on your main worship service or worship services: How many primary worship services does your church have in a week, not counting other meetings such as prayer meetings, small groups, Sunday School, and so on?

49. AUTOCODE FOR ALTERNATE SERVICE LANGUAGE

English

French

50. Is a language besides English (French) used?

51. Which language(s)?

52. Do these worship services have basically the same worship style, sermon, and other elements, or do they differ in important ways?

53. Compare the largest worship service and the worship service that is most different from it. What would you say are the main differences between those two services (PROBE FOR UP TO THREE)?

54. Thinking now of the largest worship service in terms of attendance, please tell me if the following elements are Always, Usually, Sometimes, Rarely, or Never part of that service in the last year, starting with ...

54a. A time for laity to share testimonies or prayer requests?

54b. Public speaking in tongues?

54c. Spontaneous dancing, jumping, or shouting?

54d. The collection of a monetary offering during the service?

54e. A praise band with drums and/or electric guitars?

54f. The Lords Supper or Communion?

54g. Following a liturgy or prayerbook?

54h. Dialogue between pastor and attendees, like a question-answer time?

54i. Reciting the Lords Prayer?

54j. Reciting a creed or statement of faith?

54k. Reading a Bible passage?

54l. Use of visual projection equipment like Powerpoint or video?

54m. Drama or dance?

54n. Use of non-electric organ or piano?

54o. Traditional hymns?

54p. Times of silence for prayer, meditation, etc.?

54q. Raising hands or clapping?

54r. An altar call or an invitation to receive Christ?

54s. A printed order of worship, like in a bulletin?

55. Do people in this congregation mingle and socialize informally with each other?

56. How many sermons do you typically preach in an average month?

57. How many times in the last 6 MONTHS would you say you addressed the following themes from the pulpit? Please only count the times when you spoke on the theme for more than 2 or 3 minutes. If you can't recall for sure, please just give your best estimate. The first theme is...

Devotional practices, like reading the Bible and praying

Caring for the poor or needy outside the church

Evangelizing the unconverted

Sexual moral issues, like premarital sex or same-sex marriage

The sanctity of marriage or healthy marriages, but not specifically on same-sex marriage

The negative effects of the media

Evil and suffering

Caring for the needs of others in this church

Participating in a small group

APPENDIX 227

58. I would like to ask some questions about the people who regularly participate in this church at the present time, that is, THOSE WHO ATTEND TWICE A MONTH OR MORE. Please give your best estimate if you are not sure. What per cent ...

Of those who regularly attend are under the age of 18?

Are between 18 and 29 years old?

Are between 30 and 64 years old?

What per cent are over 65 years old?

Of adults are female?

Still thinking about regular participants only, what per cent of adults, age 18 or more, have a high school education or less?

What per cent of adults have four-year college or university degrees or more?

Have a graduate school degree?

Have household incomes below $25,000?

Have household incomes greater than $100,000?

59. AUTOCODE FOR CONGREGATION MAKE-UP

French

English

60. Still thinking of REGULAR PARTICIPANTS, what percent ...

Of WOMEN volunteer in some capacity in this church?

Of MEN volunteer in some capacity in this church?

Of adults give faithfully to this church?

Of adults participate in a small group once a month or more?

Not including small groups, what per cent of adults attend Bible studies or

Sunday School classes in an average week?

What per cent of regular participants have come to Canada within the last 5 years?

Regular participants are not yet converted to Christ, in your view?

What per cent are Canadian?

Asian?

Latin American?

Black or African?

61. Besides those listed here, is there any other minority ethnic group that makes up more than 10% of your REGULAR participants?

62. What ethnic group is that?

Other (Specify)_____

63. And what per cent of your regular participants are white?

64. As you know, most churches experience conflict within the church at some point, whether over purpose and goals, finances, worship, personality tensions, etc. In the last 5 years, has this church experienced conflicts that caused a significant number of the active lay participants to leave the church?

65. Has a pastor, youth minister, music minister, or another member of the pastoral staff left over a conflict in the last 5 years?

66. Does this church have a formal procedure for handling conflict within the church?

67. In terms of overall identity or culture, how well do you feel the following terms describe this congregation? Does this term describe this congregation Very, Somewhat, or Not Very Well? The first one is ...

67a. Charismatic?

67b. Fundamentalist?

67c. Evangelical?

67d. Seeker sensitive?

67e. Missional?

67f. Emerging or emergent church?

67g. Purpose-driven church?

67h. Cell church?

67i. Liturgical?

68. How closely does this congregation identify with its denomination? Would you say...

Extremely closely, Very closely, Fairly closely, Not very closely, Not at all?

69. Here are some questions about connections that you and this church may have with other groups around you. Do you regularly meet with pastors from other churches for prayer or support?

70. IN THE PAST YEAR, has this church cooperated with any of the following organizations in your community, possibly to plan an event, a joint worship service, or an outreach into the community ...

Another Protestant church that you would consider an evangelical church?

Another Catholic or Protestant church that you would NOT consider an evangelical church?

A Jewish, Muslim, Hindu, or other congregation from a non-Christian religious tradition?

A Christian community organization other than a church?

A non-religious community organization?

NONE OF THE ABOVE?

71. I now have a set of questions where I am looking for your personal opinion, so it's what you think that matters here. As I read each statement, please tell me if you Strongly Agree, Moderately Agree, are Neutral, Moderately Disagree, or Strongly Disagree with these statements, starting with ...

71a. In general, this congregation is wary of change and innovation.

71b. The vast majority of lay people are NOT aware of the goals and direction of this church.

71c. Everyone enthusiastically participates in congregational singing.

71d. The pastors and staff of this church often scramble to complete tasks that are dropped by the lay person responsible for them.

71e. Newcomers find it hard to form friendships with people in this church.

71f. The lay leaders are committed to this church and fully endorse its mission.

71g. The participants in this church are pessimistic about its future.

71h. I think we have problems with communication between the clergy, lay leaders, and the congregation.

71i. Attendees frequently invite unconverted friends and family to this church.

71j. The contributions of our youth and children are appreciated in this church.

71k. I don't think we are doing enough for our children and youth in this church.

71l. In general, the congregation is satisfied with the quality of the programs provided for the adults in this church.

71m. The congregation is committed to praying for this church's ministry and programs.

71n. People in our church are encouraged to ask questions and challenge ideas.

71o. The laity expect the pastors and other church staff to do most of the work in this church.

71p. This church is very committed to leadership development and formation.

71q. It is often difficult to fill voluntary positions in this church.

71r. Overall, I would consider this to be a very healthy church.

71s. I am worried about the long term future of this church.

71t. This church tends to burn out its leaders.

72. Now I have some questions about you and other pastoral staff. BESIDES YOU, how many other pastoral staff, either full or part time, do you have at this church? Please include music ministers, directors of Christian education and other pastors, but not secretaries, janitors, or others not primarily engaged in religious work.

73. How many, if any, of the pastoral staff are female?

74. How many, if any, of these positions are paid?

75. Do you personally have pastoral training from a Bible college or seminary?

76. What is your highest level of pastoral training?

  Some courses or a diploma but less than a bachelor's degree
  Bachelor's degree
  Master's degree
  Doctoral degree
  Other (Specify)_____

77. Do you have any post secondary education that is NOT pastoral training, like a university degree?

78. What was your highest non-pastoral degree?

  Some courses, a diploma, but less than a bachelor's degree
  Bachelor's degree or equivalent
  Master's degree
  Doctoral degree
  Other (Specify)_____

79. Is your pastoral position full-time paid, part-time paid, or an unpaid position?

80. Do you formally serve another congregation or religious organization as well?

81. Do you work at a secular job as well?

82. In an average week, how many hours do you spend in pastoral work?

83. What year were you born? (ENTER 4 DIGITS)

84. From what part of the world do you trace your ancestry? For example, most people who think of themselves as "white" have ancestors from Europe. Would you say ...

  Africa Latin America, or Central/South America
  Asia
  Caribbean
  Europe

Pacific Islands
Aboriginal, First Nations
North America (Canadian, American)
Other (Specify)_____

85. On a scale of 1 to 10, where 1 is Completely Dissatisfied and 10 is Completely Satisfied, how would you rate your overall job satisfaction right now?

86. On the same 1 to 10 scale, where 1 is Completely Dissatisfied and 10 is Completely Satisfied, how would you rate the following areas ...

86a. Work load and work expectations?
86b. Salary and benefits?
86c. Support and encouragement from the congregation?
86d. Time off each week?
86e. Vacation time?
86f. Study leaves or sabbaticals?
86g. Relationships with the lay leaders?
86h. Relationships with other church staff?
86i. Support from the denomination, including training, conferences, financial assistance, placementassistance, regional/national leadership, and pastoral counseling?

87. On a scale of 1 to 10, where 1 is No Stress and 10 is Extremely Stressful, how stressful is your pastoral work right now?

88. Do you have close friends in your area with whom you share your personal or spiritual struggles?

89. Now I'm going to list some typical pastoral duties. Which duties from this list are you typically involved in at least monthly ...

Leading worship singing
Working with children
Sermon preparation and preaching
Teaching adults, like in Sunday school classes
Visitation
Leading small groups
Counseling
Developing a vision and goals for this church
Administrative work
Meeting or contacting newcomers
Working with youth
Other (Specify) _____
NONE OF THE ABOVE

232　APPENDIX

90. I will now read through those duties you said you were involved in at least monthly. Please identify those areas that you consider Strengths, areas of satisfaction and enjoyment, and those areas you consider Weaknesses, areas that you find draining. If the area is neither a strength nor weakness, just say "Neither." The first item is ...

90a. Leading worship singing?

90b. Sermon preparation and preaching?

90c. Visitation?

90d. Counselling?

90e. Developing a vision and goals for this church?

90f. Administrative work?

90g. Meeting or contacting newcomers?

90h. Working with youth?

90i. Working with children?

90j. Teaching adults, like in Sunday school classes?

90k. Leading small groups?

91. You consider the following as areas of weakness ... (READ LIST) Roughly what percentage of your work time do you spend on areas of weakness?

92. (ENTER PERCENTAGE OF WORK TIME SPENT ON AREAS OF WEAKNESS)

93. Has your church hired staff or positioned volunteers to help with these areas of weakness?

94. Finally, some questions about church finances. Do you have a copy of your church's financial statements from 2008 handy?
(IF YES) Great!
(IF NO) No problem, please give me your best estimate.
Approximately how much income did your congregation receive in 2008, from all sources?

95. Approximately how much money did your congregation spend in 2008, that is, its total expenditures?

96. What % of total expenditures, if any, went toward ...
　　Staff salaries and benefits
　　Foreign mission, whether support for organizations or individuals
　　Building maintenance, grounds, utilities, mortgages, insurance,
　　　and general upkeep
　　New construction or major renovations
　　Community outreach activities, those activities run by your
　　　church which benefit people in the community

APPENDIX   233

97. How would you describe your congregation's financial health
currently? Would you say it is Excellent, Good, Tight But
Manageable, in Some Difficulty, or in Serious Difficulty?
98. During the first four months of 2009, did total giving to this
church Decrease, Increase, or Remain About The Same as compared to the first four months of last year?
99. By approximately what percentage did total giving change?
100. I just have one more question. One of our mandates is to also
interview youth or children's pastors to get an overview of youth and
children's ministry in evangelical churches in Canada. Do you have a
youth pastor that has served this church for 6 months or more?
101. Do you have a children's pastor who has served this church
for 6 months or more?
Thank you very much for participating in the Canadian
Evangelical Congregations Study. If you are interested in results,
they should be coming out later this year on the EFC website. In the
meantime, if you have any questions or comments, feel free to contact the lead researchers. Their phone numbers and email addresses
were included in the emails sent to you previously. Thanks again
for your time.
    (RECORD GENDER)

B: Phone Interview with Second Pastor (Children or Youth) – CECS

1. We are calling on behalf of the Canadian Evangelical Churches
Study, which is sponsored by the Evangelical Fellowship of Canada.
Is it OK to proceed with the interview?
2. What is your official job title?
    Youth pastor
    Children's pastor
    Other (Specify)_____
3. Have you always been ( ) at this church, or did you hold another
pastoral position at this church prior to becoming ( )?
4. What year did you first join the pastoral staff at this congregation?
5. The pastor you replaced, how long was he or she serving this
church before you?
6. I would like to ask some questions about your youth and children's
programs or events. Which of the following areas do you personally
oversee ...

Ministry for children, age 12 and under
Small groups
Middle school youth ministry, typically age 13–14
Administration
High school youth ministry, typically age 15–18
Young adults or post high school ministry, typically age 18–29
Outreach/evangelism
Music for the main worship services
Anything else (Specify)_____
NONE OF THE ABOVE

7. AUTOCODE FOR CONGREGATION MAKEUP
youth
children

8. AUTOCODE FOR MINISTRY
Youth
Children's

9. Does this church have events for teenagers, age 13–18, that meet at least weekly?

10. Which of these weekly events do you have for the teens ...
Youth groups
Youth bible study groups that meet separately from the youth group
Youth choirs, bands, drama teams, or other musical or artistic
    groups
Any other type of weekly events for youth
    (Specify)_____
NONE OF THE ABOVE

11. In an average week, how many volunteers, in total, help run these youth programs?

12. How many different youth, in total, would you say participate in these events in an average week?

13. Compared with 2 years ago, that is, this time in 2007, has the number of 13- to 18-year-old youth who participate in church events in an average week Increased, Decreased, or remained about the Same?

14. How many of these youth, if any, have at least one parent who regularly attends this church?

15. How many of these youth, that is, those with at least one parent in this church, regularly attend a worship service at this church themselves?

16. How many youth, if any, would be from un-churched families?
17. How many of the un-churched youth, if any, attend a worship service at this church regularly?
18. At any time IN THE LAST 12 MONTHS, has this church sponsored, or played a major role in cosponsoring, any of following youth events or activities ...

Special outreach events, where youth invite their friends to an event to introduce them to the church or youth group

Classes that teach youth spiritual disciplines or promote private devotional habits, like prayer, Bible reading, etc.

Community service events, like helping the needy or cleaning up public property in the past 12 months

Classes that address youth issues, like peer influences, time pressures, sex, dating, consumerism, etc.

Events that address social justice issues, like participating in the 30-hour Famine or raising funds for AIDS victims

Intergenerational connections, where youth are paired with an adult in the church who is not a parent, for prayer support or mentoring

Baptism or confirmation classes for youth

Nature/ wilderness events, like camping trips, nature hikes, or fishing trips

Missions trips, where youth travel in Canada or overseas to serve others within the last year

Classes or meetings that help youth plan for the future, including occupational or educational goals

Youth Sundays, where youth play a major role in the main worship service

Classes where youth are trained for ministry, like training for outreach events, missions trips, or sharing their faith with their friends

Classes that help youth discover their spiritual gifts

NONE OF THE ABOVE

19. Has this church held any other types of events or activities for youth anytime IN THE LAST YEAR?
20. What events or activities?
21. Does your church have events for children aged 12 and under that meet at least weekly?
22. Which of these weekly events do you have for the children of

this church ...

Sunday school classes or Children's church

Midweek children events, like Team Kid, Awana, or Pioneers?

Children's choir, or other musical or artistic groups

Any other type of weekly events for children

(Specify)_____

NONE OF THE ABOVE

23. How many different children, in total, would you say participate in these events in an average week?

24. Compared to two years ago, that is, this time in 2007, has the number of children who participate in church events in an average week Increased, Decreased, or remained about the Same?

25. How many of these children would have at least one parent attending this church?

26. How many would be from un-churched homes?

27. In an average week, how many volunteers, in total, help run these children's programs?

28. Anytime IN THE LAST YEAR, has your church sponsored any of the following events for children ...

Vacation Bible school

Children Sundays, where children play a major role in the main worship service

Special outreach events, where children invite their friends to a church sponsored event

Training for the parents with children aged 12 and under

Service projects that involve kids

Christmas programs

Other (Specify)_____

NONE OF THE ABOVE

29. Now thinking about your main worship services, what percentage of those who regularly attend this church are between the ages of 13 and 18?

30. What percentage of those who regularly attend your church are children age 12 or under? Please also include those children who attend Children's church, or another children's program during a main worship service.

31. Are there specific goals for the next six months, year or two years for the youth/children's ministry in this church?

32. Are there specific ways to measure these goals, so that you can

determine whether or not the goals have been reached?

33. Are there set times or dates when leadership will evaluate the extent to which these goals have been reached?

34. Are those responsible for implementing these goals held accountable by someone or some group within the church?

35. I now have a set of questions where I am looking for your personal opinion, so it's what you think that matters here. As I read each statement, please tell me if you Strongly Agree, Moderately Agree, are Neutral, Moderately Disagree, or Strongly Disagree with these statements, starting with ...

35a. In general, this congregation is wary of change and innovation.

35b. The contributions of our youth and children are appreciated in this church.

35c. The vast majority of lay people are NOT aware of the goals and direction of this church.

35d. In general, parents are satisfied with the quality of ministry provided for youth/children in this church.

35e. The youth who participate in our church ministries remain committed to the faith in their teen years and into adulthood.

35f. I find little change in the behavior and moral views of the church youth in spite of my best efforts.

35g. The pastors and staff of this church often scramble to complete tasks that are dropped by the lay person responsible for them.

35h. New youth/children find it hard to form friendships with people in this congregation.

35i. The lay people in this church are pessimistic about its future.

35j. This church actively cooperates with local agencies and groups for purposes of evangelism and community service.

35k. I think we have problems with communication between the clergy, lay leaders, and the congregation.

35l. The church youth/children frequently invite unconverted friends and family to this church.

35m. I don't think we are doing enough for our youth/children in this church.

35n. The congregation is committed to praying for our children's and youth ministries.

35o. Youth in our church are encouraged to ask questions and challenge ideas.

35p. The laity expect the pastors and other church staff to do most of the work in this church.

35q. There are serious interpersonal tensions within this church right now.

35r. This church is committed to youth leadership development.

35s. It is often difficult to find volunteers for the youth ministries in this church.

35t. The youth in our church have no input into the decisions that affect them.

35u. When youth move away from home, this church connects them to other congregations and, in general, does a good job of helping them with the transition to post-secondary education or work.

35v. Overall, I would consider this to be a very healthy church.

35w. I am worried about the long-term future of this church.

35x. This church tends to burn out its leaders.

36. Now I have some questions about you. Do you personally have pastoral training from a Bible college or seminary?

37. What is your highest level of pastoral training?

Some courses or a diploma but less than a bachelor's degree

Bachelor's degree

Master's degree

Doctoral degree

Other (Specify)_____

38. Do you have any post secondary education that is NOT pastoral training, like a university degree?

39. What was your highest non-pastoral degree?

Some courses or a diploma, but less than a bachelor's degree

Bachelor's degree or equivalent

Master's degree

Doctoral degree

Other (Specify)_____

40. Is your pastoral position full-time paid, part-time paid, or an unpaid position?

41. How many hours a week are you paid to work?

42. Do you formally serve another congregation or religious organization as well?

43. Do you work at a secular job in addition to your pastoral responsibilities?

44. What year were you born?

45. From what part of the world do you trace your ancestry? For example, most people who think of themselves as "white" have

ancestors from Europe. Would you say ...
  Africa
  Latin America, or Central/South America
  Asia
  Caribbean
  Europe
  Pacific Islands
  Aboriginal, First Nations
  North America (Canadian, American)
  Other (Specify)_____

46. On a scale of 1 to 10, where 1 is Completely Dissatisfied and 10 is Completely Satisfied, how would you rate your overall job satisfaction right now?

47. On the same 1 to 10 scale, where 1 is Completely Dissatisfied and 10 is Completely Satisfied, how would you rate the following areas, starting with ...

47a. Work load and work expectations?
47b. Salary and benefits?
47c. Support and encouragement from the congregation?
47d. Time off each week?
47e. Vacation time?
47f. Study leaves or sabbaticals?
47g. Relationships with the lay leaders?
47h. Relationships with other church staff?
47i. Support from your denomination, including training, conferences, financial assistance, placement assistance, regional/national leadership, pastoral counseling, etc.?

48. On a scale of 1 to 10, where 1 is No Stress and 10 is Extremely Stressful, how stressful is your pastoral work right now?

49. Do you have close friends in your area with whom you share your personal or spiritual struggles?

50. In an average week, how many hours would you spend in pastoral work?

51. Now I'm going to list some typical pastoral duties. Please tell me which of these things you do at least once a month. The first item is ...
  Leading worship singing
  Teaching adults, like in Sunday school classes
  Sermon preparation and preaching

Leading small groups
Visitation
Counselling
Developing a vision and goals for the youth/children's ministry
Administrative work
Meeting or contacting newcomers
Other (Specify) _____
NONE OF THE ABOVE

52. I will now read through those duties you said you were involved in at least monthly. Please identify those areas that you consider Strengths, areas of satisfaction and enjoyment, and those areas you consider Weaknesses, areas that you find draining. If the area is neither a strength nor weakness, just say "Neither." The first item is ...

52a. Leading worship singing?
52b. Sermon preparation and preaching?
52c. Visitation?
52d. Counselling?
52e. Developing a vision and goals for the youth/children's ministry?
52f. Administrative work?
52g. Meeting or contacting newcomers?
52h. Teaching adults, like in Sunday school classes?
52i. Leading small groups?

53. You consider the following as areas of weakness ... (READ LIST) Roughly what percentage of your work time do you spend on areas of weakness?
Leading worship singing
Meeting or contacting newcomers
Sermon preparation and preaching
Teaching adults, like in Sunday school classes
Visitation
Leading small groups
Counselling
Developing a vision and goals for the youth/children's ministry
Administrative work

54. (ENTER PERCENTAGE OF WORK TIME SPENT ON AREAS OF WEAKNESS)

55. Has your church hired staff or positioned volunteers to help with these areas of weakness?

APPENDIX 241

56. Thank you very much for participating in the Canadian Evangelical Congregations Study. If you are interested in results, they should be coming out later this year on the EFC website. In the meantime, if you have any questions or comments, feel free to contact the lead researchers. Their phone numbers and email addresses were included in the emails sent to your lead pastor. Thanks again for your time.

(RECORD GENDER)

C: *Phone Interview with Denominational Leaders*

Denominational leaders were asked to discuss the following questions about general trends.

1. Demographics of the denomination
   a. Ethnic minorities – more churches or growing churches? What region? Urban centers? Interracial churches?
   b. Age – aging congregations? Where?
   c. Rural/urban – growing or shrinking?
   d. Other diversity – theological, worship style, etc.
   e. Overall patterns of growth/decline for the denomination
2. Successful churches
   a. Does your denomination use a definition or measurement of church health?
   b. Where are they?
   c. Why are they doing well?
   d. Denominational strategies for creating more successful churches?
3. Churches challenges
   a. Failed starts – where and why?
   b. Church splits – where and why?
   c. Church tensions – over what? Worship style, moral failure, theology, etc.
   d. Other challenges – finances, clarity of mission, staffing, etc.
4. Pastors
   a. Demographics – gender, age, minorities.
   b. Areas of challenge – not enough pastors, need ethnic pastors, pastoral training, etc.
   c. Any measures of pastoral health? How does the denomination do pastoral care?
5. Denomination

a. Describe connection between denomination and congregations – congregational giving to denomination, resources/services offered by denomination, etc.
b. What information would be helpful to you that could be gleaned from this research?

Notes

INTRODUCTION

1 Bibby's data show evangelical growth from 8% in 2001 to 11% in 2009 (2012, 33). However, he uses census data to show that evangelicals have held steady at 8% since 1871 to 2001, and the 2009 data are from the Canadian General Social Survey (CGSS). The differences between the two surveys and weak denominational measures may account for the apparent upswing.

2 Other terms used as descriptors for mainline Protestants include "historic Protestants" or "traditional Protestants." However, these terms also pose certain problems. For example, in what sense are evangelical Protestants not historic or traditional? Scholars have generally used mainline and evangelical to differentiate two types of Protestants in the twentieth century, as we do here.

3 Of course, not all congregations that identify as evangelical Protestant are evangelical based on our definition. The Evangelical Lutheran Church in Canada, for example, is understood as a mainline Protestant denomination.

4 Here we use a common evangelical phrase drawn from the New Testament Epistle to the Romans, 12:2.

5 Bibby argues that people will always need the spiritual products that churches offer, and that is why religion will not disappear in Canada. We agree, if by that we mean that humans tend to seek metaphysical answers to questions of meaning, belonging, and moral orientation, the sort of questions religions tend to answer. However, it does not mean that congregational participation, at least as we know it today, will not continue to decline. People may always need what religion offers, but institutional religion is not the only place to find meaning, belonging, and moral orientation. Thus, we think that the individualism, consumerism, and rationalism of society will continue to undermine institutional religion in the foreseeable future.

244 NOTES TO PAGES 9–17

6 While Catholics are more likely to overreport their attendance than Protestants, research from the United States shows similar rates of overreporting in an evangelical Protestant church (Marler and Hadaway, 1999).

7 Telephone interviews were completed by Advitek Data Collection Services (www.advitek.ca) of Toronto on our behalf in 2009.

8 The CRC pastors (43.5%) were much less likely to identify their congregations as "evangelical" than were the pastors of the other denominations. It is unclear whether this meant that they do not identify themselves as evangelical, or if the pastors thought the congregation is to be defined as "reformed" first.

9 This is based on unpublished data from "Denominations in Canada," compiled by Bruce Guenther and the Research Department of Outreach Canada. Our thanks to Bruce for making his data available to us.

10 Studies of churchgoing individuals are normally done by handing out surveys in a main worship service (Woolever and Bruce, 2002; Ammerman, 2005) or by sending surveys to a randomly selected sample of members from the congregations's records (Hoge, Johnson, and Luidens, 1994). Both methods have sampling problems, including low response rates and biases, as do all sampling strategies.

CHAPTER ONE

1 Ingrid Peritz, "As Churches Crumble, Communities Fear Loss of Heritage," *Globe and Mail*, 13 Dec. 2010, http://www.theglobeand mail.com/news/national/as-churches-crumble-communities-fear-loss-of-heritage/article1320111/

2 The Canadian General Social Survey (CGSS) places the 2008 number at 18.3% weekly attendance, down from 30.8% in 1986. For reasons of sample size and representativeness, these are probably the most accurate Canadian numbers available. For more information, see Eagle (2011).

3 Reginald Bibby's Project Canada 1985 and 2005 datasets are used here. Note the slight wording change from people in charge of "the church" (1985) and people in charge of "religious organizations" (2005) is unlikely to make much difference. We use Bibby's Project Canada data often in this book because Bibby uses a denominationally based definition of evangelicals as we do here. Our thanks to Bibby for allowing us access to his data.

4 See http://www12.statcan.gc.ca/nhs-enm/2011/dp-pd/dt-td/Rp-eng.cfm? LANG=E&APATH=3&DETAIL=0&DIM=0&FL=A&FREE=0&GC =0&GID=0&GK=0&GRP=1&PID=105399&PRID=0&PTYPE=10 5277&S=0&SHOWALL=0&SUB=0&Temporal=2013&THEME=95 &VID=0&VNAMEE=&VNAMEF.

5 For this study, we consider evangelicals and conservative Protestants to

be the same, based on a denominational definition of evangelicals. However, by conservative, we do not mean that evangelicals represent a single block when it comes to politics and political parties. Most, however, share similar "conservative" social values.

6 Outreach Canada is an evangelical organization that tracks the number of congregations from denominational reports. Data are available at http://www.churchmap.ca/. Bibby estimates there are about 30,000 congregations in Canada (2006, 194). Based on data from the *Yearbook of American and Canadian Churches*, Bibby estimates there are 9,800 evangelical congregations, more congregations than either Roman Catholics or mainline Protestants (2004, 134–5). Brownlee et al. (2005, vi) estimate that there are 31,000 religious organizations in Canada, which are either congregations or families of congregations (denominations). They claim that the CRA data capture 94% of all religious organizations (it is unclear how they derived this figure).

7 United Church of Canada (UCC) official website, http://www.united-church.ca/organization/statistics. Miner (2010) of the *London Free Press* states that the declining attendance has resulted in the closure of some 400 churches over the previous decade, just under one a week.

8 This information is from the "Vision 2019" document from the Anglican Church of Canada's official website, http://archive.anglican.ca/v2019/.

9 David Ewart, "United Church of Canada Trends – How We Got Here," 5 Dec. 2007, http://www.davidewart.ca/2007/12/united-church-0.html, linked to the UCC official website; also avalabile at http://www.davidewart.ca/UCCan-Trends-How-Did-We-Get-Here.pdf

10 There are a disproportionate number of evangelical congregations in the United States as well. Conservative Protestants make up roughly 25% of the American population but account for 56% of the congregations (Chaves, 2004, 28).

11 It is possible that the link between pro-social behaviours and congregational participation is partly explained by selection effects. In other words, churches attract (select) people who are already generous, not that churches make people generous. Yet, we emphasize religious networks and congregations because they provide venues and impetus for generosity. Also, religious socialization by congregations is part of what makes current attendees generous.

CHAPTER TWO

1 Of course, the phrase "born again Christians" likely conjures images of American-style evangelicalism, which many Canadians view as both intolerant and politically conservative to the extreme, two qualities that are patently un-Canadian. Much to the chagrin of Canadian evangelicals,

they are often painted with the same brush. Such caricatures, of both American (Smith, 2000) and Canadian evangelicals (Reimer, 2003), are inaccurate.

2 Gerardo Marti (2008) captured this well in his study of a Hollywood mega-church where evangelicals attempted to navigate the tensions between their understanding of faith and the entertainment industry.

3 The thinking here is consonant with "critical realism," which argues, among other things, that social realities are emergent as lower-level realities interact to form higher-level realities. It rejects, however, hard social constructionism, where social reality is no more than a social construction (see Smith, 2010; Sayer, 2000).

4 Quebec is a case in point. In 2007, after months of controversy over religion and the reasonable accommodation of minority groups, the provincial government established the Consultation Commission on Accommodation Practices Related to Cultural Differences. Two well-known intellectuals, Gérard Bouchard and philosopher Charles Taylor, held townhall meetings throughout the province. The public consultation was meant to provide a forum to establish a process for religious and social change without alienating religious or ethnic minorities. Pauline Côté (2008, 63) argues that while "the Commission has failed in providing elements to structured, focused public deliberation," ongoing reflection, especially with how other states are wrestling with these issues, needs to occur.

5 Hiemstra, Rick, "How Is the Church in Canada Doing?" Powerpoint presentation for the Evangelical Fellowship of Canada meetings, Moncton, New Brunswick, 2112. Hiemstra uses Statistics Canada data from Lindsay (2008) in his presentation.

6 The data Eagle (2011) uses do not allow him to distinguish between evangelical and mainline Protestant attendance, but Eagle speculates about the possibility of evangelical congregational attendance propping up declining mainline Protestant attendance when the two are aggregated.

7 Angus Reid panel data from 2006 and 2011 give figures higher or lower than 50% depending on how you count. If we include those categories that likely contain a good number of evangelicals but without specific denominational affiliations ("non-denominational," "Christian," "charismatic," etc.), we would conclude that about 44% of evangelicals attend weekly. If we remove these groups, we get figures above 55%, which is what we report above. We do this to be consistent with the other traditions, where respondents give a specific denomination or tradition. Those who claim a generic "Christian" denomination are less likely to attend, for example. Our thanks to Andrew Grenville of Angus Reid for making these data available.

8 Recent immigration patterns also affect weekly attendance, since immigrants are more likely to attend. Of course, immigrants also affect

market share. Statistics Canada (2003) reports that 23% of immigrants arriving in the 1990s were Catholic, while only 11% were Protestant.

9 Both the supply-side and the demand-side arguments are valid, depending on place and time. This is not a safe compromise position as much as a conviction that the social world is a complex reality. That is, the combination of factors that contribute to any social outcome is too complex and diverse for all-encompassing, "either-or" theories to be right in all social contexts. A myriad of influences in all sorts of complex configurations influence the relative success or vitality of religious groups, influences that vary by place and time. Yet, social patterns exist, and certain theories (especially those with some flexibility) are more adequate than others, as we suggest below.

10 Of course, the ways evangelical congregations adjust or react to the larger Canadian context is important, but we focus on factors from within evangelicalism (a subculture), but not from the larger Canadian culture. In addition, the explanations we seek are primarily at the congregational level, not the individual level. Thus, explaining why *individual* evangelicals are religiously committed – like a private religious conversion experience, or having religiously committed parents – is not our purpose, except as these individual-level factors relate to congregations. Finally, we focus on factors that likely increase congregational retention in other traditions, but only if they are distinct or more prevalent in evangelical congregations than in other Christian traditions.

11 A similar expression of "moralistic, therapeutic deism" was used by Smith and Denton to describe the Christianity of American teens (2005).

12 Tamney argues against Smith (1998) that evangelical subcultural boundaries are not just changing, but are becoming increasingly blurred as individuals have more choice to believe and act as they wish. Of course, it is difficult to empirically show whether change is due to "redefining" boundaries or "softening" boundaries.

13 According to Bibby's Project Canada 1995 data, evangelicals (73.3%) are much more likely to disagree (disagree or strongly disagree) with the statement, "What's right or wrong is a matter of personal opinion" than are mainline Protestants (53.4%), Catholics in Quebec (33.0%), or Catholics outside Quebec (54.3%). In addition, disagreement with the statement is correlated with church attendance in Canada. Similarly, Bibby's data show that evangelicals (58.1%) are much more likely to disagree with the statement "everything's relative" than other traditions (mainline Protestants, 25.9%; Quebec Catholics, 21.7%; Catholics outside Quebec, 33.5%), and rejecting relativism is significantly correlated with church attendance.

14 According to Bibby's Project Canada 2005 data, evangelicals average 2.0 children per respondent compared with the national average of 1.76. While Statistics Canada's fertility rate is closer to 1.5, the data

248   NOTES TO PAGES 63–73

still suggest that evangelicals have slightly higher fertility rates. In 1975 they also had a slight edge, with 2.4 children on average compared with 2.2 nationally.

15 Notions of congregational health or vitality are difficult to define. Since our data are taken largely from interviews with pastors, they do not give a fully rounded picture of vitality. Nonetheless, some interesting findings are published in Reimer, "Congregational Vitality among Evangelical Churches in Canada" (2012).

16 Of course, their uncritical embrace of technology also opens them up to influences that undercut their distinctiveness. The individualist nature of technology undermines an "external locus of authority" as well as volunteerism.

CHAPTER THREE

1 We are not suggesting that evangelism is inconsequential. In fact, we think evangelism contributes to congregational vitality in ways that are beyond numerical growth. Our point here is that it is not the primary reason for growth or decline.

2 Hiemstra (2008) has noted that some evangelicals are likely captured in the "other Christian" category, but it likely captures non-evangelicals as well. Our best reading of the Statistics Canada report is that the fertility rate for the "other Christian" category is probably around 1.75, Protestant about 1.6, and the national average 1.57 (in 2000). http://www.statcan.gc.ca/pub/91-209-x/91-209-x2003000-eng.pdf 2012

3 Thanks to Rick Hiemstra for providing CRA data and creating this table. For more information about these data, see chapter 8. Inflation is based on the Consumer Price Index, reported by the government, and available at http://www5.statcan.gc.ca/cansim/pick-choisir?lang=eng&p2=33&id=1760003

4 Some data are from the Anglican Church of Canada website, as the yearbook data seem to switch between parishes (several congregations can be under one parish, as in a multi-congregation rural charge) and congregations. Data from http://www.anglican.ca/help/faq/number-of-anglicans/statistical-archive/. They have not collected data past 2001 (in spite of what the yearbook suggests).

5 The membership data are taken from Clarke and MacDonald (2011); 2010 attendance data are from the UCC website.

6 When comparing mainline and evangelical denominations, it is noteworthy that the largest evangelical denominations now have similar numbers of attendees, even though the mainline Protestants have many more affiliates and congregations. This is shown previously in Table 1.2. For example, the UCC claims 174,660 average weekly attendees

and the PAOC claims 154,134, although the UCC has roughly three times as many congregations. Similarly, the Presbyterian Church in Canada claims 64,250 average attendance in 899 congregations compared with 85,855 in 430 congregations for the CMA. Clearly, fuller pews in fewer buildings are an asset as building costs are debilitating for some mainline congregations.

7 The denominations rely on their congregations reporting every year. Some congregations do not keep accurate statistics, and sometimes they neglect to update their information. In addition, denominations do not all count membership in the same way (e.g., some count children as official members and others do not).

8 The yearbook also reports inclusive membership. In keeping with the congregational growth rates, inclusive membership over four decades for the Baptists (132,003 to 135,844) and the CRC (70,747 to 78,460) shows little change, while the MB (17,982 to 33,916), CMA (31,355 to 125,945), and PAOC (92,132 to 234,385) grew substantially in membership. In each case, however, data show less growth in the past decade. We wonder about the usefulness of inclusive membership data, since definitions of "membership" are not consistently applied across denominations or across time, and membership says less about congregational vitality than does attendance. In addition, the accuracy of the data is in question. For example, the PAOC website shows that denomination has not grown in number of congregations nor in attendance in the past five years. Furthermore, data we received from a denominational representative suggest that their total adherents and number of congregations had levelled off by the early 1990s. Regardless of their veracity, in every case the data show less growth in the past decade, and some show decline.

9 We used yearbooks from the following years: 1970, 1971, 1975, 1980, 1981, 1983, 1984, 1989, 1991, 1992, 1993, 1999, 2001, 2003, 2007, 2011, 2012.

10 http://www12.statcan.gc.ca/census-recensement/2011/as-sa/98-310-x/98-310-x2011001-eng.cfm. Accessed 25 June 2012.

11 The reader will notice that for the CRC and MB, the number of congregations reported increased while the membership did not. This may be partly explained by one popular strategy for growth with all five denominations, particularly in the last two decades of church planting. Lately, denominational leaders are encouraging congregations to plant new congregations themselves, rather than hiring planters to start congregations from scratch. About 22% (N = 150) of congregations in our sample have started a new congregation. In addition, another 7 per cent of congregations have started another site (or campus) of their congregation. In total, 150 congregations in our sample say they have started another congregation or site, with 67 starting more than one.

250   NOTES TO PAGES 76–86

12 In comparison, Posterski and Barker (1993) estimate that over half of Protestant congregations have fewer than 75 attendees on average, a figure that would include mainline Protestant congregations (it is not clear how they derived this figure).

13 Using the hyper-network sampling method, Chaves (2004) asked a random sample of Americans which congregation they attended, then proceeded to interview the pastors of the congregations. The random sample allowed him to find the size of the congregation that the average American attended was much larger than the average congregation. Chaves does not give the figures for conservative Protestant congregations, which we retrieved from his data (the National Congregations Study of 1998).

14 Urban and rural congregations were distinguished based on the area codes given in the denominational data. Note that congregations in small towns are given an urban designation based on area codes, just like those that exist in big cities. New Brunswick area codes have been urbanized (see Hiemstra, 2010), so the New Brunswick congregations were coded urban and rural based on addresses and recommendations by a local academic and Baptist minister (since the majority of the congregations were Baptist).

15 Somewhat surprisingly, the age of the congregation is not related to its size. We predicted that older congregations would be smaller because they tend to be rural and have elderly participants, but this prediction did not fit the data.

16 The perception that the urban, old congregations are wealthy, often true of Protestant congregations in the United States, does not appear to be true of Canadian evangelical congregations. Older urban congregations do not have higher total congregational incomes than younger urban congregations.

17 Reimer (2003) notes that while good published data on the number of evangelicals in Quebec are hard to find, there seems to be agreement that they are less than 1 per cent of the population. An evangelical leader in Quebec gave us the 0.5 per cent figure, although he noted that some evangelicals in Quebec do not attend evangelical worship services, so the proportion of evangelicals in Quebec is probably closer to 1 per cent.

18 Outreach Canada appears to be updated based on information from denominations and with some congregations added by authorized users of the website. For comparable use of these data, see Hiemstra (2010).

19 Bibby's Project Canada 2005 dataset shows that evangelicals have a lower average age (44.7) than mainline Protestants (52.1) and than Catholics inside (49.8) and outside (47.3) Quebec.

20 For example, the PAOC reported that nearly all of their new congregations that started in the 1990s were new immigrant congregations. See Wilkinson, *The Spirit Said Go* (2006).

NOTES TO PAGES 87–92   251

21 Overall, these numbers may suggest that the CECS has too few ethnic congregations. For example, the CMA has 89 Chinese, 20 Vietnamese, and 12 Korean, or 28% Asian congregations. We sampled 16 Asian (17%) congregations. The PAOC claim 90 Aboriginal congregations (8%) and we sampled 2 (2%). The MB indicate that they have 16 Chinese congregations and 4 other Asian congregations (8%), whereas we sampled 3 (3.5%). However, it could also mean that denominations use looser definitions for ethnic congregations than the 80% cut-off we used. Furthermore, we found many multiracial congregations based on pastors' reports, some of which may be considered ethnic congregations based on different definitions.

22 This finding is based on logistic regression analysis, used for dependent variables with two possible outcomes (e.g., multiracial or not multiracial).

CHAPTER FOUR

1 Media often conflate the "religious right" with evangelicalism, or American evangelicalism with its Canadian counterpart, or suggest that Stephen Harper's Conservatives have successfully won over the congregations to their agenda, mobilizing them into political activists. See M. McDonald, *The Armageddon Factor* (Toronto: Random House, 2011); Bob Hepburn, "Religious Right a Force for Harper," *Toronto Sun*, 13 April 2011, http://www.thestar.com/opinion/editorialopinion/article/974432—hepburn-religious-right-a-force-for-harper; Judith Timson, "Still Questioning Same-Sex Love? Sorry, I Thought this Was the 21st Century," *Globe and Mail*, 12 Jan. 2012, http://www.theglobeandmail.com/life/relationships/still-questioning-same-sex-love-sorry-i-thought-this-was-the-21st-century/article1358281/

2 Jonathan Malloy, "Playing to His Base: Two Books Track the Rise of Christian and Social Conservatism in Harper's Ottawa," *Literary Review of Canada* (July/Aug. 2010), http://www.jonathanmalloy.com/armageddon-factorlosing-control-review.html

3 Recent surveys from Angus Reid have shown a tendency for evangelicals to vote for the Conservative Party, a trend that is strengthened by church attendance. In 2011, for example, upwards of three-quarters of evangelicals who attend church weekly or more often voted Conservative, compared with just over 40% of evangelicals who never attend. Yet, overall, evangelicals tend to follow the voting behaviours of their region, and we think the current move toward voting conservative is more a symptom the Liberal party alienating voters than a galvanized "Christian Right" (Hutchinson and Hiemstra, 2009).

4 Malloy (2011) notes that some religiously conservative lobby groups,

252 NOTES TO PAGES 99–115

like the 2005 group called Equipping Christians for the Public Square, did promote certain candidates, but these groups seem to be localized and short-lived.

5 Alpha Canada provides resources for congregations who operate the program. See http://www.alphacanada.org/

6 Urban and rural congregations were distinguished based on the area codes given in the denominational data. Note that congregations in small towns are given an urban designation based on area codes, just like those that exist in big cities. New Brunswick area codes have been urbanized (see Hiemstra, 2010), so the New Brunswick congregations were coded urban and rural based on addresses and recommendations by a local academic and Baptist minister (since the majority of the congregations were Baptist).

7 See www.ncdcanada.com/ for details; accessed 23 Nov. 2012.

8 It is not surprising that congregations high on these orientations tend to also be high on pastors' ratings. Note that pastors had to have said that certain priorities were "very high priority" for their congregations on these items for them to be high on any of the scales, which is in itself a positive endorsement. It is more surprising that the fundamentalist orientation is not higher on the pastors' opinion scale at all.

9 See Mark Cartledge, *Testimony in the Spirit* (2010), for a study on the role of testimony in a charismatic congregation.

CHAPTER FIVE

1 According to its website, "Awana Canada helps churches and parents worldwide raise children and youth to know, love and serve Christ. Awana is a broad-based ministry. Scripture memory and weekly children's clubs are just one aspect of what we offer. We feature seven core benefits that will help churches and parents raise children and youth to know, love and serve Christ for a lifetime: Fully integrated programs for ages 2 to 18; the best evangelism tools to reach unsaved children, youth and families; teaching that builds an enduring biblical faith; resources that bring churches and parents together to disciple the next generation; initial and ongoing volunteer training; healthy mentor and peer relationships; irresistible fun for children, teens and adults alike!" See http://awanacanada.ca/about/ for details about Awana; accessed 12 Nov. 2012.

2 Cell groups are qualitatively different than a small group based upon affinity. Typically, cell groups contain a mandate to evangelize, disciple, and multiply. The term "cell" is borrowed from biology and assumes an organic nature. Leaders of cells are often recognized as leaders or pastors in congregations. The "cell church" is especially prominent outside North America. For example, see Paul (David) Yonggi Cho,

Successful Home Cell Groups (Alachua, FL: Bridge Logos, 1987).

3 Mission trip training is also highly correlated with the number involved in the congregation's children's ($r = .246^{***}$) and youth ($r = .318^{***}$) religious education classes. Short-term mission trips are common among youth ministries in evangelical churches.

4 Partial correlation $r = .158^{***}$. Regression results show other factors are related to number of programs. Using a scale created by combining eighteen items in table 5.1 (alpha = .722), we used as our dependent variable the total number of programs offered by a church. Only 2 churches had fewer than 4 of these programs, and 9 had all 18. As noted above, the number of internal programs is highly correlated with the size of the church ($r = .370^{***}$), so we control for average attendance in the regression. Other factors, listed in order of predictive strength, that increase the number of programs include increasing attendance (growth), "missional" identity, "purpose driven" identity, and percentage of attendees with graduate degrees. The adjusted $R2$ was .346, indicating a fairly robust model. For the regression table, contact the authors.

5 The MB average 31.75 volunteers per congregation, which is a significantly higher number than the evangelical average, even when we control for congregation size. Congregations with women pastors, congregations that are predominately white, are larger, have a higher percentage of poor attendees, and espouse the "emergent church" label, are more likely to have more volunteers, even when we control for congregation size.

6 The miscellaneous category includes seniors' ministry (4.0%), clothing banks (3.1%), camp for kids (2.9%), movie nights (2.5%), assisting immigrants/refugees (2.3%), special needs ministry (1.5%), etc. Note again here lots of activity in the community or reaching out to the community. Congregations that have government funding are more likely to be in British Columbia (22, or 22.7% of all BC congregations in the sample) and urban, and government funding is positively correlated with services like food pantry/soup kitchen, daycare/preschool/after school programs, substance abuse programs, language training/educational programs, and community workshops. Eight of the twelve Maritime congregations with government funding are Baptist in the sample.

7 See http://www.wycliffe.ca/wycliffe/about_us/?overview for details about Wycliffe in Canada; accessed 13 Nov. 2012.

8 See http://www.ywamcanada.org/faith.html for details about YWAM, Canada; accessed 13 Nov. 2012.

9 This pastor's view may represent a small minority. While it was not possible for us to assess from our data the level of disagreement with the "missional" or "emergent" church theologies, there are a number of publications that illustrate the tension among evangelicals about

254   NOTES TO PAGES 130–9

these movements. For example, see D.A. Carson, *Becoming Conversant with the Emerging Church* (Grand Rapids, MI: Zondervan, 2005); Gary L.W. Johnson and Ronald L. Gleason, eds., *Reforming or Conforming? Postconservative Evangelicals and the Emerging Church* (Wheaton, IL: Crossway Books, 2008); Grant Richison, *Certainty: A Critique of the Emergent Church of Postevangelicals* (Pickering, ON: Castle Quay, 2010). Also see the doctoral dissertation by Robert L. Elkington, "A Model for the Growth of the Evangelical Churches in Canada," Potchefstroom Campus of the North-West University, South Africa, 2010.

10 For details, see www.purposedrivenchurch.com; accessed 23 Nov. 2012.

CHAPTER SIX

1   Karen Pauls, *Christian Week*, 18 Dec. 2001. http://www.christian week.org/stories.php?id=1214

2   Joe Friesen, "Clergy Shortage Affecting All Denominations in Canada," *Globe and Mail*, 15 Dec. 2010. http://www.theglobeand mail.com/news/national/clergy-shortage-affecting-all-denominations-in-canada/article1320247/

3   Ministerial training for the PAOC predominately occurs at the undergraduate level with the vast number of new pastors attending one of the many Pentecostal Bible colleges in Canada, like Summit Pacific College in British Columbia or Master's College in Ontario. Canadian Pentecostal Seminary operates as a member of the Associated Canadian Theological Schools Schools (ACTS) at Trinity Western University, Langley, BC. Master's Seminary offers courses toward degrees at Tyndale Seminary, Toronto.

4   Our thanks to Chris Meinzer at ATS for running and sending these data. There were thirty-eight seminaries in 2001 and thirty-nine in 2011. A seminary is considered evangelical if the president is part of the Fellowship of Evangelical Presidents. ATS do not send out a list of schools under each category. Some seminaries in Canada are not directly affiliated with ATS because they are part of larger consortiums or are new and independent. It is safe to say that ATS data capture the majority of seminarians in Canada. ATS data tables are available at http://www.ats.edu/Resources/PublicationsPresentations /Documents/AnnualDataTables/2011-12AnnualDataTables.pdf

5   Our thanks to Bruce Guenther, president of Mennonite Brethren Biblical Seminary Canada, for sending us these data. E-mail communication 13 June 2012.

6   Personal e-mail communication from Bruce Guenther.

7   Jim Coggins, "Guess Who's Coming to Seminary?" *Christian Week*, 1 Feb. 2011, 1ff.

8 This information based on the official denominational websites or conversations with denominational leaders. We heard that the CMA voted to ordain women during the writing of this manuscript.

9 The exception is Larson and Goltz (1993), which was sponsored by the EFC's task force on the family. For more information, see Wiseman (1998a; 1998b).

10 For the "relationships with church staff" item, the sample is 312, as only those pastors who have other staff responded. For the other items, the sample is 477.

11 This difference is statistically significant, but substantively it is not very large. The mean is 7.58 for those who did not have help in their areas of weakness, compared with 7.98 for those who did have help (p = .009).

12 There is a medium strong and statistically significant correlation between having a confidant and pastoral satisfaction (r = .184).

13 All the job satisfaction items were included except "relationships with church staff," which was left out to maintain sample size. One-third of the sampled pastors work in situations where they are the only staff. The 9-item scale ranges from 9 to 90 and has an alpha of 0.798 (which means the items are well suited to be combined into one scale).

14 French-language Protestant congregations tend to be small and their pastors poorly paid. A francophone evangelical leader noted that many of their congregations have between twenty and forty members, and he knows of one full-time pastor making $20,000 a year, and several others making around $30,000.

15 Regression results suggest that the most important factor for job satisfaction is the congregation, and when the "congregation" factor is included in the regression, the effect of age is very weak. In other words, once we account for the congregation, young pastors and older pastors have nearly identical job satisfaction.

16 For the 100 youth pastor interviews, we asked first to interview a youth pastor or the pastor that had youth ministry as part of his or her larger job description, then a children's pastor. So, the higher than expected age of the youth pastors is likely due to the fact that we had some associate pastors that had youth ministry as part of their larger portfolio.

17 The 13 items are 1, 2, 4, 7, 8, 10, 11, 13, 15, 17, 18, 19, 20 listed above. The scale (Opinion2) has an alpha of 0.831 for youth pastors and 0.816 for lead pastors.

18 Since the (normally) young youth pastor is evaluating the same congregation as the (normally) older lead pastors, their scores were positively correlated (r = 0.446***). However, the gap between youth and lead pastor Opinion2 scores for the same congregation is sometimes surprising, and the differences range from −15 (a negative score means the youth pastor rates the congregation healthier than the lead pastor) to +23 (positive means the senior pastor gives a more positive score),

256   NOTES TO PAGES 154–63

which indicates the subjective nature of this evaluation. There are 39 negative scores, and 56 positive scores (5 scores are identical). However, the gap between the lead pastor and the youth pastor's opinion scores is not correlated with the age gap. So, negative evaluations of the congregation from younger pastors do not seem to be due to difficulties of working with a much older lead pastor, but with the youthfulness of the youth pastors.

19 Ancillary analysis shows that youth pastors are no more negative about their congregations than lead pastors of the same age. In other words, it's an age effect, not a youth-pastor-vs.-senior-pastor effect.

CHAPTER SEVEN

1 We asked lead pastors if they had Christian education classes for teens, in addition to youth group; 73% of pastors with congregations over 100 people said "yes." We can conclude from the youth pastor interviews that more would have youth group meetings than Christian education classes for youth.

2 *The Spirit of Generation Y* report (Mason, Singleton, and Webber, 2007), studying Australia, found similarly low levels of identification with Christianity among youth, where 51% said they believed in God and 46% considered themselves Christian. The youth of Britain also have shown little recent interest in Christianity. Only about 5% of British teens are found attending a worship service on a given Sunday (Brierley, 2006). In the United States, seven in ten church-attending high school Protestant seniors have a year or more of religious inactivity by the time they are 23 years old (Stetzer, 2009). Smith with Denton (2005) label the de facto dominant faith of American youth as "Moralistic Therapeutic Deism," a version of Christianity focused on self-fulfilment (171). It has five key tenets: God exists and watches over the created world; God wants people to treat each other with kindness and fairness as taught by most religions; one's purpose is to be happy and self-fulfilled; God is absent from everyday life, except when needed in the midst of crisis; and morally good people (regardless of beliefs) go to heaven when they die. Smith and Denton predict that Moralistic Therapeutic Deism "may be the new mainstream American (and western) religious faith for our culturally individualistic, mass-consumerist society" (171).

3 Spiritual gifts are those special talents that evangelicals believe are given by God to each individual uniquely, to enable her or him to better serve in the church and beyond. These gifts are empowered by the Holy Spirit so that their use allows the young person to do a task particularly well. For example, some are gifted to be teachers, which allows them to teach (in the congregation and elsewhere) particularly

well. Others may be given gifts of mercy or compassion, allowing them to work well with the less fortunate.

4 For more information, see www.30hourfamine.org

5 We heard from youth leaders that the two-year turnover figure was commonly cited, but they thought that the average tenure of youth pastors is longer than that. Our data suggest that is probably true.

6 These negative and significant relationships hold up in regression analysis, when we control for age and gender, hours worked per week, whether or not the pastor has a confidant with whom to share his or her struggles, and time spent in areas of weakness. None of these control variables reached standard levels of significance.

7 While we have confidence in the general findings of this report, the panel data may somewhat underestimate retention rates. First, we know that young adults are in a period of life when they are less likely to participate in religious institutions, and that some (but probably a clear minority) will increase their religious participation once they have settled into family life. Second, the panel somewhat underrepresents immigrant young adults (who tend to be more religious; see Bibby (2012) or Penner et al. (2012)), and were slightly more likely to be urban, highly educated, female, and fully employed. There was also a small non-response bias, with fewer religious service attendees than non-attendees filling out the survey. Also note that respondents had to be "raised Christian" or convert to Christianity post childhood in order to participate in the survey but their religious participation and parental dedication varied considerably, as we shall see below. Overall, it is important to remember that all sample data have weaknesses, and there is good reason to have confidence in these data once these minor underrepresentations are considered. Angus Reid works diligently to ensure its online panel matches demographic characteristics like region and religious affiliation. A respectable 71% of those invited completed the survey. The Appendix in Penner et al. (2012) gives more detail on the panel characteristics and the project's methodology.

8 Young adults were considered "raised Christian" if they identified as "Christian" to the question: "Which one of the following best describes the religious identity of your family, when you were a child of public school age?" and they attended church "seldom" or more often as a child (options were "more than once a week, once a week, once or twice a month, a few times a year, seldom, never"). "Raised evangelical" refers to those who identify as Christian, identify with an evangelical denomination, and attend "seldom" or more.

9 Sometimes, difficult experiences actually drive a young person toward a faith community amid deep questioning of God. This was the experience of one young adult that led to his whole family finding and joining an evangelical congregation:. "When my cousin committed suicide it impacted me ... how can God take away someone that you care

258   NOTES TO PAGES 181–7

about so much? How can He let that happen?"
A self-proclaimed childhood agnostic, this person became a regularly attending evangelical in late elementary school after the suicide: "That's the reason we started going. So at the time I had a problem with God because it felt like he took my cousin. So yeah. But as time passed on you eventually learn that it was his choice to do what he did, and God just, he's there to guide you and try to help you, and that's what he did with my cousin, but other circumstances ... blinded him to the fact that God was there." Incidentally, as a teen he stopped attending the congregation (largely over his inability to reconcile the young earth creation his congregation taught and the old earth evolutionary account learned from science teachers in Grade 11).

10 We tested the relative predictive strength of the parental religiosity, youth leader modelling, faith came alive at camp, faith came alive on a mission trip, parental attendance decline, and friends are mostly Christian, in linear regression and ordinal regression models. The relative strength of the predictors, based on standardized Beta and Wald coefficients, showed the same order of predictive strength. The Beta scores are parental religiosity (.335), youth leader model (.190), friends were committed Christians (.138), faith came alive on a mission trip (.118), and parents' attendance declined (–.106). The model predicted about 25% of the total variance (Adjusted $R2$ = .246).

CHAPTER EIGHT

1 We suspect that the differences between the CSGVP data and income tax claims are related to (1) couples pooling their giving on one return for tax benefits, (2) some donations are not reported on income tax (often donations below $10.00 or so are not receipted by charities), and (3) some overreporting on surveys. Other reasons may exist. See Statistics Canada, Table 111-0001, Summary of Charitable Donations, http://www5.statcan.gc.ca/cansim/a26?lang=eng&retrLang=eng&id= 1110001&paSer=&pattern=&stByVal=1&p1=1&p2=37&tabMode= dataTable&csid= Accessed 7 October 2011.

2 It should be noted that some are required by their organizations to volunteer, which is not uncommon among high schools and universities. Young people were more likely to report required volunteering (Vézina and Crompton, 2010), and there is some evidence that required volunteering does not necessarily translate into greater volunteerism later in life (Henderson et al., 2007).

3 The United States is also experiencing a decline in giving to churches, not in actual dollars, but in percentage of income. Between 1968 and 2009, giving to a sample of eight Evangelical denominations fell from 6.17% to 3.90%, while giving to mainline Protestant churches fell

more slowly, from 3.31% to 2.78% over the same period. Most of this money went toward congregational expenses; only about 15% of these monies going toward missions or local outreach (Ronsvalle and Ronsvalle, 2011).

4 This is the Statistics Canada figure representing before tax income from all sources for economic families for 2010. Accessed 3 July 2012 at http://www.statcan.gc.ca/tables-tableaux/sum-som/l01/cst01/famil108a-eng.htm.

5 We computed this from Turcotte (2012) tables by dividing the median yearly donation for all donors by the midpoint of the income category.

6 Data computed from OECD, see, e.g., http://www.thefactfile.com/2012/01/20/foreign-aid-on-the-cheap-u-s-spending-on-foreign-assistance-among-the-lowest-in-the-oecd

7 For reports from this study, see www.faithcommunitiestoday.org. The Holy Toll report is available for free download at http://faith communitiestoday.org/sites/faithcommunitiestoday.org/files/HolyToll Report.pdf; accessed 16 Dec. 2011.

8 See http://www.cra-arc.gc.ca/ebci/haip/srch/advancedsearch-eng.action and Barbara Brownlee, Glenn Gumulka, Cathy Barr, and David Lasby. "Understanding the Capacity of Religious Organizations: A Synthesis of Findings form the National Survey of Nonprofit and Voluntary Organizations and the National Survey of Giving, Volunteering and Participating." *Imagine Canada* (2005), vi.

9 "Registered Charity Information Return (version t3010-1-10e), http://www.cra-arc.gc.ca/E/pbg/tf/t3010-1/t3010-1-10e.pdf, accessed 17 August 2012.

10 http://www.cra-arc.gc.ca/ebci/haip/srch/advancedsearch-eng.action

11 We were unable to match only 12 (2.5%) churches in our CECS sample to CRA data, indicating that the CRA dataset contains nearly all the evangelical churches, even though a small number may not file directly. Readers should also note that there have been five versions of the T3010 from 2000 to 2010, but changes are minor, and data were carefully matched to provide continuity over time.

12 While the CECS data show considerably higher income (median $204,345) and expenditures ($201,206), this has to do with the sampling strategy of the CECS and the differences can be completely reconciled (see Appendix). The two data sources give nearly identical allocations of expenditures, giving us more confidence in our data. Both show an identical median of 45% allocated to compensation expenditures in evangelical congregations. The percentages spent on occupancy costs were also nearly identical. Based on CECS data, evangelical congregations spent 10% on foreign mission and only 5% on community outreach (both medians).

13 Many of these congregations likely no longer have paid staff, but some of them may simply have failed to fill in an amount on this line. Thus,

260   NOTES TO PAGES 199–219

we did not impute amounts (a zero) where there was missing data.

14 To be precise, these churches do not pay for staff themselves. It could be that there are staff at these churches who are being paid by another church (like in a multi-church charge) or by the denomination, etc.

CONCLUSION

1 For comparisons between American and Canadian evangelicals, see Noll (1992; 1997), Noll, Bebbington, and Rawlyk (1994), Rawlyk and Noll (1994), and Reimer (2003). One difference is that only 1.3% of mega-churches are in Canada (roughly 20 churches), below what would be expected based on population (about 10 to 1). Even the largest churches in Canada do not compare in size to Lakewood Church in Houston (43,500), which is the size of some of the largest evangelical denominations in Canada; this database has 1,638 churches listed as of 31 December 2012 and is available at http://hirr.hartsem.edu/megachurch/database.html. About 70% of these mega-churches are evangelical.

2 While Dickerson's concern for the trajectory of evangelical churches in the United States is well founded, we find a lack of solid data and methodological rigour in the book. As a result, we think he exaggerates the degree and speed of any decline that may be approaching.

APPENDIX

1 While CRA information has been made available since 2000, a revision that came into effect for the 2003 reporting year substantially improved the quality of the data. It is our view that the data prior to 2003 are too dissimilar to what came after to offer valid or useful comparisons.

2 These scripts used an application of the Levenshtein edit distance algorithm to suggest preliminary matches.

3 The Anglican Network in Canada (ANiC) was coded as evangelical on the basis of its affiliation with the Evangelical Fellowship of Canada.

4 Canada Post has urbanized New Brunswick postal codes. There are many congregations in a rural setting in New Brunswick, but the general rule was followed for the analysis in our research rather than trying to make an independent determination of which New Brunswick congregations were urban and which were rural.

References

Adams, M. 2006. *Sex in the Snow: The Surprising Revolution of Canadian Social Values*. Toronto: Penguin.

Aechtner, T. 2012. "Standing at the Crux: Pentecostalism and Identity Formation in an African Diaspora Christian Community." In *Global Pentecostal Movements*, ed. Michael Wilkinson, 171–94. Leiden: Brill.

Ammerman, N.T. 1987. *Bible Believers: Fundamentalists in the Modern World*. New Brunswick, NJ: Rutgers University Press.

– 1997. *Congregation and Community*. New Brunswick, NJ: Rutgers University Press.

– 1998. "Culture and Identity in Congregations." In *Studying Congregations: A New Handbook*, eds. Nancy Ammerman, Jackson W. Carroll, and Carl S. Dudley, 78–104. Nashville, TN: Abingdon.

– 2005. *Pillars of Faith: American Congregations and Their Partners*. Berkeley, CA: University of California Press.

Angus Reid Global. 2014. "Electoral Forecasts since 2007." http://www.angus reidglobal.com/wp-content/uploads/2014/04/Electoral-Record-06.17.pdf

Anderssen, E. 2011. "Who Will Replace the Faith-Based Donors?" *Globe and Mail*, 1 Dec.

Anderson, A. 2013. *Pentecostalism and the Transformation of World Christianity*. Oxford: Oxford University Press.

Arnett, J.J. 2004. *Emerging Adulthood: The Winding Road from the Late Teens through the Twenties*. Oxford: Oxford University Press.

Arnett, J.J., and L.A. Jensen. 2002. "A Congregation of One: Individualized Religious Beliefs among Emerging Adults." *Journal of Adolescent Research* 17(5): 451–67.

Association of Theological Schools. 2011. http://www.ats.edu/Resources/ PublicationsPresentations/Documents/AnnualDataTables/2011-12 AnnualDataTables.pdf

Bader, C., and S. Desmond. 2006. "Do As I Say and as I Do: The Effects of Consistent Beliefs and Behaviors upon Religious Transmission." *Sociology of Religion* 67(3): 313–29.

Bardoel, E.A., L. Morgan, and C. Santos. 2007. "Quality Part-Time Work in Australian Organizations: Implications for HRD." *Human Resources Development International* 10(3): 281–99.

Barna, G. 1993. *Today's Pastors*. Ventura, CA: Regal.

Baum, J.A.C., and J.V. Singh. 1994. "Organizational Niches and the Dynamics of Organizational Mortality." *American Journal of Sociology* 100(2): 346–80.

Bean, L., M. Gonzalez, and J. Kaufmann. 2008. "Why Doesn't Canada Have an American-Style Christian Right? A Comparative Framework for Analyzing the Political Effects of Evangelical Subcultural Identity." *Canadian Journal of Sociology* 33(4): 899–943.

Bebbington, D. W. 1989. *Evangelicalism in Modern Britain*. New York: Routledge.

Becker, P.E. 1999. *Congregations in Conflict: Cultural Models of Local Religious Life*. New York: Cambridge University Press.

Bedell, K. B., ed. 1993. *Yearbook of American and Canadian Churches*. Nashville, TN: Abingdon.

Bedell, K. B., and A. M. Jones, eds. 1992. *Yearbook of American and Canadian Churches*. Nashville, TN: Abingdon.

Bélanger, A. 2006. "Report on the Demographic Situation in Canada, 2003 and 2004." Statistics Canada, Catalogue no. 91-209-XIE. http://publications.gc.ca/Collection/Statcan/91-209-X/91-209-XIE2003000.pdf. Accessed 15 June 2012.

Bellah, R., R. Madsen, W. Sullivan, A. Swidler, and S. Tipton. 1985. *Habits of the Heart: Individualism and Commitment in American Life*. Berkeley, CA: University of California Press.

Berger, I. E. 2006. "The Influence of Religion on Philanthropy in Canada." *Voluntas* 17: 115–32.

– 2006. "The Influence of Religion on Philanthropy in Canada." *Voluntas* 17: 115–32.

Berger, P. 1969. *A Rumor of Angels: Modern Society and the Rediscovery of the Supernatural*. New York: Doubleday.

Berton, P. 1965. *The Comfortable Pew*. Toronto: McClelland and Stewart.

Beyer, P. 1993. "Roman Catholicism in Quebec: The Ghosts of Religion Past." In *The Sociology of Religion: A Canadian Focus*, ed. W.E. Hewitt, 133–56. Toronto: Butterworths.

– 1997. "Religious Vitality in Canada: The Complimentarity of Religious Market and Secularization Perspectives." *Journal for the Scientific Study of Religion* 36: 272–88.

– 2005. "The Future of Non-Christian Religions in Canada: Patterns of Religious Identification among Recent Immigrants and their Second Generation, 1981–2001." *Studies in Religion* 34: 165–96.

– 2008. "Appendix: The Demographics of Christianity in Canada." In *Christianity and Ethnicity in Canada*, eds. Paul Bramadat and David Seljak, 437–40. Toronto: University of Toronto Press.

Bibby, R. W. 1983. "Circulation of the Saints Revisited: A Longitudinal Look at Conservative Church Growth." *Journal for the Scientific Study of Religion* 22(3): 253–62.

– 1987. *Fragmented Gods: The Poverty and Potential of Religion in Canada.* Toronto: Irwin.

– 1993. *Unknown Gods: The Ongoing Story of Religion in Canada.* Toronto: Stoddart.

– 1994. "Circulation of the Saints, 1966–1990: New Data, New Reflections." *Journal for the Scientific Study of Religion* 33(3): 273–80.

– 1995a. *Evangeltrends.* Waterloo, ON: Vision 2000 Canada.

– 1995b. *There's Got to Be More! Connecting Churches and Canadians.* Toronto: Novalis.

– 2002. *Restless Gods: The Renaissance of Religion in Canada.* Toronto: Stoddart.

– 2004. *Restless Churches: How Canada's Churches Can Contribute to the Emerging Religious Renaissance.* Ottawa: Novalis.

– 2006. *The Boomer Factor: What Canada's Most Famous Generation Is Leaving Behind.* Toronto: Bastian.

– 2009. *The Emerging Millennials: How Canada's Newest Generation Is Responding to Change and Choice.* Lethbridge: Project Canada.

– 2011. *Beyond the Gods and Back.* Lethbridge: Project Canada.

– 2012. *A New Day: The Resilience and Restructuring of Religion in Canada.* Lethbridge: Project Canada.

Bibby, R. W., and M. B. Brinkerhoff. 1973. "Circulation of the Saints: A Study of People Who Join Conservative Churches." *Journal for the Scientific Study of Religion* 12: 273–83.

Bielo, J. 2011. *Emerging Evangelicals: Faith, Modernity and the Decline of Authenticity.* New York: New York University Press.

Blau, P.M. 1970. "A Formal Theory of Differentiation in Organizations." *American Sociological Review* 35: 201–18.

Boddie, S.C., and R. Cnaan, eds. 2007. *Faith-based Social Services: Measures, Assessments, and Effectiveness.* New York: Routledge.

Bowen, J. 2010. *Growing Up Christian: Why Young People Stay in Church, Leave Church and (Sometimes) Come Back to Church.* Vancouver, BC: Regent College.

Bowen, K. 1999. *Religion, Participation, and Charitable Giving: A Report.* Toronto: Canadian Centre of Philanthropy and Volunteer Canada.

– 2004. *Christians in a Secular World: The Canadian Experience.* Montreal and Kingston: McGill-Queen's University Press.

Bowler, C. 2010. "From Far and Wide: The Canadian Faith Movement." *Church and Faith Trends* 3(1): 1–6.

– 2013. *Blessed: A History of American Prosperity Gospel.* New York: Oxford University Press.

Bradshaw, M., and C. Ellison. 2009. "The Nature-Nurture Debate Is Over, and Both Sides Lost! Implications for Understanding Gender

Differences in Religiosity." *Journal for the Scientific Study of Religion* 48(2): 241–51.

Bramadat, P., and D. Seljak, eds. 2005. *Religion and Ethnicity in Canada.* Toronto: Pearson.

– 2008. *Christianity and Ethnicity in Canada.* Toronto: University of Toronto Press.

Brenner, P. 2012. "Identity as a Determinant of the Overreporting of Church Attendance in Canada. *Journal for the Scientific Study of Religion* 51(2): 377–85.

Brierley, P. 2006. *Pulling Out of A Nose Dive: A Contemporary Portrait of Churchgoing – What the 2005 English Church Census Reveals.* London: Christian Research.

Brownlee, B., G. Gumulka, C. Barr, and D. Lasby. 2005. "Understanding the Capacity of Religious Organizations: A Synthesis of Findings from the National Survey of Nonprofit and Voluntary Organizations and the National Survey of Giving, Volunteering and Participating." Imagine Canada. Available at http://nonprofitscan.imaginecanada.ca/files/en/ misc/understanding_capacity_religious_orgs_report.pdf

Brubaker, R., M. Loveman, and P. Stamatov. 2004. "Ethnicity as Cognition." *Theory and Society* 33(1): 31–64.

Bruce, S. 2011. *Secularization.* Oxford: Oxford University Press.

Canada Revenue Agency. http://www.cra-arc.gc.ca/ebci/haip/srch/advancedsearch-eng.action

Canales, A. 2006. "Models for Adolescent Ministry: Exploring Eight Ecumenical Examples." *Religious Review* 101(2): 204–32.

Cartledge, M. J. 2010. *Testimony in the Spirit: Rescripting Ordinary Theology.* Surrey, UK: Ashgate.

Carroll, J. 2006. *God's Potters: Pastoral Leadership and the Shaping of Congregations.* Grand Rapids, MI: Eerdmans.

Chang, P.M.Y. 2003. "Pulpit Supply: A Clergy Shortage?" *Christian Century,* 29 Nov, 28–30.

Chaves, M. "Religious Organizations: Data Resources and Research Opportunities." *American Behavioral Scientist* 45: 1523–49.

– 2003. "Religious Authority in the Modern World." *Society* (Mar./Apr.): 38–40.

– 2004. *Congregations in America.* Cambridge, MA: Harvard University Press.

– 2010. "Rain Dances in the Dry Season: Overcoming the Religious Congruence Fallacy." *Journal for the Scientific Study of Religion* 49(1): 1–14.

– 2011. *American Religion: Contemporary Trends.* Princeton, NJ: Princeton University Press.

Christie, N., and M. Gauvreau. 1996. *A Full-Orbed Christianity: The Protestant Churches and Social Welfare in Canada, 1900–1940.* Montreal and Kingston: McGill-Queen's University Press.

REFERENCES   265

Clarke, B. 1996. "English-Speaking Canada from 1854." In *A Concise History of Christianity in Canada*, eds. T. Murphy and R. Perin, 261–360. Toronto: Oxford University Press.

Clarke, B., and S. Macdonald 2010. "Working Paper – Anglican Church of Canada Statistics." http://individual.utoronto.ca/clarkemacdonald/ clarkemacdonald/Welcome_files/anglicanchurch.pdf

– 2011. "Working Paper – United Church of Canada Statistics." http://individual.utoronto.ca/clarkemacdonald/clarkemacdonald/ Welcome_files/unitedchurch.pdf

Clark, S.D. 1948. *Church and Sect in Canada*. Toronto: University of Toronto Press.

Clark, W., and G. Shellenberg. 2006. "Who's Religious?" *Canadian Social Trends*. Summer. http://www.statcan.gc.ca/pub/11-008-x/2006001 /pdf/9181-eng.pdf.

Clydesdale, T. 2007. *The First Year Out: Understanding American Teens after High School*. Chicago, IL: University of Chicago Press.

Cnaan, R., R.J. Wineburg, and S.C. Boddie. 1999. *The Newer Deal: Social Work and Religion in Partnership*. New York: Columbia University Press.

Cnaan, R., S.C. Boddie, F. Handy, G. Yancey, and R. Schneider. 2002. *The Invisible Caring Hand: American Congregations and the Provision of Welfare*. New York: New York University Press.

Coggins, J. 2011. "Guess Who's Coming to Seminary?" *Christian Week*, 1 Feb., 1ff.

Cornwall, M. 1988. "The Influence of Three Agents of Religious Socialization: Family, Church and Peers." In *The Religion and Family Connection: Social Science Perspectives*. Vol. 16 edited by Darwin L. Thomas, 207–31. Provo, UT: Brigham Young University Press.

Côté, Pauline. 2008. "Quebec and Reasonable Accommodation: Uses and Misuses of Public Consultation. In *Religion and Diversity in Canada*, eds. Lori G. Beaman and Peter Beyer, 41–66. Leiden: Brill.

Dart, J. 2008. "Survey Shows that Pastoral Posts still Attract and Satisfy." *Christian Century* 125(4): 15–16.

Davidson, J.D. 2003. "Fewer and Fewer: Is the Clergy Shortage Unique to the Catholic Church?" *America* 1: 10–13.

Dean, K.C. 2010. *Almost Christian: What the Faith of Our Teenagers Is Telling the American Church*. Oxford: Oxford University Press.

DeYoung, C.P., M.O. Emerson, G. Yancey, and K.C. Kim. 2004. *United by Faith: The Multiracial Congregation as an Answer to the Problem of Race*. New York: Oxford University Press.

Dickerson, J. S. 2013. *The Great Evangelical Recession: 6 Factors that Will Crash the American Church… and How to Prepare*. Grand Rapids, MI: Baker.

Dueck, A.J., B.L. Guenther, and D. Heidebrecht. 2011. *Renewing Identity and Mission: Mennonite Brethren Reflections after 150 years*. Hillsboro, KS: Kindred.

Durkheim, E. 1995 [1912]. *The Elementary Forms of Religious Life.* Translated and with an Introduction by Karen E. Fields. New York: Free Press.

Eagle, D. 2011. "Changing Patterns of Attendance at Religious Services in Canada, 1986–2008." *Journal for the Scientific Study of Religion* 5(1): 187–200.

Ebaugh, H.R., and J.S. Chafetz, eds. 2000. *Religion and the New Immigrants: Continuities and Adaptations in Immigrant Congregations.* Walnut Creek, CA: Altamira.

Ebaugh, H.R., and J. Saltzman. 2002. *Religion across Borders: Transnational Immigrant Communities.* Walnut Creek, CA: Altamira.

Eckersley, R. 2005. "Is Modern Western Culture a Health Hazard?" *International Journal of Epidemiology* 35(2): 252–8.

Edgell, P. 2006. *Religion and Family in a Changing Society.* Princeton, NJ: Princeton University Press.

Eliasoph, N., and P. Lichterman. 2003. "Culture in Interaction." *American Journal of Sociology* 108(4): 735–94.

Emerson, M.O., and C. Smith. 2000. *Divided by Faith: Evangelical Religion and the Problem of Race in America.* New York: Oxford University Press.

Emerson, M.O., and R.M. Woo. 2006. *People of the Dream: Multiracial Congregations in the United States.* Princeton, NJ: Princeton University Press.

Ewart, D. 2010. "United Church of Canada Trends – How We Got Here." http://www.davidewart.ca/UCCan-Trends-How-Did-We-Get-Here.pdf

Farrell, J. 2011. "The Young and the Restless: The Liberalization of Young Evangelicals." *Journal for the Scientific Study of Religion* 50(3): 517–32.

Fichter, J. 1968. *America's Forgotten Priests: What They Are Saying.* New York: Harper.

Finke, R. 1994. "The Quiet Transformation: Changes in Size and Leadership of Southern Baptist Churches." *Review of Religious Research* 36: 3–22.

Finke, R., and R. Stark. 1992. *The Churching of America, 1776–1990: Winners and Losers in Our Religious Economy.* New Brunswick, NJ: Rutgers University Press.

Francis, L., P. Hills, and P. Kaldor. 2009. "The Oswald Clergy Burnout Scale: Reliability, Factor Structure and Preliminary Application among Australian Clergy. *Pastoral Psychology* 57(5): 243–52.

Francis, L.J., P. Hills, and C.J.F. Rutledge. 2008. "Clergy Work-Related Satisfactions in Parochial Ministry: The influence of Personality and Churchmanship. *Mental Health, Religion and Culture* 11(3): 327–39.

Frenk, S.M., S.L. Anderson, and N. Martin. 2011. "Assessing the Validity of Key Informant Reports about Congregation's Social Composition."

Sociology of Religion 72(1): 78–90.

Froese, P., and C. Bader. 2010. *America's Four Gods: What We Say about God – and What that Says about Us*. New York: Oxford University Press.

Gallagher, S. 2007. "Children as Religious Resources: The Role of Children in the Social Reformation of Class, Culture and Religious Identity." *Journal for the Scientific Study of Religion* 46(2): 169–83.

Gauvreau, M. 1991. *The Evangelical Century*. Montreal and Kingston: McGill-Queen's University Press.

Goetz, D.L. 1997. "Why Pastor Steve Loves His Job." *Christianity Today* 41(4): 12–16.

Grant, J.W. 1988. *The Church in the Canadian Era*. Burlington, ON: Welch.

Greeley, A. 1972. *The Catholic Priest in the United States: Sociological Investigations*. Washington, DC: United States Catholic Conference.

Greeley, A., and M. Hout. 2006. *The Truth about Conservative Christians: What They Think and What They Believe*. Chicago, IL: University of Chicago Press.

Grenville, A. 2000. "'For by Him All Things Were Created ... Visible and Invisible': Sketching the Contours of Public and Private Religion in North America." In *Rethinking Church, State and Modernity*, eds. D. Lyon and M. Van Die, 211–27. Toronto: University of Toronto Press.

Guder, D.L., ed. 1998. *Missional Church: A Vision for the Sending of the Church in North America*. Grand Rapids, MI: Eerdmans.

Guenther, B. 2008a. "'From the Edge of Oblivion': Reflections on Evangelical Protestant Denominational Historiography in Canada." *Historical Papers* (June): 153–74.

– 2008b. "Ethnicity and Evangelical Protestants in Canada." In *Christianity and Ethnicity in Canada*, eds. Paul Bramadat and David Seljak, 365–414. Toronto: University of Toronto Press.

Gushee, D. P. 2008. *The Future of Faith in American Politics: The Public Witness of the Evangelical Center*. Waco, TX: Baylor University Press.

Hadaway, C.K. 2011. "FACTs on Growth: 2010." Hartford Institute for Religious Research. http://faithcommunitiestoday.org/sites/faithcommunitiestoday.org/files/FACTs%20on%

Hadaway, C.K., and P.L. Marler. 1997. "Religion in a Canadian County: A Case Study of Church Attendance Overreporting." Presented at the Conference of the Association for the Sociology of Religion, Toronto, Canada.

Hadaway, C.K., and Roozen, D.A. 1993. "Denominational Growth and Decline." In *Church and Denominational Growth: What Does (and Does Not) Cause Growth and Decline*, eds. D.A. Roozen and C.K. Hadaway, 37–46. Nashville, TN: Abingdon.

Hamilton, M.S. 2000. "More Money, More Ministry: The Financing of American Evangelicalism since 1945." In *More Money, More Ministry:*

Money and Evangelicals in Recent North American History, eds. L. Eskridge and M.A. Noll, 104–40. Grand Rapids, MI: Eerdmans.

Hannan, M.T., and J. Freeman. 1977. "The Population Ecology of Organizations. *American Journal of Sociology* 82(5): 929–64.

Hannan, M.T., G.R. Carroll, and L. Polos. 2003. "The Organizational Niche." *Sociological Theory* 21: 309–40.

Haskell, D. 2007. "News Media Influence on Non-Evangelicals' Perceptions of Evangelical Christians: A Case Study. *Journal of Media and Religion* 6(3): 153–79.

Henderson, A, S.D. Brown, S.M. Pancer, and K. Ellis-Hale. 2007. "Mandated Community Service in High School and Subsequent Civic Engagement: The Case of the 'Double Cohort' in Ontario, Canada." *Journal of Youth and Adolescence* 36 (7): 849–60.

Herzog, P.S. 2011. "Contextual Inequalities in Religious Youth Programming." *Review of Religious Research* 53: 227–46.

Hiebert, R. 2001. "Mr Berton, You Were Wrong." *Alberta Report* 28(18): 45.

Hiemstra, J. 2002. "Government Relations with Faith-Based Non-profit Social Agencies in Alberta." *Journal of Church and State* 44(1): 19–45.

Hiemstra, R. 2007. "Counting Canadian Evangelicals." *Church and Faith Trends* 1(1): 1–10.

– 2008. "Evangelicals and the Canadian Census." *Church and Faith Trends* 1(2): 1–15.

– 2009. "Evangelical Giving and Volunteering." *Church and Faith Trends* 2(2): 1–10.

– 2010. "Canadian Evangelical Congregational Income, 2003–2008." *Church and Faith Trends* 3(1): 1–21.

– 2011. "Canadian Evangelical Congregational Full-Time and Part-Time Staffing Complements, 2003–2009." *Church and Faith Trends* 4(1): 1–19.

Hills, P., L.J. Francis, and C.J.F. Rutledge. 2004. "The Factor Structure of a Measure of Burnout Specific to Clergy, and Its Trial Application with Respect to Some Individual Personal Differences." *Review of Religious Research* 46(1): 27–42.

Hodgkinson, V.A., and M.S. Weitzman. 1992. "From Belief to Commitment: The Community Service Activities and Finances of Religious Congregations in the United States. Findings from a National Survey." Washington, DC: Independent Sector.

Hoge, D.R., J.J. Shields, and D.L. Griffin. 1995. "Changes in Satisfaction and Institutional Attitudes of Catholic Priests, 1970–1993." *Sociology of Religion* 56(2): 195–213.

Hoge, D.R., J.J. Shields, and M.J. Verdieck. 1988. "Changing Age Distribution and Theological Attitudes of Catholic Priests, 1970–1985." *Sociology of Religion* 49(3): 264–80.

Hoge, D., B. Johnson, and D. Luidens. 1994. *Vanishing Boundaries: The Religion of Mainline Protestant Baby Boomers*. Louisville, KY: John Knox Press.

Holmes, P. M.S. 2009. "Ministering Women in the Pentecostal Assemblies of Canada: A Feminist Exploration." In *Canadian Pentecostalism: Transition and Transformation*, ed. Michael Wilkinson, 171–96. Montreal and Kingston: McGill-Queen's University Press.

– 2010. "Acts 29 and Authority: Towards a Pentecostal Feminist Hermeneutic of Liberation." In *A Liberating Spirit: Pentecostals and Social Action in North America*, eds. Michael Wilkinson and Steven Studebaker, 185–212. Eugene, OR: Wipf and Stock.

Hopewell, J.F. 1987. *Congregation: Stories and Structures*. Philadelphia, PA: Fortress Press.

Hout, M., A.M. Greeley, and M.J. Wilde. 2001. "The Demographic Imperative in Religious Change." *American Journal of Sociology* 107: 468–500.

Hunter, J.D. 1983. *American Evangelicalism: Conservative Religion and the Quandary of Modernity*. New Brunswick, NJ: Rutgers University Press.

Hutchinson, D. and R. Hiemstra. 2009. "Canadian Evangelical Voting Trends by Region, 1996-2008." Church and Faith Trends 2 (2): 1-10. http://files.efc-canada.net/min/rc/cft/V02I03/Evangelical_Voting_Trends_1996-2008.pdf

Hutchinson, M., and J. Wolffe. 2012. *A Short History of Global Evangelicalism*. Cambridge: Cambridge University Press.

Iannaccone, L. 1992. "Sacrifice and Stigma: Reducing Free-riding in Cults, Communes, and Other Collectives." *Journal of Political Economy* 100: 271–91.

Iannaccone, L.R., D. Olson, and R. Stark. 1995. "Religious Resources and Church Growth." *Social Forces* 74: 705–31.

Inskeep, K.W. 1993. "A Short History of Church Growth Research." In *Church and Denominational Growth*, eds. C.K. Hadaway and D.A. Roozen, 135–48. Nashville, TN: Abingdon.

Jacquet, C. H., Jr. 1970. *Yearbook of American and Canadian Churches*. New York: National Council of Churches.

– 1971. *Yearbook of American and Canadian Churches*. National Council of Churches.

– 1975. *Yearbook of American and Canadian Churches*. Nashville, TN: Abingdon.

– 1980. *Yearbook of American and Canadian Churches*. Nashville, TN: Abingdon.

– 1981. *Yearbook of American and Canadian Churches*. Nashville, TN: Abingdon.

– 1983. *Yearbook of American and Canadian Churches*. Nashville, TN: Abingdon.

– 1984. *Yearbook of American and Canadian Churches*. Nashville, TN: Abingdon.

Jacquet, C. H., Jr., and A. M. Jones, eds. 1989. *Yearbook of American and Canadian Churches*. Nashville, TN: Abingdon.

- 1991. *Yearbook of American and Canadian Churches*. Nashville, TN: Abingdon.
James, W. C. 2011. *God's Plenty: Religious Diversity in Kingston*. Montreal and Kingston: McGill-Queen's University Press.
Jenkins, S.R., and C. Maslach. 1994. "Psychological Health and Involvement in Interpersonally Demanding Occupations: A Longitudinal Perspective." *Journal of Organizational Behavior* 15(2): 101–27.
Ji, C.C., and T. Tameifuna. 2011. "Youth Pastor, Youth Ministry and Youth Attitude toward The Church." *Review of Religious Research* 52(3): 306–22.
Jinkins, M. 2002. "Great Expectations, Sobering Realities: Findings from a New Study on Clergy Burnout." *Congregations* 28(3): 11–13, 24–7.
Jud, G.J., E. Mills, and G.W. Burch. 1970. *Ex-pastors: Why Men Leave the Parish Ministry*. Philadelphia, PA: Pilgrim.
Keller, R.S., and R.R. Ruether, eds. 2006. *Encyclopedia of Women and Religion in North America*. Bloomington: University of Indiana Press.
Kelley, D.M. 1972. *Why Conservative Churches Are Growing*. New York: Harper and Row.
Larson, L., and J.W. Goltz. 1993. *Clergy Families in Canada: An Initial Report*. Unpublished manuscript, retrieved from https://www.evangelicalfellowship.ca/.
Lehr, F. 2006. *Clergy Burnout: Recovering from the 70-Hour Work Week … and Other Self-Defeating Practices*. Minneapolis, MN: Augsburg Fortress.
Linder, E.W., ed. 1999. *Yearbook of American and Canadian Churches*. Nashville, TN: Abingdon.
- 2001. *Yearbook of American and Canadian Churches*. Nashville, TN: Abingdon.
- 2003. *Yearbook of American and Canadian Churches*. Nashville, TN: Abingdon.
- 2007. *Yearbook of American and Canadian Churches*. New York: Abingdon.
- 2011. *Yearbook of American and Canadian Churches*. New York: Abingdon.
- 2012. *Yearbook of American and Canadian Churches*. New York: Abingdon.
Lindsay, C. 2008. "Canadians attend weekly religious services less than 20 years ago." Statistics Canada. http://www.statcan.gc.ca/pub/89-630-x/2008001/article/10650-eng.htm
Luckmann, T. 1967. *The Invisible Religion: The Problem of Religion in Modern Society*. New York: Macmillan.
Luhrmann, T. 2012. *When God Talks Back: Understanding the American Evangelical Relationship with God*. New York: Vintage.
Lyon, D. 2000. "Introduction." In *Rethinking Church, State, and*

Modernity, eds. D. Lyon and M. Van Die, 3–22. Toronto: University of Toronto Press.

Lyon, D., and M. Van Die, eds. 2000. *Rethinking Church, State, and Modernity: Canada between Europe and America*. Toronto: University of Toronto Press.

MacArthur, J.F. 2010. *Ashamed of the Gospel: When the Church Becomes like the World*. Wheaton, IL: Crossway.

Maclean's Special Report. 1993. "God Is Alive." *Maclean's*, 12 Apr., 32–50.

Malenfant, É. C., A. Lebel, and L. Martel. 2010. "Projections of the Diversity of the Canadian Population, 2006 to 2031." www.statcan.gc.ca/pub/91-551-x/91-551-x2010001-eng.htm

Malloy, J. 2011. "Between America and Europe: Religion, Politics and Evangelicals in Canada." *Politics, Religion and Ideology* 12(3): 315–31.

Marler, P. L., and C. K. Hadaway. 1999. "Testing the Attendance Gap in a Conservative Church." *Sociology of Religion* 60 (2): 175–86.

Marsden, George. 1984. "Introduction" in *Evangelicalism and Modern America*, ed. George Marsden. Grand Rapids, MI: Eerdmans, vii–xvi.

Marti, G. 2008. *Hollywood Faith: Holiness, Prosperity, and Ambition in a Los Angeles Church*. New Brunswick, NJ: Rutgers University Press.

– 2009. *A Mosaic of Believers: Diversity and Innovation in a Multiethnic Church*. Bloomington: Indiana University Press.

Maslach, C., and S.E. Jackson. 1981. "The Measurement of Experienced Burnout." *Journal of Occupational Behavior* 2: 99–113.

Mason, M., A. Singleton, and R. Webber. 2007. *The Spirit of Generation Y: Young People's Spirituality in a Changing Australia*. Mulgrave: John Garratt.

Mata, F. 2010. "Religion-Mix Growth in Canadian Cities: A look at 2006–2031." http://ir.lib.uwo.ca/wmc/2011/posters/11/

McGuire, M. 2008. *Religion: The Social Context*. Belmont: Wadsworth.

McKeown, L., D. McIver, J. Moreton, and A. Rotondo. 2004. *Giving and Volunteering: The Role of Religion*. Toronto: Canadian Centre of Philanthropy.

McKnight, S. 2007. "Five Streams of the Emerging Church." *Christianity Today* http://www.christianitytoday.com/ct/2007/february/11.35.html

McLaren, B. 2004. *A Generous Orthodoxy*. Grand Rapids, MI: Zondervan.

McMullen, M. 2011. "Insights Into: Attracting and Keeping Members." *Faith Communities Today*. http://faithcommunitiestoday.org/sites/faithcommunitiestoday.org/files/Attracting%20and%20Keeping%20Members.pdf

McNally, H. 1987. "Women in Ministry." *Atlantic Baptist* (Apr.). Reprinted in *Priscilla Papers* (Winter 1997), with the title "Let's Keep on Ordaining Women."

McPherson, J. M., and Thomas Rotolo. 1995. "Measuring the Characteristics of Voluntary Association: A Multitrait-Multimethod

Analysis." *Social Forces* 73: 1097–1115.

Mentzer, M.S. 1991. "The Validity of Denominational Membership Data in Canada." *Sociological Analysis* 52(3): 293–99.

Miller, D. E. 1997. *Reinventing American Protestantism*. Berkeley, CA: University of California Press.

Miller, D. E., and T. Yamamori. 2007. *Global Pentecostalism: The New Face of Christian Social Engagement*. Berkeley, CA: University of California Press.

Miller, A. S., and R. Stark. 2002. "Gender and Religiousness: Can Socialization Explanations Be Saved? *American Journal of Sociology* 107: 1399–1423.

Milner, M., S. Sterland, and M. Dowson. 2006. "Coping with Ministry: Development of a Multidimensional Measure of Internal Orientation to the Demands of Ministry." *Review of Religious Research* 48(2): 212–30.

Miner, J. 2010. "Predeceased by their churches." *London Free Press*, 21 May. Available at http://www.lfpress.com/news/london/2010/05/18/13993046.html

Mueller, C.W., and E. McDuff. 2004. "Clergy-Congregation Mismatches and Clergy Job Satisfaction." *Journal for the Scientific Study of Religion* 43(2): 261–73.

Murphy, T. 1996. "Epilogue." In *A Concise History of Christianity in Canada*, eds. T. Murphy and R. Perin, 361–9. Toronto: Oxford University Press.

Myers, S. 1996. "An Interactive Model of Religious Inheritance: The Importance of Family Context." *American Sociological Review* 61: 858–66.

National Church Life Survey (NCLS). 2006. *Church Life Profile*. Sydney South, NSW.

Neibuhr, H. R. 1929 [1957]. *The Social Sources of Denominationalism*. New York: Meridian.

Noll, M. 1992. *A History of Christianity in the United States and Canada*. Grand Rapids, MI: Eerdmans.

– 1997. *Turning Points: Decisive Moments in the History of Christianity*. Grand Rapids, MI: Baker.

– 2006. "What Happened to Christian Canada?" *Church History* 75(2): 245–73.

Noll, M., D. Bebbington, and G. Rawlyk, eds. 1994. *Evangelicalism: Comparative Studies of Popular Protestantism in North America, the British Isles, and Beyond, 1700–1990*. Oxford: Oxford University Press.

Noll, M., and L. Eskridge, eds. 2000. *More Money, More Ministry: Money and Evangelicals in Recent North American History*. Grand Rapids, MI: Eerdmans.

O'Dea, T. 1961. "Five Dilemmas in the Institutionalization of Religion." *Journal for the Scientific Study of Religion* (1): 30–39.

Olson, D.V.A. 1993. "Fellowship Ties and the Transmission of Religious

Identity." In *Beyond Establishment: Protestant Identity in a Post-Protestant Age*, eds. J.W. Carroll and W.C. Roof, 32–53. Louisville, KY: John Knox Press.

Outreach Canada. 2010. "ChurchMap Canada." http://en.outreach.ca/Resources/Research/tabid/5233/ArticleId/6686/ChurchMap-Canada.aspx

Patrick, M.L. 2011. "Playing for Keeps: The Evangelical Fellowship of Canada in the Public Sphere, 1983–2006." Unpublished PhD dissertation, University of Waterloo.

Pauls, K. 2001. "New Billboards Call Men to Ministry." *Christian Week*, 18 Dec. http://www.christianweek.org/stories.php?id=1214

Penner, J., R. Harder, E. Anderson, B. Désorcy, and R. Hiemstra. 2012. *Hemorrhaging Faith: Why and When Are Canadian Young Adults Leaving, Staying, and Returning to Church*. Ottawa: Evangelical Fellowship of Canada.

Pipes, P.F., and H.R. Ebaugh. 2002. "Faith-Based Coalitions, Social Services, and Government Funding." *Sociology of Religion* 63(1): 49–68.

Plaxton, D. 1997. "'We Will Evangelize with the Whole Gospel or None': Evangelicalism and the United Church of Canada." In *Aspects of the Canadian Evangelical Experience*, ed. G. Rawlyk, 106-22. Montreal and Kingston: McGill-Queen's University Press.

Poloma, M. 1989. *The Assemblies of God at the Crossroads*. Knoxville, TN: University of Tennessee Press.

Poloma, M., and J. Green. 2010. *The Assemblies of God: Godly Love and the Revitalization of American Pentecostalism*. New York: New York University Press.

Posterski, D., and I. Barker. 1993. *Where's a Good Church?* Windfield: Wood Lake.

Posterski, D., J. McAuley, and M. Penner. 2011. *What's Happening: The State of Youth Ministry in Canada*. Toronto: Leadership Studio.

Powell, R., J. Bellamy, and P. Kaldor. 2011. "Core Qualities to Foster in Vital and Healthy Churches." Unpublished paper.

Powell, W.W., and P.J. DiMaggio, eds. 1991. *The New Institutionalism in Organizational Analysis*. Chicago, IL: University of Chicago Press.

Pupo, N., and A. Duffy. 2000. "Canadian Part-Time Work into the Millennium: On the Cusp of Change." *Community, Work and Family* 3(1): 81–101.

Putnam, R.D. 2000. *Bowling Alone: The Collapse and Revival of American Community*. New York: Simon and Schuster.

Putnam, R.D., and D.E. Campbell. 2010. *American Grace: How Religion Divides and Unites Us*. New York: Simon and Schuster.

Randall, K.J. 2004. "Burnout as a Predictor of Leaving Anglican Parish Ministry." *Review of Religious Research* 46(1): 20–6.

Rawlyk, G.A. 1996. *Is Jesus Your Personal Saviour? In Search of Canadian Evangelicals in the 1990s*. Montreal and Kingston: McGill-

Queen's University Press.

Reed, P. 2001. "Generosity in Canada: Trends in Personal Gifts and Charitable Donations over Three Decades, 1969 to 1997." *Information and Insights for the Nonprofit Sector* (4): 1–6. Ottawa: Statistics Canada.

Regnerus, Mark D., and C. Smith. 1998. "Selective Deprivatization among American Religious Traditions: The Reversal of the Great Reversal." *Social Forces* 76(4): 1347–72.

Reimer, S. 2003. *Evangelicals and the Continental Divide*. Montreal and Kingston: McGill-Queen's University Press.

– 2007. "Class and Congregations: Class and Religious Affiliation at the Congregational Level of Analysis." *Journal for the Scientific Study of Religion* 46(4): 583–94.

– 2011. "Civility without Compromise": Evangelical Attitudes toward Same-Sex Issues in Comparative Context." In *Faith, Politics and Sexual Diversity in Canada and the United States*, eds. D. Rayside and C. Wilcox, 71–86. Vancouver: UBC Press.

– 2012. "Congregational Vitality among Evangelical Churches in Canada." *Church and Faith Trends* 5(1): 1–17.

Reimer, S., and M. Wilkinson. 2010. "A Demographic Look at Evangelical Churches." *Church and Faith Trends* 3(2): 1–21.

Ronsvalle, J. L., and S. Ronsvalle. 2011. *The State of Church Giving through 2009*. Champaign, IL: Empty Tomb.

Roof, W.C. 1993. *A Generation of Seekers: The Spiritual Journeys of the Baby Boom Generation*. San Francisco, CA: Harper.

Roozen, D.S., and C.K. Hadaway 1993. *Church and Denominational Growth: What Does (and Does Not) Cause Growth and Decline*. Nashville, TN: Abingdon.

Roozen, D. A., and J. R. Nieman, eds. 2005. *Church, Identity, and Change*. Grand Rapids, MI: Eerdmans.

Rouhlkepartain, E.C., and P.C. Scales. 1995. *Youth Development in Congregations: An Exploration of the Potential and Barriers*. Minneapolis, MN: Search Institute.

Rugenstein, K. 2005. "Clergy Dissatisfaction: Denominational Hierarchy as a Salient Factor." *Journal of Pastoral Care and Counseling* 59 (1–2): 79–86.

Rutledge, C.F.J., and L. Francis. 2004. "Burnout among Male Anglican Parochial Clergy in England: Testing a Modified Form of the Maslach Burnout Inventory." *Research in the Social Scientific Study of Religion* 15(1): 71–93.

Sayer, A. 2000. *Realism and Social Science*. London: Sage.

Segers, M., ed. 2003. *Faith-Based Initiatives and the Bush Administration*. Lanham, MD: Rowman and Littlefield.

Selbee, L.K., and P.B. Reed. 2000. *Patterns of Volunteering over the Life Cycle*. Report from the Nonprofit Sector Knowledge Base Project. Ottawa: Statistics Canada.

Scheitle, C.P. 2007. "Organizational Niches and Religious Markets: Uniting Two Literatures." *Interdisciplinary Journal of Research on Religion* 3(2): 1–29.

Scheitle, C.P., and K.D. Dougherty. 2008. "Density and Growth in a Congregational Population: Reformed Churches in New York, 1628–2000." *Review of Religious Research* 49(3): 233–50.

Scheitle, C.P., J.B. Kane, and J. Van Hook 2011. "Demographic Imperatives and Religious Markets: Considering the Individual and Interactive Roles of Fertility and Switching in Group Growth." *Journal for the Scientific Study of Religion* 50(3): 470–82.

Scheitle, C.P., and B.G. Smith. 2011. "A Note on the Frequency and Sources of Close Interreligious Ties." *Journal for the Scientific Study of Religion* 50(2): 410–21.

Scholte, J. A. 2005. *Globalization: A Critical Introduction*, 2nd ed. New York: Palgrave.

Schwadel, P., and K.D. Dougherty. 2010. "Assessing Key Informant Methodology in Congregational Research." *Review of Religious Research* 51(4): 366–79.

Schwarz, C. 2000. *Natural Church Development: A Guide to Eight Essential Qualities of Healthy Churches*. Carol Stream, IL: ChurchSmart Resources.

Schwartz, K. D., B. Warkentin, and M. Wilkinson. 2008. "Faith-Based Social Services in North America: A Comparison of American and Canadian Religious History and Initiative." *Social Work and Christianity: An International Journal* 35(2): 123–47.

Scott, N. 2007. "Secular Mobilization? The Evolving Effects of Religion on Canadian Civic Engagement, 1982–2001." Paper prepared for Paul Reed with assistance from Kevin Selbee, Carleton University and Statistics Canada.

Sider, R. 1999. *Good News and Good Works*. Grand Rapids, MI: Baker.

Sider, R.J. 2005. *Scandal for the Evangelical Conscience: Why Christians Are Living Just Like the Rest of the World*. Grand Rapids, MI: Baker.

Simpson, J. H. 2000. "The Politics of the body in Canada and the United States." In *Rethinking Church, State, and Modernity*, eds. D. Lyon and M. van Die, 263–82. Toronto: University of Toronto Press.

Smith, C. 1998. *American Evangelicalism: Embattled and Thriving*. Chicago, IL: University of Chicago Press.

– 2000. *Christian America? What Evangelicals Really Want*. Berkeley, CA: University of California Press.

– 2003. "Theorizing Religious Effects among American Adolescents." *Journal for the Scientific Study of Religion* 42(1): 17–30.

– 2010. *What is a Person? Rethinking Humanity, Social Life, and the Moral Good from the Person Up*. Chicago, IL: University of Chicago Press.

Smith, C., K. Christoffersen, H. Davidson, and P. Snell Herzog. 2011. *Lost in Transition: The Dark Side of Emerging Adulthood*. Oxford: Oxford University Press.

Smith, C., with M. Denton. 2005. *Soul Searching: The Religious and Spiritual Lives of American Teenagers*. Oxford: Oxford University Press.

Smith, C., and M.O. Emerson, with P. Snell. 2008. *Passing the Plate: Why American Christians Don't Give Away More Money*. New York: Oxford University Press.

Smith, C., with P. Snell. 2009. *Souls in Transition: The Religious and Spiritual Lives of Emerging Adults*. Oxford: Oxford University Press.

Smith, G.S. 2000. "Evangelicals Confront Corporate Capitalism: Adverstising, Consumerism, Stewardship, and Spirituality, 1880–1930." In *More Money, More Ministry*, eds. L. Eskridge and M.A. Noll, 38–80. Grand Rapids, MI: Eerdmans.

Solomon, L. 2003. *In God We Trust? Faith-Based Organizations and the Quest to Solve America's Social Ills*. Lanham, MD: Lexington.

Stackhouse, J. G. 1993. *Canadian Evangelicalism in the Twentieth Century*. Toronto: University of Toronto Press.

– 2000. "Bearing the Witness: Christian Groups Engage Canadian Politics Since the 1960s." In *Rethinking Church, State, and Modernity*, eds. D. Lyon and M. Van Die, 113–30. Toronto: University of Toronto Press.

– 2007. "Defining Evangelical." *Church and Faith Trends* 1(1): 1–5.

Stark, R., and W.S. Bainbridge.1985. *The Future of Religion*. Berkeley, CA: University of California Press.

Stark, R., and R. Finke. 2000. *Acts of Faith: Explaining the Human Side of Religion*. Berkeley, CA: University of California Press.

Statistics Canada. 2003. *2001 Census: Religions in Canada*. Catalogue no. 96F0030XIE2001015.

– 2012. Caring Canadians, Involved Canadians: Tables Report, 2010. http://www.statcan.gc.ca/pub/89-649-x/89-649-x2011001-eng.pdf.

Steensland, B., and P. Goff, eds. 2013. *The New Evangelical Social Engagement*. New York: Oxford University Press.

Stetzer, E. 2009. *Lost and Found: The Younger Unchurched and the Churches That Reach Them*. Nashville, TN: B&H.

Stewart, A.S. 2012. "Quenching the Spirit: The Transformation of Religious Identity and Experience in Three Canadian Pentecostal Churches." Unpublished PhD dissertation, University of Waterloo, Waterloo, Ontario.

Studebaker, S., and L. Beach. 2012. "Emerging Churches in Post-Christian Canada." *Religions* 3: 862–79.

Swidler, A. 2001. "What Anchors Cultural Practices?" In *The Practice Turn in Contemporary Theory*, eds. T. Schatzki, K. Knorr Cetina, and E. von Savigny, 74–92. London: Routledge.

Tamney, J.B. 2002. *The Resilience of Conservative Religion: The Case of Popular, Conservative Protestant Congregations*. Cambridge: Cambridge University Press.

Thiessen, J. 2010. "Churches are not Necessarily the Problem: Lessons Learned from Christmas and Easter Affiliates." *Church and Faith Trends* 3(3): 1–24.

– 2011. "Active and Marginal Religious Affiliates in Canada: Describing the Difference and the Difference It Makes." PhD Dissertation. University of Waterloo.

– 2012. "Marginal Religious Affiliates in Canada: Little Reason to Expect Increased Church Involvement." *Canadian Review of Sociology* 49(1): 69–90.

Thiessen, J., and L. Dawson. 2008. "Is There a 'Renaissance' of Religion in Canada? A Critical Look at Bibby and Beyond." *Studies in Religion* 37(3–4): 389–415.

Tocqueville, A. de. 1945 [1863]. *Democracy in America*. Cambridge: Sever and Francis.

Todd, D. 2001. "Canada's Congregations Facing Clergy Shortage." *Christian Century*, 10 Oct., 13.

Towler, R., and A. Coxon. 1979. *The Fate of the Anglican Clergy: A Sociological Study*. London: Macmillan.

Trovato, F. 2009. *Canada's Population in a Global Context: An Introduction to Social Demography*. Toronto: Oxford University Press.

Turcotte, M. 2012. "Charitable Giving by Canadians." *Canadian Social Trends* 93: 17–36.

Uecker, J., M. Regenerus, and M. Vaaler. 2007. "Losing Your Religion: The Social Sources of Religious Decline in Early Adulthood." *Social Forces* 85(4): 1667–92.

Uslaner, E. M. 2002. "Religion and Civic Engagement in Canada and the United States." *Journal for the Scientific Study of Religion* 41(2): 239–54.

Vaidyanathan, B. 2011. "Religious Resources or Differential Returns? Early Religious Socialization and Declining Attendance in Emerging Adulthood." *Journal for the Scientific Study of Religion* 50(2): 366–87.

Vaidyanathan, B., J.P. Hill, and C. Smith. 2011. "Religion and Charitable Financial Giving to Religious and Secular Causes: Does Political Ideology Matter?" *Journal for the Scientific Study of Religion* 50(3): 450–69.

Vaidyanathan, B., and P. Snell. 2011. "Motivations for and Obstacles to Religious Financial Giving." *Sociology of Religion* 72(2): 189–214.

Vaisey, S. 2008. "Reply to Ann Swidler." *Sociological Forum* 23(3): 619–22.

Verba, S., K.L. Schlozman, and H.E. Brady 1995. *Voice and Equality: Civic Voluntarism in American Politics*. Cambridge, MA: Harvard University Press.

Vézina, M., and S. Crompton. 2012. "Volunteering in Canada." *Canadian Social Trends* 93: 37–55.

Voas, D. 2010. "Explaining Change over Time in Religious Involvement." In *Religion and Youth*, eds. S. Collins-May and P. Dandelion, 25–32.

Aldershot, UK: Ashgate.

Warkentin, B.M. 1998. "Models of Church-Agency Relationship in Church-Affiliated Social Service Agencies in the Region of Waterloo." Unpublished Master's thesis, Wilfrid Laurier University, Waterloo, Ontario.

Warren, R. 1995. *The Purpose Driven Church*. Grand Rapids, MI: Zondervan.

Warner, R.S. 1988. *New Wine in Old Wineskins: Evangelicals and Liberals in a Small-Town Church*. Berkeley, CA: University of California Press.

– 1993. "Work in Progress toward a New Paradigm for the Sociological Study of Religion in the United States." *American Journal of Sociology* 98(5): 1044–93.

– 1994. "The Place of Congregations in the Contemporary American Religious Configuration." In *American Congregations: New Perspectives in the Study of Congregations*, vol. 2, eds. J.P. Wind and J.W. Lewis, 54–99. Chicago, IL: University of Chicago Press.

Warner, R.S., and J.G. Wittner, eds. 1998. *Gatherings in Diaspora: Religious Communities and the New Immigration*. Philadelphia: Temple University Press.

Weber, M. 1993 [1922]. *The Sociology of Religion*. Boston, MA: Beacon.

– 1968. *Economy and Society*. G. Roth and C. Wittich, editors. New York: Bedminster.

Webber, R., A. Singleton, M. Joyce, and A. Dorrisa. 2010. "Models of Youth Ministry in Action: The Dynamics of Christian Youth Ministry in an Australian City." *Religious Education* 105(2): 204–15.

Welch, M.R., D.C. Leege, K.D. Wald, and L.A. Kellstedt. 1993. "Are the Sheep Hearing the Shepherds? Cue Perceptions, Congregational Responses, and Political Communication Processes." In *Rediscovering the Religious Factor in American Politics*, eds. D.C. Leege and L.A. Kellstedt, 235–54. Armonk, NY: M.E. Sharpe.

Wilkinson, M. 2000. "The Globalization of Pentecostalism: The Role of Asian Immigrant Pentecostals in Canada." *Asian Journal of Pentecostal Studies* 3: 219–26.

– 2006. *The Spirit Said Go: Pentecostal Immigrants in Canada*. New York: Peter Lang.

– 2007. "Faith-Based Social Services: Some Observations for Assessing Pentecostal Social Action." *Transformation: An International Journal of Holistic Mission Studies* 24(2): 71–9.

– ed. 2009. *Canadian Pentecostalism: Transition and Transformation*. Montreal and Kingston: McGill-Queen's University Press.

– 2010. "Globalization and the Environment: Assessing a Pentecostal Response." In *A Liberating Spirit*, eds. M. Wilkinson and S. M. Studebaker, 213–30. Eugene, OR: Wipf and Stock.

Wilkinson, M., and S. M. Studebaker. 2010. *A Liberating Spirit: Pentecostals and Social Action in North America*. Eugene, OR: Wipf and Stock.

Wilson, J. 2006. *Why Church Matters: Worship, Ministry and Mission in Practice*. Grand Rapids, MI: Brazos.

Wilson, J., and M. Musick. 1997. "Who Cares? Toward an Integrated Theory of Volunteer Work." *American Sociological Review* 62: 694–713.

Wiseman, R. 1998a. "Beyond Burnout." *Faith Today* (May/June). http://www.christianity.ca

– 1998b. "Holy Burnout." *Faith Today* (May/June). http://www.christianity.ca

Wolfe, A. 2003. *The Transformation of American Religion*. Chicago, IL: University of Chicago Press.

Wood, R. 2003. "Religion, Faith-Based Community Organizing, and the Struggle for Justice." In *Handbook of the Sociology of Religion*, ed. M. Dillon, 385–99. Cambridge: Cambridge University Press.

Woolever, C., and D. Bruce. 2002. *A Field Guide to US Congregations: Who's Going Where and Why*. Louisville, KY: John Knox Press.

Wuthnow, R. 1987. *Meaning and Moral Order: Explorations in Cultural Analysis*. Berkeley, CA: University of California Press.

– 1988. *The Restructuring of American Religion*. Princeton, NJ: Princeton University Press.

– 1991. *Acts of Compassion: Caring for Others and Helping Ourselves*. Princeton, NJ: Princeton University Press.

– 1994. *Sharing the Journey: Support Groups and the Quest for Community*. New York: Simon and Schuster.

– 1998. *After Heaven: Spirituality in America Since the 1950s*. Berkeley, CA: University of California Press.

– 2004. *Saving America? Faith-Based Services and the Future of Civil Society*. Princeton, NJ: Princeton University Press.

– 2007. *After the Boom: How Twenty-and Thirty-Somethings Are Shaping the Future of American Religion*. Princeton, NJ: Princeton University Press.

– 2009. *Boundless Faith: The Global Outreach of American Churches*. Berkeley, CA: University of California Press.

Wuthnow, R., and John H. Evans, eds. 2002. *The Quiet Hand of God: Faith-Based Activism and the Public Role of Mainline Protestantism*. Berkeley, CA: University of California Press.

Yancey, G.A. 2003. *One Body, One Spirit: Principles of Successful Multiracial Churches*. Downers Grove, IL: InterVarsity Press.

Zuidema, J., ed. 2011. *French-Speaking Protestants in Quebec*. Leiden: Brill.

Zylstra, S.E. 2009. "Caring for the Caregivers." *Christianity Today* (May): 1.

Index

abortion, 10, 18, 55, 59
activism, 5–6, 10, 26, 42, 101, 104,
111–12
affiliates, marginal, active, 4, 16–19,
50, 57–9, 62, 79, 86, 171
Alpha Program, 35, 95–6, 119,
123–4, 224, 252
Ammerman, Nancy, 7–8, 12, 40–1,
131, 244
Anglican Church of Canada, 5–6,
19, 46, 49, 72–3, 140, 218–19,
245, 248
Associated Canadian Theological
Schools, 254
attendance, 3, 29, 35, 42, 76, 89,
121, 132, 137, 143, 186–7, 192–3,
196, 203, 206; weekly vs. monthly,
8–24; changes in, 45–50, 57–8,
70, 72–4; priorities and,106,
108, 110; youth/children and,
166, 171, 173–5, 177–9, 180–1
attitudes, 10, 12, 23, 37, 63, 90,
148, 161, 203
authenticity, 112, 133
authority, moral, 6, 46–7, 51,
160–1, 202; of Pastor, biblical,
external locus of, 17, 42–3, 54–9,
61–2, 67, 189, 204, 209, 248

Bebbington, David, 6, 42, 101, 208,
260
beliefs, 5–7, 12, 16–18, 22, 23, 40,
43–4, 47, 53, 55, 57–61, 104,
175, 185–6, 203, 256
Berton, Pierre, 46, 134
Beyer, Peter, 47, 52, 69, 81, 86, 206
Bibby, Reginald, 3–5, 8, 10, 15–18,
24, 26, 37, 48–52, 57, 63, 68–71,
79, 83, 85–6, 91, 103, 109, 137,
159–61, 185, 189, 220, 243–5,
247, 250, 257
Bible, 5–6, 17, 32–3, 35, 42–3,
59–61, 93–4, 111–12, 114–19,
121, 123–5, 131–2, 162–3,
178–9, 181
biblicism, authority of Bible, 6, 17,
42–3, 55–6, 59, 204, 209
birth rates, 52, 63, 65, 69, 206–7
Bowen, Kurt, 17, 24–5, 44, 48, 69,
83–5, 160, 186, 188
Bowler, Kate, 103
Bramadat, Paul, 47–8, 85
Buddhism, 3, 16, 69
buildings, facilities, 13, 19, 28–9,
33, 35–6, 103, 105, 108, 119,
164, 209–10, 221, 225, 232,
249; age of, 64, 80; costs of,
89,182, 191, 195, 199–200

Canada Revenue Agency, 14, 71, 72,
81–2, 144, 190, 192–7, 200, 211,
213–15, 218, 245, 248, 259–60
Canada Survey of Giving, Volunteering and Participating, 85, 183

Catholics: church participation of, 3–5, 15–19, 45–50, 204–5, 216–19, 228, 244–5, 247, 250; demographics of, 81, 85, 89; leadership of, 127, 130; clergy, 134, 136–8, 140, 143–4, 155; youth/children and, 159, 161, 169–74, 178; finances, 182, 191, 196–200

charisma, charismatic movement, 129–32, 202, 208, 228, 246, 252

charitable giving, 14, 22–5, 44, 81–2, 183–6, 190, 198–9, 216, 258

Chaves, Mark, 7, 9, 12, 23, 25, 77, 84, 91, 139, 171, 182, 189, 206, 245, 250

Church and Faith Study of Young Adults, 159–60, 169, 211, 219

church growth, 4, 13–14, 19, 29, 31, 52, 59, 62–75, 79, 88–9, 97–9, 107–9, 115, 119, 128, 133, 158, 166, 171, 192, 203–9, 241, 243, 248–9

Church health, 63, 97, 107, 130, 150–7, 209–10

circulation of the saints, 68–70, 89

civil society, 22, 25, 37–8

clergy shortage, 134–6, 139, 142, 144, 155, 205, 254

congregational studies, 7, 12

conversion, conversionism, 5–6, 42–3, 52, 61, 71, 77, 86, 109–10, 146, 174, 202, 206, 247

cooperation, 6, 13, 47, 101–8, 113, 119, 126–7, 133, 203, 225

crucicentrism, 5–6

culture of congregations, 7–8, 12–13, 20–3, 37

Dawson, Lorne, 16

demographics, 21, 68, 77, 79, 83, 89, 136, 139, 205, 220

discipleship, spiritual disciplines, spiritual formation, 8, 32, 33, 95–6, 105–6, 110, 114, 118, 126, 128, 164–5, 179, 223, 225, 235

distinctiveness, 8, 37–8, 46, 54, 59, 67, 110, 133, 248

Eagle, David, 9, 15–16, 48–9, 69, 244, 246

education, 43, 46–8, 60, 62, 92, 161; of congregants, 12, 77, 79, 83–5, 108, 204; church programs for, 7, 25, 60, 90–3, 116–18, 121, 132, 136, 200, 222–3, 253, 256; of clergy; 11–12, 142–3, 146, 151, 168

emergent, emerging church, 20, 36, 40, 51, 112–13, 128–31, 159–60, 170, 200, 228, 246, 253

ethnic congregations, 11, 74, 83, 86–8, 206, 212, 225, 227, 241, 246, 251

ethnicity,13, 29, 36, 48, 102–4, 115, 121, 139–41,152, 155

Evangelical Fellowship of Canada, 5–6, 47, 92, 26, 233, 241, 246, 255

evangelical quadrilateral, 6, 42

evangelical subculture, 6, 8, 12–13, 133, 160, 203, 206, 208, 247; congregations and, 20–1, 36–7, 39–40, 42–9, 103–4, 109–14, 203–4; North American, 24, 42; vitality of, 53, 55, 57, 60–1, 65–7

evangelism, 10, 30, 38, 202, 223, 225, 234, 237, 248, 252; priority of; 6, 42, 68–9, 89, 91–7, 101–2, 104–7, 109; programs for,112–13, 115–16, 118, 123, 126, 130, 133; youth/children and, 165, 168

experience, religious, 6, 18, 42–3, 55, 60–1, 110, 174–6, 180–1, 202, 247

family, 8, 14, 27, 32, 34, 185, 220, 225, 229, 255, 257; traditional views of, 42–3, 57–8, 60, 101; demographics of, 62, 77–84; prioritizing the, 92, 94, 101, 103, 109; pastors and, 146–7; youth/children and, 159, 168,

176, 178
Finke, Roger, 51–2, 59, 65, 79–80, 136
food bank, 119–20, 253
fundamentalism, religious right, 53, 90–1, 101, 108, 129–31, 228

gender, 84–5, 111, 117, 132, 139, 150, 155, 233, 241, 257
globalization, 13, 30, 33, 207
Guder, Darrel, 112
Guenther, Bruce, 6–7, 85, 104, 139, 244, 254

Hiemstra, Rick, 14, 17–19, 24, 48, 83, 118, 144
Hinduism, 16, 47, 69, 85, 126, 228
Holmes, Pamela, 140
homosexuality, 10, 18, 38

identity, 101, 104, 228, 253; evangelical, 7–9, 13, 16, 46–7, 69, 111, 113, 120, 204; congregational, 8, 40, 44, 127, 129, 130–2; religious, 46, 53, 55, 57, 59
immigrants, 220, 247, 250, 257; recent, 3, 14, 16, 46–7, 50, 65–6, 74, 78–9, 84–8, 119, 141, 206–8; outreach to, 30, 33–4, 36
incarnational ministry, 29, 31, 33, 96, 129, 133
individualism, 22, 38, 54–5, 58, 61, 67, 136, 146, 160, 189, 243
Islam, 3, 16, 47, 69, 85, 126, 205, 228
isomorphism, 43, 110, 113

James, William Closson, 69
job satisfaction, pastors', 145–57, 168, 239, 255

Lutheran Church of Canada, 19–20, 72, 140, 207, 218, 243
Lyon, David, 91

mainline Protestantism, 3–6, 13, 16–19, 24–5, 46, 49–50, 55–7,

205–7, 216–19, 243–50, 258; demographics of, 60, 72, 85, 88–9; priorities and, 98, 108, 127; leadership and, 135, 137, 144, 155; children and, 159, 161, 169–73, 178; money and, 182, 191, 195–200
Marsden, George, 6, 131
Marti, Gerardo, 86, 246
McLaren, Brian, 112
McMaster Divinity College, 129
mega-church, 11, 32, 112, 246, 260
Mission Possible, 119
missional, 13–14, 29–31, 63, 104–9, 112–13, 127–33, 228, 253
missions, short-term, missionary work, 92, 95, 97, 118, 123–5, 130, 182, 189, 191, 224, 235, 259
multicultural congregations, multiculturalism, 28, 46, 86
music, worship, 25, 27, 34–5, 40–3, 47, 54, 61–2, 79, 91, 116, 162–3, 168, 223, 230, 234, 236
Mustard Seed, Calgary, 119

National Church Life Survey, Australia, 63, 97
Natural Church Development, Christian Schwartz, 63, 107
Noll, Mark, 45–6, 209, 260

ordination of women, 128, 139
orthodoxy, 15, 37, 41
orthopraxy, 15, 37, 41–2
Outreach Canada, 18, 81, 138, 244–5, 250

Penner, James, 14
pluralism, 46–7, 51, 67, 90, 160
political views, politics, 26, 45–6, 90–2, 206, 245
post-Christian, 13, 45–7, 112, 129, 133
practices, 61, 93–4, 140, 179, 185–6, 203, 226
Presbyterian Church of Canada, 6, 20, 44, 49, 72, 140, 218–19, 249

Prosperity Gospel, 103
pro-social effects, 23–4, 31, 118, 120, 133, 161, 185, 245

race, 11, 65, 80, 83, 85, 87–8, 132, 139, 230, 238
Rawlyk, George, 5, 17, 85, 260
Regent College, 138
relational embeddedness, 60
reverse mission, 207
Roman Catholic Church.
   See Catholics

Salvation Army, 30, 118, 197, 217
secular, secularism, secularization, 3, 22, 25, 31, 38, 43, 51–3, 59, 62, 112–13, 134, 144, 147, 183, 186, 207
Seljak, David, 47–8, 85
sex, sexuality, 10, 16–18, 38, 43, 54–5, 59, 62, 90, 93–4, 160, 163, 203, 206, 226, 235, 251
Sikhism, 16, 47, 69, 85
Simpson, John, 55, 91
small groups, cell groups, home groups, 32, 34, 56, 79, 93, 113–18, 123–4, 128, 132, 150, 168, 181, 222, 224–8, 231, 252
Smith, Christian, 24, 53, 60–1, 67, 90, 160, 188, 246–7, 256
social concerns, 7, 22, 30, 128
socialization, 60–1, 114, 180, 185–6, 245
Stackhouse, Jr, John G., 5–6, 43, 91–2
Stark, Rodney, 51–2, 59, 80, 84, 136
Stewart, Adam, 55, 104
Studebaker, Steven, 118, 129, 133
Sunday school, 28, 43, 56, 60, 62, 72–3, 112, 114–15, 150, 158, 162, 164–5, 205, 222, 225, 227, 231–2, 236, 239–40, 256

tension, religious, organizational, 26, 37, 41, 46, 51–3, 55–6, 59, 64, 90, 111, 135, 188

theological education, Bible College, seminary, 27, 43, 63, 136–9, 141–2, 227, 230, 238, 254
Thiessen, Joel, 16, 57–8
traditional, 104–8, 113, 118, 129, 133, 135, 162, 225–6, 243; worship, 54–5, 202; family, 60, 92; beliefs and morals, 17, 43, 47, 101–2
transdenominational, 6, 13, 42, 130, 132
Tyndale University College and Seminary, 43, 126, 138, 254

United Church of Canada, 5–6, 19, 20, 44–5, 49, 72–3, 140, 218, 245
United States, comparisons with evangelicals, 22, 24–5, 42, 54, 58, 83, 85, 90–2, 134, 160, 171, 188, 190, 194, 206–7, 245, 250, 256, 260

Vacation Bible School, 114–15, 123–4, 164–5, 224, 236
vitality, institutional strength, 4, 6, 12, 21, 26, 33, 44, 74, 203–5, 210, 247–8; theories of 51–3, 63, 66–9; priorities and, 97, 99, 103, 107–10, 132–3; pastors and, 153, 157; money and,182, 191–2, 196, 199
voluntarism, generosity, 9, 14, 26, 38, 44, 143, 182–8, 204, 245, 249

Warner, R. Stephen, 7, 12, 85
Warren, Rick, 96, 130
Wilson, Jonathan, 23, 39
World Vision, 43, 125, 163
Wuthnow, Robert, 6, 23, 91, 117–18, 160, 189
Wycliffe Bible translators, 125–6, 253

Yonge Street Mission, 119
Youth with a Mission, 125–6, 253